An

ECONOMIST'S OUTLOOK

Essays by John H. Makin from a Transformative Era

THE AEI PRESS

Publisher for the American Enterprise Institute
Washington, DC

ISNB-13: 978-0-8447-5036-1   Hardback
ISNB-13: 978-0-8447-5037-8   Paperback
ISNB-13: 978-0-8447-5038-5   eBook

American Enterprise Institute
1789 Massachusetts Avenue, NW
Washington, DC 20036
www.aei.org

Content

Acknowledgments

The idea of publishing a selection of the *Economic Outlook* written by John Makin for the American Enterprise Institute originated with John himself. Unfortunately, it was an idea he was not able to see to fruition.

The essays included in this book are selected from hundreds he wrote. They provide unique insights into economic events and policy decisions from 1992 to 2014, a tumultuous, transformative period beginning with the end of the Cold War. His commentary about this period remains relevant to the downstream economic changes we see in the world today.

This book is not intended to be a comprehensive history, but rather a perspective on the important and outstanding economic events of these years as they were experienced, analyzed, and evaluated in real time. John saw them as components of deeply intertwined and iterative trends with long-term repercussions. The purpose of this book, therefore, is to provoke thought, raise questions, and provide a broader framework for examining current and future economic events. Above all, I hope that John's insights will inspire and embolden young economists to break from the herd, analyze data carefully and thoroughly, fuse their analysis with the challenges facing lawmakers around the world, draw carefully constructed conclusions, and speak with independent voices, just as John did.

A scholar of economics and well versed in historical trends and events, John wrote in a penetrating and thoughtful style, rooted in realities of the day and the strong economic analytic skills he acquired earning his PhD from the University of Chicago. His experience in academia, the think tank and policy worlds, and the financial markets, coupled with his understanding of economic history, enabled him to interpret economic and political events through a uniquely multifaceted lens. He was known for his astute analysis and objectivity, which earned respect from both sides of the political spectrum and from readers and colleagues worldwide. Never one to "talk his book," John called it like he saw it, no matter the repercussions. He was the first to admit when he got it wrong, quipping that "when the facts change, I change my mind," a quote he attributed to John Maynard Keynes.

I would like to thank the ever-brilliant team at the American Enterprise Institute for bringing John's dream to reality and publishing this collection. From the interns and research assistants, especially Wendy Morrison, who doggedly scanned endless documents and amassed and organized John's writings as far back as the 1970s, to Véronique Rodman, Stan Veuger, Michael Strain, and the creative editing and design team, especially Director of Editing Services Sarah Bowe, they have been a wonderful group with which to work.

The book would not be a reality, however, without the commitment and energy of my dear friend Karlyn Bowman. I am grateful to her for her tireless efforts to find an editor, remarkable attention to detail, and wisdom. I will long remember our endless conversations, lengthy email chains, and marathon session of reading and editing at my kitchen table. John admired and respected her greatly and would have loved working with her.

Thanks also to Tony Mecia, who's good-natured patience and serious, dedicated editing has made all the difference. His introductions are thoughtful and thorough. I am grateful, too, for Carmen and Vincent Reinhardt's excellent foreword, which provides the book with valuable context. Colleagues and friends of whom John thought highly, the Reinhardts made an important contribution, linking John's work to the present.

And thanks to the friends who provided important ideas, encouragement, and advice, especially Charles Nelson, Kevin Hassett, Peter Joers, Lyric Hale, Phil Davies, Jon Morgan, Jim Haskell, Peter and Mary Sue Fisher, Peter and Jean Richards, and Maneesh Shanbhag.

This book is dedicated to Jane Makin and Rahul Mehta.

Gwendolyn van Paasschen
April 2021

Foreword

The global pandemic is a generational stress test to the market system and financial order. It is also a stress test of economic understanding. How do we put reasonable predictive bounds on economic outcomes when two-thirds of the population was instructed for a time not to participate in normal market activity? What do we make of fiscal initiatives that are almost an order of magnitude larger than precedent and with no apparent consequence put to the resulting fiscal dynamics of deficits piling on debt? What follows when monetary policymakers cross established boundaries into fiscal finance? And where might stresses emerge among the patchwork of existing trade and exchange-rate systems that were cobbled together by political opportunism rather than designed from economic logic?

This is not just about now. Two hundred years from now, economists and other social scientists will still be debating the events of 2020, presumably applying finer-resolution microscopes given, we hope, the progress of science. This means that the analyses of the moment represent the first drafts of history.

We would have more confidence that those first drafts would make progress in tackling these crucial questions if John Makin were among the authors. Reading this volume of his real-time, flinty-eyed assessments of the high crimes and misdemeanors of economic policymakers and of investors' market swings from giddiness to despair and back again reminds us of our loss.

We both knew John back in the day as an academic at the University of Washington in the late 1980s, and he was an office neighbor for one of us at the American Enterprise Institute a decade ago. In between and since, our paths crossed multiple times, with John serving as a combative, compelling, and always collegial colleague in various forums.

We miss his *Economic Outlook*, especially for the four themes he reliably addressed that are especially relevant to our once-in-a-generation shock.

First, borders are open, so understanding domestic circumstances, both the outlook and the risks to that outlook, requires appreciating the multiple roles of international trade in goods, services, and assets. Think of what John would have made of the first half of 2020 as witness to the most coincident contraction among world economies since the 1930s. The cratering of global trade volumes would have produced multiple clarion calls from AEI's offices on the corner of 17th and Massachusetts streets in Northwest DC. And he would have been among the earliest mapping the lowness of US Treasury yields back to negative yields in Europe and Japan.

Second, woven through this book is a mistrust of official "solutions." (Of note, this was always about policy and not people. At various stages in our careers, we sat across the table from John as representatives of either the Federal Reserve or International Monetary Fund. The badge title never mattered for the quality of the interaction.) Pride of place is his criticism of the single currency of the euro area. Readers of the *Economic Outlook* learned early that this was a leap into the unknown to establish a currency union without a fiscal transfer system among a citizenry with wildly different attitudes toward fiscal deficits, government debt, and inflation. Even with this urge to unify, local officials could not wean themselves away from protecting national financial champions, especially in finance. How would John view the recent late-hour move by European Union leaders to create a fiscal transfer mechanism with common debt in an opaque and undemocratic fashion? We are not sure if it would be sorrow, bemusement, or anger. But we are sure the missing commentary would be bracing.

Third, John was a consummate financial market professional but never one to retreat to platitudes about the "wisdom of crowds." He knew from experience that investors did the round trip from exuberance to panic and back again. His preferred policy solutions relied on market mechanisms, not because of confidence in market participants but rather from a lack of confidence in any other alternative. How many flags would he have raised now that equity prices are at all-time highs even as the global economy is in a deep recession and its recovery will be measured in years? John would not have mistaken rebound—the cyclical bounce back of market economies from a deep blow—for sustained recovery. And he would have been deeply suspicious of the role of central banks in propping up the financial edifice with inflated balance sheets. As for one of the consequences, concerns about inflation sound old-fashioned right now, but John was old-fashioned in a good way.

Lastly, another theme of the economic bio-system temporarily in suspended animation is government debt. According to the International Monetary Fund, the world economy is likely to pile on about 20 percentage points of gross general debt relative to nominal income within three years. Someone who spent his career expressing concern about government debt dynamics would have the gravity to address this.

John Makin was that person. He is missed.

Carmen Reinhart and Vincent Reinhart
July 24, 2020

Carmen Reinhart is vice president and chief economist at the World Bank Group. She is on public service leave from the Harvard Kennedy School, where she is the Minos A. Zombanakis Professor of the International Financial System. Vincent Reinhart is the chief economist and macro strategist at Mellon.

PART I

ECONOMICS 101, APPLIED

1

THE ECONOMY: AN OVERVIEW

The Global Economy After the Cold War

OCTOBER 1992

We begin our exploration of John Makin's extensive writings in 1992. In this prescient essay from October 1992, Makin assessed the challenges Western economies faced at the close of the Cold War. Many of the themes he identified in Japan, Europe, and the United States eventually became topics of some of the most consequential debates in economics in the 1990s and beyond.

At the inception of Japan's "lost decade," Makin identified many of the policy blunders that would lead the county's previously booming economy to suffer long-term damage throughout the 1990s.

As Europe began the challenge of integrating former Soviet-bloc countries, Makin chronicled some of the persistent challenges that policymakers encountered with exchange rates—a problem that was eventually addressed by the creation of the European Central Bank and the introduction of the euro in 1999.

As early as 1992, Makin noted some of the themes that have played out in the United States in recent years, including what he termed "the impotence of monetary policy," the surprising lack of correlation between deficits and interest rates, and the costs of mandated health care. He correctly predicted the resurgence of economic growth in the US in the 1990s, and he foresaw that President Bill Clinton—who wasn't even elected at the time this essay was written—would be forced to cut taxes on capital to get the economy moving. That happened in 1997.

Ironically, while the collapse of the Soviet Union was providing one of history's most powerful demonstrations of the dangers of ignoring basic principles of economics, Western governments continued to pursue political goals inconsistent with both economics and common sense. The triumph of economic power over military power has been accompanied by illogical efforts in Europe, Japan, and America to pursue mistaken economic policies that have precipitated a wrenching, rapid disinflation, which has proceeded much further and faster than anyone envisioned. The only remaining question is whether recent forced abandonments of such policies first in Japan and then in Europe have come soon enough or are decisive enough to avoid a dangerous crossover from global disinflation to global deflation and economic collapse.

Today's dangerous deflationary policies began in the aftermath of the stock market crash of October 1987. Rightly, central banks interrupted programs of inflation control following the crash and provided a surge of liquidity to world financial markets, aimed at avoiding a self-reinforcing market collapse of the sort that occurred in global stock markets after October 1929. After providing what was, in retrospect, too much liquidity for world financial markets in the six months following the October 1987 crash, the world's major central banks in the United States, Japan, and Germany, each for different reasons, began to pursue disinflationary policies.

Japan's Disinflationary Policies

In Japan, the onset of concerted disinflationary policies was marked by a change of leadership at the Bank of Japan (BOJ). An accommodative BOJ head, Gov. Satoshi Sumita, was replaced by Gov. Yasushi Mieno, a BOJ stalwart dedicated to deflating the speculative bubbles in Japanese real estate and stock markets. Mieno aimed to disinflate those bubbles gradually, a delicate operation. In retrospect, he moved too aggressively, bringing money growth down from 13 percent in 1990 to a 3–4 percent range in 1991 and most recently to virtually zero. Such a rapid tightening of monetary policy caused a virtual collapse in the Tokyo stock market, with prices plummeting more than 60 percent, from highs around 39,000 early in 1990 to a low below 15,000 in August 1992.

Mieno's disinflationary goal for Japan was laudable enough. Soaring land prices had put homeownership well out of reach of most Japanese families. The land and stock market bubbles had created a disconcerting bipolar wealth distribution in Japan, which the Japanese government saw as potentially destabilizing. It feared, probably with some justification, for a loss of the famous Japanese work ethic in an economy where land and stock speculators were rewarded with wealth unimaginable to the Japanese salary men[1] who make up the hard core of the Japanese labor force.

Gov. Mieno's mistake was to hold monetary policy too tight too long. He actually began to cut interest rates in the middle of 1991 and pushed the official discount rate down rapidly from 6 percent to 3.25 percent in the summer of 1992. But ominously, while interest rates were falling, money growth was falling even more rapidly, suggesting that disinflationary forces were operating more rapidly than could be offset by normal reductions in interest rates.

Close behind the collapse in equity prices was a collapse in land prices in major cities such as Tokyo and Osaka. Land prices fell at rates of more than 30 percent a year, while the Japanese government pretended that because there were no land transactions—or at least no widely reported transactions—land prices were stable.

The collapse of land prices has sharply hampered the ability of Japan's banks to operate as financial intermediaries, creating a situation similar to the impaired position of US banks over the past several years. When banks do not want to lend because they are attempting to restore impaired capital positions, while borrowers do not want to borrow because of falling stock and real estate prices and the uncertainty that they engender, monetary policy becomes impotent as a potential stimulus for the economy. This has been painfully true in the United States over the past two years and has emerged as a difficult reality for the Japanese over the past year.

In keeping policy too tight for too long, Japanese decision makers overlooked the basic dynamics of every business cycle. Japan's expansion was driven by rapid investment. In turn, the rapid investment was driven by a soaring stock market, which allowed the financing of huge investments at a cost of only about 1 percent. The low cost of capital meant that capital investment far exceeded its normal level when the cost of capital runs its usual 6 or 7 percent.

When the collapse of the Japanese stock market raised the cost of capital for Japanese firms to 7 percent, they began to realize too late that they had overinvested in capital, partly because the cost of capital was driven artificially low by the boom in the stock market and partly because the

BOJ's disinflationary efforts had erased wealth by inducing a sharp drop in stock and property prices. Until late in the spring of 1992, the Japanese government continued to insist that the signs of an economic slowdown were no more than a normal inventory correction whereby companies were gradually cutting production to avoid inventory buildup.

The reality was different. The jump in the cost of capital meant that firms were quickly realizing they had bought too much capital equipment even in light of Japan's chronic labor shortage. Excess capacity ballooned in export industries such as automobiles and electronics. The strong investment that had been driving the Japanese economy since 1987 was cut to zero.

One of the problems with business cycle dynamics is that investment cannot be cut below zero. Companies cannot lay off capital they have already purchased. Rather, they must hold it as excess capacity and continue to service the debt utilized to finance its acquisition. This problem results in more pressure to lay off labor, which, in turn, reduces consumer confidence and income even further.

Currently, Japan is at the stage where both investment and consumption are being rapidly curtailed.

The Collapsing European Exchange Rate Mechanism

In Europe, another troubled part of the global economy, the collapse of the European Exchange Rate Mechanism (ERM)[2] actually represents an encouraging step toward avoiding a serious global economic slowdown. Countries like Britain, now free from the yoke of currency overvaluation—yes, the pound sterling *was* overvalued—can lower real interest rates and allow a modest economic recovery. If central banks in the countries with newly floating currencies like Britain and Italy are made independent of their treasuries, as the German Bundesbank is, inflation need not result from devaluation.

The collapse of the European ERM was predetermined by a combination of events largely unforeseen by its founders and advocates. German unification—and with it an unrealistic exchange rate between the German mark and the former East German currency—produced a huge surge in consumer demand during 1990. As Germans were to discover by the end of 1991, unification meant they had agreed to give approximately 5 percent of their annual income to East Germany. The citizens in the east, long deprived of consumer goods, rapidly spent the transfers, creating powerful inflationary pressures in a German economy led by a central bank determined to avoid inflation.

Germany, in effect, followed the combination of easy fiscal and tight monetary policy used by the United States in the early 1980s. The combination of tight money and easy fiscal policy resulted in a rapid appreciation of the dollar in the 1980s.

There were two differences between the German policy combination of the early 1990s and the American policy in the 1980s. First, instead of a large budget deficit resulting from tax cuts that would lead to capital formation and eventually more rapid growth in the American case, the German budget deficit resulted largely from huge transfers from the former West Germany to the former East Germany. The budget deficit in Germany resulted from a heavy subsidy to consumption rather than a subsidy to capital formation, as it had in the United States.

The other difference, painfully demonstrated by the recent collapse of the European ERM, was the pegging of European currencies to the deutsche mark[3] while they were free to float against the appreciating American dollar. The high real US interest rates that resulted from its easy fiscal-tight money configuration therefore were not transmitted to other economies. By pegging their currency to the deutsche mark as real rates rose in Germany during and after unification, other European economies were forced to follow tighter money policies.

At first, when the pound was pegged to the deutsche mark in October 1990, three months after German unification had ensured high real interest rates in Germany, markets were impressed by Britain's apparent commitment to tight money, and inflation and interest rates fell. Eventually, however, it became clearer that the exchange rate of 2.95 deutsche marks per pound sterling overvalued sterling. The symptoms were plain. The British economic recovery never arrived, and the economy grew weaker. Even as the British economy was experiencing negative growth, its external trade deficit was rising, suggesting that even if the British economy did recover, the trade deficit would rise so rapidly as to cast serious doubts on the viability of the exchange rate.

John Major's election victory in April 1992 provided a brief respite with British financial markets celebrating a quick economic recovery after British voters had validated Major's ill-advised policy of pegging the sterling to the deutsche mark. Continued inflation pressures in Germany plus the return to a weak economy in the United Kingdom and the weakening economic conditions in Japan and the United States eventually produced unbearable strains on overvalued Italian and British currencies.

Slow US Growth

Alongside the contracting economies of Japan and Europe, in the United States an unlikely combination of events has produced a prolonged economic slowdown, with growth averaging only about 0.3 percent per year since 1989. The combination of unexpected impotence of monetary policy as an economic stimulant, the uncertainty engendered by the onset of the Persian Gulf conflict in August 1990,[4] and the ill-timed effort to cut the deficit in October 1990, just as the economy was slipping into recession, has produced low US growth.

The impotence of monetary policy and the failure of either money growth or the economy to respond to cuts of more than 6 percentage points in short-term interest rates by the Federal Reserve are a manifestation of the same problem that Japan faces: Banks do not want to lend and households do not want to borrow until they have reduced their debts to manageable levels. Disinflation that has progressed further and faster than most households and businesses anticipated adds to the burden of debts and, in the short run, accelerates the economic slowdown.

The idea that simply reducing the budget deficit in a slowing economy would help revive it was decisively disproved after October 1990, when Congress, with the blessing of President George H. W. Bush, cut the deficit when it should have been cutting taxes. Although the deficit-reduction effort was modest—about $35 billion—the actual mistake was larger, since the difference between a $35 billion tax increase and a needed $50 billion tax cut is $85 billion, or about 1.5 percent of gross domestic product (GDP). Had tax cuts to stimulate investment replaced efforts to reduce the budget deficit, the American economy might not have slipped into the sharp slow-down that followed in late 1990 and early 1991.

A broader truth about the deficit, politics, and the economy emerges from the experience of the Bush administration. The deficit itself has not been nearly as damaging to the economy as many have claimed. During 1992, when the deficit has approached 6 percent of GDP, interest rates have fallen to the lowest levels in nearly a quarter of a decade. Deficits per se therefore do not result in high interest rates, which hurt the economy. The economy has been so weak that large deficits could be absorbed with falling interest rates.

One of the major reasons for the weakness of the American economy over the past several years has been the sharp increase in the cost of hiring American labor. Congress, prevented by deficit fears from direct increases in discretionary spending, has mandated sharp increases in health and retirement benefits. These mandates, added to the 15.4 percent payroll tax, have pushed the federal tax on hiring American labor to more than 20 percent of wages. In a slowing economy, where congressional mandates have added to the cost of hiring labor, it is little wonder that employment growth and, with it, economic growth have been tepid.

The high cost of mandated health care and retirement benefits and the 15.4 percent payroll tax have pushed hiring abroad. Large corporations with global operations have tended to relocate production facilities in low-cost labor areas in Latin America and Asia. As a result, a large infusion of capital has caused emerging economies in those parts of the globe to boom while American employment languishes. The solution of this problem is *not* to attempt to force American multinational firms to pay American labor at wages inclusive of benefits that make it impossible for them to compete in the world economy. The solution, rather, is a sharp reduction in payroll tax rates, as members of Congress on both sides of the aisle have proposed.

Unfortunately for America's small businesses and for the growth of American employment, small enterprises cannot relocate to escape the high marginal costs of hiring American labor. They therefore must curtail their activities or go out of business in the face of rapidly escalating labor costs in a weak economy.

Most unfortunately, the Bush administration has abetted the rising cost of hiring American labor by going along with the rapid growth of mandated benefits that originated in the Congress. The president who served as vice president during the two Ronald Reagan administrations, in which small business was the major engine of American job growth, and who later witnessed the collapse of Communism in the Soviet Union, a testimony to the folly of putting politics before economics, ought to have known better.

Bush's failure to learn the importance of sound economic policy emanating from Washington may cost him a second term as president. The great irony may be that the Democratic candidate with the backing of the Democratic Leadership Council has learned the lessons of the Reagan economic policies better than George Bush has. The result may be a Clinton presidency and a healthy resurgence of American economic growth, an outcome doubly galling to conservative Republicans.

A Brief Look Ahead

The first step toward solving a problem is to acknowledge that mistakes have been made. With their modest expansionary package, the Japanese have acknowledged that with monetary policy rendered impotent by heavy losses on bank portfolios and a high level of indebtedness, some fiscal expansion is necessary. If they discover that the current program is inadequate, some reduction in marginal income tax rates would go a long way toward increasing labor effort in an economy already saturated with capital.

Germany's internal problems, together with the reluctance of its central bank to accommodate inflation, mean that real interest rates in Germany will remain high for some time and that countries with less inflationary environments would be ill-advised to peg their currencies to the deutsche mark if they wish to see economic growth during 1993. The British and the Italians have learned this lesson the hard way. If they come away from the experience determined to allow their currencies to float, while they reduce interest rates to levels commensurate with reduced inflation rates in their countries, then at least some of the European economies can begin to recover by the middle of 1993.

The American contribution to a more robust global economy in 1993 may take the form of another irony in American political and economic history. Just as a conservative Republican, Richard Nixon, was the one who initiated contact with China, a moderate Democrat, like Bill Clinton, may be required to initiate tax cuts on capital that help get the US economy growing again.[5]

These measures—European, Japanese, and American—by no means assured at this point, could help renew economic growth in 1993 without stimulating inflation. In the 1990s, a renewal of economic growth could help avoid the dangerous transition from disinflation to deflation, rather than serve as a harbinger of higher inflation, as it did during the 1970s and 1980s.

Notes

1. The term "salary man" refers to salaried white-collar workers in Japan.

2. The European Exchange Rate Mechanism was established in 1979 to stabilize exchange rates before the integration of European currencies and the introduction of the euro. Eurostat, "Glossary: Euro," December 19, 2014, https://ec.europa.eu/eurostat/statistics-explained/index.php?title=Glossary:Euro.

3. The euro replaced the deutsche mark in 2002 as the official currency of the Federal Republic of Germany.

4. The conflict in the Persian Gulf was precipitated by Iraqi President Saddam Hussein's invasion of Kuwait, a move to acquire its oil reserves and simultaneously cancel its debt to Kuwait. Condemned by the United Nations, the United States and its allies undertook military procedures to liberate Kuwait.

5. In 1997, President Bill Clinton signed into law a bill passed by the Republican Congress that cut the capital gains tax from 28 percent to 20 percent and reduced other taxes.

2

MONETARY POLICY

What Should Central Banks Do?

OCTOBER 1999

Leaders of central banks, Makin noted, often face vexing challenges as they try to guide their countries' monetary policy. Is their mission to keep inflation low? To prevent deflation? Prevent bubbles? Stop boom-and-bust cycles? In this piece, drawing on history, Makin explained what it means when some of these goals seem to be in conflict—and how bankers should react when facing new combinations of circumstances.

Writing in 1999, Makin was one of the few at the time who expressed concern about deflation. This era wound up being important in US economic history: The tech bubble was about to burst, which would soon lead to the 2001 recession and profoundly affect the economy for years. Undershooting, as opposed to overshooting, inflation targets has been central banks' main concern in most countries in the Organisation for Economic Co-operation and Development.

Wake a central banker out of a sound sleep and ask him what he should try to achieve with monetary policy. "Stable prices" would be the quick, instinctive answer from most. But the answer merely prompts harder questions.

"Do you mean zero inflation, which is what would be required for stable prices?" "Well," goes the usual response, "it is probably best to shoot for inflation between 0 and 2 percent, given measurement error and the danger of overshooting to negative inflation or deflation." Falling prices can be associated with liquidity traps, and those can cause real problems. A liquidity trap defines a situation wherein monetary policy can't affect aggregate demand. Deflation can get out of hand. The images of contemporary Japan, not to mention the Great Depression in the United States, flicker across the central banker's mind. But still, he will often add quickly that low inflation is the best target because low inflation is stable inflation, and stable inflation means the economy will function better because the messages that prices convey to households and businesses, as they allocate demand and resources, are easier to read when inflation is low.

One presses a little harder. "Is there anything else a central banker should do when setting monetary policy?" Now he is fully awake and starting to perspire. "Well, we do have to maintain orderly financial markets." "What do you mean by orderly financial markets?" "I mean financial markets that do not interfere with the functioning of the 'real' economy where goods and services are actually produced and exchanged, as distinct from the financial sector that prices claim on the assets of the real economy."

One presses harder still. "So central bankers should avoid asset market bubbles on the one hand and financial panic on the other. Of course, panics often follow bubbles, so avoiding bubbles is a good idea. But that is difficult, since a bubble is usually defined only by looking back after a financial panic has occurred."

The central banker is wide awake and looking especially uncomfortable. It's time for the kill. "What if stock prices or other asset prices keep going up without any inflation? If your main goal is to keep inflation low and stable, then low and stable inflation shouldn't trigger any response from the central bank. But if financial market bubbles, or suspected bubbles, can be followed by financial panics, shouldn't the central bank do something to deflate a bubble, even if there is no inflation?"

The central banker is anxiously searching for a way to end the conversation. The disconcerting fact is that central banks weren't founded primarily to fight inflation. Rather, they were established to maintain order in the financial sector and prevent financial panics or booms from harming the real sector of the economy where goods and services are produced. They have just adopted the objective of low inflation as a good way to achieve order in financial markets and, thereby, they hope, avoid bubbles and panics. But things have not always worked out as they hoped.

Central Banks in the 20th Century

In the United States, the financial panic of 1907 was barely staunched by the extraordinary efforts of JPMorgan. Fear that the country could not always count on such a fortuitous and timely presence launched the movement toward the formation of the Federal Reserve System, which came into being in 1913.

The financial sector, where stocks and bonds are traded and priced, exists to smooth out spending and earnings streams in a way that allows the swapping of purchasing power over time. A producer may wish to undertake a profitable expansion of capacity by making an outlay for capital equipment that cannot be funded out of current cash flow or assets. So he issues a claim to a lender whose current assets or cash flow exceed his current needs. The borrower must pay for the accommodation by the lender, usually with an interest rate on a bond or through some sharing of the prospective returns on capital by issuing to the lender an ownership claim on those returns.

The financial sector is both crucial and fickle. But central banks can't actually say that their main purpose is to prevent booms or panics in the financial sector that might interfere with the performance of the "real" economy—in part because financial bubbles and panics are quite unusual events. It would be awkward for central banks to spend long periods of time awaiting a boom or a panic—with which they might not be able to deal anyway. The record is not good. Look at the United States in 1929, the United Kingdom in 1989, and Japan in 1989–90.

So central banks adopted the idea that securing low inflation is a good proximate objective; properly undertaken, it should prevent booms or panics. Much of the postwar period has kept central banks busy just achieving the goal of low inflation. In Germany, the Bundesbank was created as a bulwark against a reemergence of the ruinous inflation of the 1920s. Right after World War II, the Federal Reserve maintained orderly functioning of the market for US government bonds, the stock of which had surged to over 100 percent of gross domestic product (GDP) during the war. When the Korean War threatened to overheat the economy during the 1950s, the Fed tightened monetary policy and ended the postwar policy of always accommodating government borrowing. Low and attendant stable inflation was maintained until the mid-1960s.

But by 1967 the Vietnam War and the Great Society in combination elevated total demand too rapidly, and a 13-year period of accelerating inflation began, punctuated by several oil crises, rising commodity prices—remember the silver-price bubble?[1]—and a massive boom in real estate. That resurgence of inflation, largely a result of inattention to the basic principles of monetary policy, gave the Federal Reserve and its two great chairmen—Paul Volcker (1979–87) and Alan Greenspan (1987–present)[2]—a solid proximate challenge: reduce inflation.

Other major central banks, particularly those in Germany, Japan, and the United Kingdom, fought similar battles with inflation after the mid-1960s, sometimes exceeding, sometimes falling short of the Fed's performance. But they focused broadly on the easily defined goal of bringing down inflation—and, broadly, they succeeded. The Bundesbank remained the most consistently successful opponent of inflation, to a degree that inflation faded as a major concern in Germany. By January 1999, the German people were—or perhaps one should say the German government was—prepared to let the Bundesbank cease to control German monetary policy and be replaced by a European Central Bank (ECB), proximately modeled after the Bundesbank.

The Bank of Japan tackled the first major postwar equity market and real estate bubble in 1989, when there was no inflation in Japan. The resulting collapse of equity and real estate values has erased about $18 trillion of Japanese wealth, or about four years of national income. Japan's problem in the aftermath of this catastrophe (in fairness, not attributable entirely to monetary policy) is now a tendency toward deflation—and the danger that monetary policy, thanks to a liquidity trap, cannot arrest it. Japan now confronts the reality that central banks are better at eradicating inflation than they are at eradicating deflation, though the latter is arguably more dangerous to the real and financial sectors of the economy.

After Low Inflation, What?

With inflation low and stable (or gone entirely), the major central banks, like parents who have worked hard to raise their now-grown children, are left with the tricky combination of a diverse set of new problems and no clear sense of how to address them. The Fed has little inflation to contend with, yet stock prices are 40 percent above where they normally would be, given current interest rates and earnings prospects. The Bank of Japan has pushed short-term interest rates virtually to zero, yet the only demand growth is coming from massive government spending programs that have lifted Japan's government debt to well over 100 percent of GDP. The new ECB has encountered no inflation; prices are rising about 1 percent annually in most of Europe. The ECB cut short-term interest rates by half a percent, to 2.5 percent, in April, while grousing, perhaps wistfully, about the need to be vigilant on inflation. The German economy, about a quarter of the new ECB's enlarged European responsibility, has yet to resume growth, while unemployment remains high and budget deficits threaten to rise.

It is worth asking how central banks have achieved, or overachieved, their goal of largely eliminating inflation. Most central banks operate by targeting an interest rate, usually a short-term interest rate that the central bank can manage by raising and lowering the rate at which it lends overnight to commercial banks in the system. If the inflation rate (or the expected inflation rate) is above the target level, the central bank raises interest rates, hoping to slow the growth of demand and, thereby, slow inflation. If, simultaneously, the economy is growing faster than the central bank's estimate of "capacity growth," the interest rate may be raised somewhat further, although the primary response of the central bank is to remove deviations of the inflation rate above or below its target level. That is the so-called Taylor rule, named after the Stanford University economist John Taylor.

Meanwhile, not much thought has been given, until recently, to the problem of inflation that is too low—deflation. That may be so because the process of bringing the inflation rate down from a high level—say 10 percent or more, to 1 or 2 percent—can take a long time. When inflation had reached double-digit levels in the United States by the end of the 1970s, the Federal Reserve raised interest rates sharply and simultaneously restricted the flow of liquidity available to the economy. By the end of 1982, the Fed had brought inflation down from a frightening 13.3 percent at the end of 1979 to a tame 3.8 percent, an incredible accomplishment. There was no stock market crash because the stock market had already been depressed by the disruptions associated with rising and more volatile inflation. The real estate market stopped rising and fell in some areas, although the associated balance-sheet problems were left to be addressed a decade later.

In general, central banks have been quite successful at reining in double-digit inflation insofar as they have been able to get it back into single digits, and then low single digits, without bursting financial bubbles or causing financial panics. The problems arise after the banks have achieved the low-inflation target and especially as financial markets celebrate the success of eliminating inflation.

When Central Bankers Meet

At the annual meeting of the central banks at Jackson Hole, Wyoming,[3] in late August, the matters of principal concern were, first, the experience of the Federal Reserve and other central banks in meeting their inflation targets and, second, determining what to do about financial market bubbles, panics, and deflation. The conference was aptly titled "New Challenges for Monetary Policy," and its nominal focus was on how to maintain the low inflation and stable prices that are now being enjoyed by the US and European economies. The discussion summarized a good deal of what we currently know about how central banks operate (or should operate) to achieve the proximate target of price stability; there was discussion as well of how to deal with deflation and a liquidity trap in Japan.

Despite the great proximate success in bringing down inflation rates, the persistent subtext at the conference was how responsive the Federal Reserve should be to the behavior of the US stock market. The formal papers argued that the Fed should concentrate on targeting expected inflation, not on responding directly to movements in the stock market. But two nagging questions remained: Is the US stock market a bubble? And what should the Fed do if the bubble bursts and stock prices drop sharply?

Bank of Japan Deputy Governor Yutaka Yamaguchi gave an eerie account of conditions in Japan during the late 1980s, just before the bursting of the Japanese equity and real estate bubbles that began in 1990. The conditions he described, such as zero inflation, rapid investment growth, and talk of a new era of unlimited prosperity, reminded the audience of current conditions in the US economy.

One of the papers at the conference suggested through modeling that, by 1989 to 1990, the Bank of Japan ought to have raised interest rates to 8 percent—well above the 4–6 percent rates then prevailing. The increase was warranted by the roaring expansion that was underway and the rapid rise in stock prices that had swelled the balance sheets of households and businesses and led to a borrowing boom. But Yamaguchi reminded a somewhat discomforted audience that it would have been difficult for the Bank of Japan to set short-term rates at 8 percent, given the zero inflation at the time and the primary stated goal of achieving low inflation.

Chairman Greenspan Speaks

In a discussion of the current possible "bubble" situation facing the Fed, one prominent economist at the conference suggested that, while targeting inflation was a good general policy rule for the Fed and other central banks to follow, the rule did not address what the Fed should do if the stock market begins to drop rapidly with no inflation in sight. Federal Reserve Chairman Greenspan responded to this comment with a remarkably candid statement about Fed policy and asset markets. The chairman maintained that the Fed would react to offset rapidly falling or rapidly rising asset market prices, but that if changes in asset prices were gradual, the Fed would not react and would continue to focus on changes in expected inflation when setting interest rates and monetary policy. In his statement, Chairman Greenspan was perhaps rationalizing the Fed's passive stance on the US stock market since his "irrational exuberance" comments in December 1996. But since then, the US stock market, measured by the S&P 500 index, has risen at an average annual rate of 25 percent—well above the average 14 percent annual growth rate since the start of the great US bull market in August 1982.

Before Greenspan's "irrational exuberance" comment, the US stock market had been rising at a 15 percent annual rate since the start of the current expansion early in 1991, quite close to the post-1982 average of

14 percent, though still robust. The acceleration thereafter to a 25 percent annual growth rate apparently has not struck the chairman as too rapid.

Clearly what Chairman Greenspan has in mind when he speaks of the need for the central bank to react to a rapid drop in equity prices is the impact of a sharp drop in the stock market—over, say, several days—that seriously damages the balance sheets of households and businesses and thereby threatens to cause liquidity to dry up as everyone rushes for the safety of short-term Treasury securities. (The events of October 1987 come to mind.) The chairman is harkening back to the fundamental reasons behind the founding of the Federal Reserve System in 1913: Disorderly financial markets are to be avoided, especially if their condition threatens the performance of the "real" economy.

But even the chairman's unusually explicit discussion of the Fed's possible reaction to changes in the US equity market left conference participants uneasy. If the central bank is prepared to allow asset prices to rise steadily at a brisk 25 percent pace, yet is still prepared to support the stock market if it falls (more) rapidly, it is hardly surprising that a "buy on the dips" mentality has emerged over the past several years and has resulted, in turn, in higher and higher equity prices.

The Fed's Looming Choices

The Fed, like the Bank of Japan a decade ago, may be forced by circumstances to increase interest rates steadily—and, in so doing, to test severely the resiliency of the stock market. Part of the reason for the rapid growth without inflation in the United States over the past 18 months has been an unusual desynchronization of the global business cycle. The Asian crisis, the Russian collapse and the associated Long-Term Capital Management crisis,[4] and the emergence of deflation in Japan after the ill-timed tax increase in spring 1997 have all produced a remarkably benign atmosphere within which the US investment-led recovery has been able to flourish without placing strains on real resources or generating inflation.

Now, with the emergence of the European Monetary Union[5]—and lower interest rates in Europe accompanied by somewhat higher growth—the reemergence of expansion in most of Asia, perhaps even in Japan (though this remains in question), and the unwinding of the Asian debt crisis, US inflation may not rise spectacularly but simply by enough to put heavy pressure on current valuation in US equity markets.

A Scenario for the Banks

What, then, *should* central banks do, now that inflation is low but the United States may be facing a stock market bubble and Japan may be facing more deflation? Probably, the Fed should keep inflation low by responding to the recent modest uptick in inflation with appropriate modest tightening. The Bank of Japan, simultaneously, needs more than ever to be easing aggressively by printing more money. That might stem the recent deflationary appreciation of the yen while helping offset the negative global liquidity effects of a modest Fed tightening.

In short, the Fed should tighten a little, and the Bank of Japan should ease a lot. And both should pray.

Notes

1. The silver bubble burst in 1980.
2. This article was written in 1999. Alan Greenspan served from 1987 to 2006.
3. The Federal Reserve Bank of Kansas City has hosted an annual economic symposium for central bankers, academic economists, financial economists, and other attendees in Jackson Hole, Wyoming, since 1981.
4. Discussed at length in Part II, "The Fed Didn't Cause the Stock Market Bubble (October 2002)."
5. The European Monetary Union refers to a set of policies that has facilitated the integration of the economies, a process that began in 1957. In addition to establishing a common central bank for Europe, it also resulted in the adoption of the euro.

3

INTEREST RATES

Understanding Interest Rates

SEPTEMBER 1999

Interest rates are integral to the banking industry, of course, but they also have a big ripple effect into the housing market, business investment and growth, and government finances. But how are interest rates set? That was a theme Makin returned to repeatedly—busting myths about the factors that affect interest rates and clarifying their origins. In this piece from 1999, Makin drew on history and real-world experience—from the economic upheaval of the late 1970s and into the early 1980s, when the federal funds rate peaked at nearly 20 percent, through the following two decades.

Interest-rate behavior is maddeningly difficult to understand, yet it is crucial to nearly every area of the economy, including households, businesses, and governments. What determines interest rates and where they are going? If you think you know the answer, think again. Events in the real world regularly demolish what many market participants take to be a profound understanding of interest-rate behavior.

Government Financial Activity Doesn't Set Rates

Whatever determines interest rates (the main subject of this essay); the level of government bond issue, or the lack thereof; and government deficits or surpluses are *not* key factors. Don't forget, of course, that while the

US fiscal picture in the early 1980s was deteriorating at what was termed "an alarming pace," US interest rates were falling steadily from their highs in the inflationary apex year of 1980.

Based on the broad experience of Japan in the late 1990s and the United States in the early 1980s, "deteriorating" fiscal positions of central governments, where debt and deficits rise rapidly relative to gross domestic product (GDP), can coincide with significant drops in interest rates. During the years since 1993, when Japan has put forward larger and larger spending programs and the budget deficit has exploded, interest rates have fallen from their highs of around 5 percent in 1994 to below 1 percent in the fall of 1998, and they have since risen to about 1.9 percent on signs of economic recovery in Japan. Meanwhile, in the early 1980s, while US bond yields were volatile, interest rates dropped from their highs of around 15 percent in 1980–81 to a far more benign 8 percent by 1986, amid cries of $300 billion budget deficits "as far as the eye can see."

There are two basic reasons why government finances have so little to do with determining interest rates. First, borrowing and lending activities by any single government, even a government as large as the US or Japanese government, are only a small portion of the total supply of the world's interest-rate instruments. And second, most of the movement in interest rates is determined by changes in inflation expectations, which, in turn, operate on perceptions about central bank actions to determine short-term interest rates.

Government is not the major borrower in the United States. Corporations are. While total government debt (federal and state) has fallen relative to GDP from a peak of about 65 percent in 1994 to around 57 percent today, corporate debt has risen from 38 percent of GDP in 1994 to over 42 percent today. And since corporate debt is larger than government debt, the stock of total nonfinancial debt to GDP has risen from about 63 percent of GDP in 1993–94 to about 68 percent today. Putting the same thing another way, the sum of US corporate and government debt has grown 5 percent faster than the economy (GDP) during a half decade of rapid GDP growth. Yet interest rates fell during most of that period.

Governments typically do not dominate the supply side of global debt markets, and supply in debt markets does not fully explain interest rates. We must also consider demand conditions in debt markets. Both borrowers and lenders, when they agree on the interest rate on a bond of a certain maturity—say, 10 years—are thinking about the conditions that will affect that bond's value. Those conditions are primarily the return on alternative assets and the expected rate of inflation, because that rate determines the purchasing power of the principal and the interest paid on the bond over its life.

The Fisher Equation and the Real Determinants of Rates

Two factors—the underlying real return on the bond, tied to the real return on alternative assets, and the expected rate of inflation—are the major determinants of the interest rate demanded by borrowers and lenders as they meet in the credit markets. With a large and heterogeneous supply of debt available in the market, on which the maturities range from overnight to upward of 30 years in the government sector and upward of 100 years in the corporate sector, it turns out that interest rates are far more sensitive to the prospect of inflation than they are to returns on alternative assets like equities, which, in turn, mirror the real returns from investing.

One of the best-known descriptions of the proximate determinants of interest rates is the so-called Fisher equation, named after the famous economist Irving Fisher, who theorized extensively about interest rates during the first third of the 1900s. The Fisher equation sets the market or "nominal" interest rate equal to the sum of a so-called real rate of return and anticipated inflation. For precision, the simple Fisher equation would need to be adjusted for taxes and possible risk premiums, but the Fisher equation in its simplest form is an adequate basis for understanding much of the behavior of interest rates.

Of course, governments can affect the behavior of interest rates in the terms represented by the Fisher equation to the extent that they can cause changes in expected inflation. The persistence of the belief that larger budget deficits lead to higher interest rates can be traced to cases in history in which large budget deficits that have pushed up government debt have forced governments to print money to pay the interest on debt rather than to raise the money by raising taxes. The case of Latin American countries during the inflationary 1980s (and 1990s) comes to mind, as does the case of Russia in the 1990s. Countries with large stocks of debt that cannot be financed by tax revenues have no alternative but to print money, thereby pushing up expected inflation and the rates at which people are willing to lend money denominated in a currency that is expected to depreciate against goods.

The most dramatic cases of high interest rates are associated with the hyperinflationary period of the early 1920s when the German government, faced with massive reparations payments to the victorious allies, had no alternative but to print money to pay its bills. Of course, by printing money it devalued the currency against goods and thereby caused people to hold less money. The stock of money that citizens are willing to hold constitutes the tax base in an environment where printing money is the means to raise revenue. The inflation rate is the tax rate. As the government pushes up the inflation rate or the tax rate on money holdings, individuals want to hold less and less, and so, to raise an equivalent amount of money, the government has to push up the inflation rate even faster. This is the route to hyperinflation that ends with individuals rushing to spend wheelbarrow loads of virtually worthless government notes before they depreciate even more rapidly in the next round of inflation.

Once a hyperinflation renders it worthless as a store of value, money can't serve as a medium of exchange because it can't store purchasing power over time and space. Such hyperinflationary episodes usually end in a barter economy, in which people elect to use alternative media— such as cigarettes or other portable, readily acceptable, fairly standard items—that can serve, however imperfectly, the requirements of a medium of exchange.

Although governments can affect interest rates by affecting the supply of debt instruments and inflationary expectations, it is better to view interest rates as part of a broad asset-pricing process: Borrowers and lenders come together to agree on an interest rate in the context of considerations about the return on other assets, including equities and real assets, the return on assets denominated in different currencies, and the outlook for inflation. The underlying, riskless real interest rate is determined by a broad spectrum of factors that set the rate at which it is *possible* to exchange purchasing power today for purchasing power tomorrow and, simultaneously, the rate at which individuals are *willing* to exchange purchasing power today for purchasing power tomorrow. In a world where the expected inflation is zero, the rate of exchange between current and future goods (the real interest rate) has typically averaged between 2 and 3 percent. Most variations in interest rates around that level have been determined by changes in inflationary expectations, but the rates may also be altered from time to time by higher expected returns on real investments.

By comparing the movements in market interest rates with the movements in interest rates on instruments that are indexed to inflation (and so protect the investor against inflation by a formula that increases the payment on the bond by the increase in inflation), it is possible to disentangle the movements in interest rates that are a consequence of changes in real returns and those that are attributable to changes in expected inflation.

The extraordinary behavior of Japanese interest rates is easier to understand with the help of the Fisher equation. Governments can also affect interest rates with deflationary policies. As the yen appreciated in the fall of 1998 while a global financial crisis emerged, rising Asian deflation and heavy government bond buying pushed Japanese long-term interest rates down to 0.7 percent. When they rose to 2.4 percent by February 1999, the Bank of Japan pushed short-term rates to zero, but the Japanese economy was so weak that deflation expectations remained intact. So rates fell back to 1.3 percent. Subsequent rate rises to 1.9 percent reflect expectations of recovery and reflation in Japan following a surge in first-quarter growth to an 8 percent annual rate.

Bear in mind that Japan has interest rates on 10-year notes below 2 percent—and presents one of the worst fiscal pictures for an industrial country since World War II. Here, again, government fiscal policy is not the determining factor for Japanese interest rates. It is, rather, the presence of few attractive investment opportunities (low real returns) in Japan, which is still burdened with huge excess capacity.

While the Fisher equation helps explain the past behavior of interest rates, it provides little help to those who must predict the rates' future behavior. The components of the Fisher equation—the real rate of return on assets alternative to bonds and the expected inflation rate—are not directly observable variables. Only by constructing a measure of expected inflation from the year-over-year consumer price index—or from a comparison between market rates and interest rates on indexed bonds—can we decompose interest-rate changes into changes in real rates and changes in expected inflation rates. This decomposition can be a useful guide in determining the path of the economy and, in some cases, providing feedback to policymakers, but it is not a forecasting tool.

The Federal Reserve can affect short-term interest rates by setting the federal funds rate, the rate at which it lends overnight to banks. Short-term rates determine the carrying costs of longer-term interest-rate instruments and indicate the Fed's assessment of where the economy is going. These factors, in turn, may affect people's calculations of the expected inflation rate or real return. For example, when the Federal Reserve Open Market Committee[1] raised interest rates by 25 basis points at its meeting late in June but indicated that it was "neutral" about the future path of the federal funds rate, the bond market rallied, probably on the surmise that the Fed expected inflation to ease.

Interest rates can also be a useful guide to an evolving economic scenario when viewed with other important economic variables, such as exchange rates and stock prices.

These adjustments of interest rates, equity prices, and the dollar will continue until markets discover a combination that is consistent with sustainable "clearing" of markets. If interest rates start to fall again and the stock market rises, US spending will rise, and the amount that the United States will have to borrow from the rest of the world will rise as well. If foreign economies grow strong, the terms on which the United States can undertake borrowing from abroad will worsen, and US interest rates will rise.[2]

We are, as always, brought back to the primary reality that a major determinant of US interest rates, irrespective of government announcements about buybacks and long-ranging discussions about surpluses as far as the eye can see, is expected inflation and its determinants, which include exchange rates, growth, and messages from the Fed. Markets will have to learn some new tricks at the mature stages of a supply-side or an investment-led recovery because they are more accustomed to pricing events associated with the end of a demand-side expansion.

Notes

1. The Federal Reserve Open Market Committee is comprised of members of the Fed's Board of Governors, the president of the Federal Reserve Bank of New York, and four of the remaining 11 Reserve Bank presidents. Meeting eight times a year, it is responsible for assessing economic and financial conditions, making decisions on monetary policy, and evaluating risks to its long-run goals of price stability and sustainable economic growth.

2. In fact, much of the developed world slipped into recession in the early 2000s, and US interest rates fell.

—⚍—

What Determines Interest Rates

JANUARY 2005

In this piece from 2005, Makin illustrates the principles of monetary policy by examining the market for US bonds and shows how, contrary to the arguments made by "deficit bemoaners," interest rates can stay low even as deficits rise. That's especially true, he writes, in the United States, which has a stable political and economic system that attracts foreign capital.

The article reflects Makin's view that people around the world were beginning to look for a means to store wealth—often in foreign countries such as the US. This had an effect on rates on US Treasury bills and the nation's financial health and stability. This view has been vindicated as US interest rates have remained at historical lows despite rapidly rising debt levels and large budget deficits, as demand for safe assets has continued to grow.

The pundits who have been predicting higher interest rates based on large US budget and current account deficits have some explaining to do. Beyond the fact that little systematic empirical evidence exists of a close link between deficits of any kind and interest rates, many high-profile commentators such as Robert Rubin and Pete Peterson, not to mention

PIMCO's Bill Gross,[1] have consistently warned that long-term interest rates would rise as America's budget and current account deficits rose. Actually, US long-term interest rates have been falling—from 4.8 percent in early June to 4.1 percent at year-end. Despite this stellar performance, Gross has even gone so far as to suggest that US government liabilities should be downgraded from their top rating of AAA to AA.

It is odd that the broad field of US deficit bemoaners, including a former Treasury secretary, an immensely successful investor, and the manager of the world's largest bond fund, have chosen to mislead the public on the major determinants of interest rates. To rationalize the awkward fact that interest rates on 10-year Treasury notes have gone down this year, the disaster that these pundits are calling for in the bond market has to be "looming" in the future. The consequences, it is assumed, are visible only to the prognosticator and somehow are invisible to the bond market. For the benefit of this distinguished group and the rest of us who need to have some idea where interest rates are going, I offer here a basic primer on the determinants of interest rates.

Proximate Determinants of Interest Rates

I shall focus primarily on a typical government security, the 10-year US note. The first thing to remember about a Treasury note is that it serves to store wealth over time. The interest rate on that note, which must compete with all other means of storing wealth, is roughly determined by the sum of the real (adjusted for inflation) interest rate and expected inflation over the life of the bond. The real interest rate on 10-year Treasury notes over the long run varies as real returns on alternative assets vary. If, other things equal, the stock market is rising as a reflection of rapidly rising investment opportunities, then the real return on stocks (an alternative financial asset to bonds) will rise, and, other things equal, the return on bonds will rise. It is no accident then that during the rapid run-up in the stock market from 1998 to 2000, the yield on 10-year Treasury notes rose from just above 4 percent to 6.5 percent. In effect, bonds had to compete with a rapidly rising stock market and therefore had to pay a higher real (inflation-adjusted) rate of return.

The other major determinant of interest rates on Treasury notes is the expected rate of inflation over the life of the Treasury instrument. Since the interest on US Treasury notes is paid in dollars, expected inflation measures the rate at which dollars depreciate against goods over the life of the bond. Therefore, an expectation of higher inflation, which will depreciate the value of interest payments and the principle on a 10-year Treasury note, means that an investor must earn a higher interest rate to compensate for the loss of purchasing power that higher expected inflation would entail. In effect, higher inflation makes a bond that is paying fixed interest a less attractive way to store wealth. Therefore, higher and more volatile inflation depresses bond prices while boosting the yield, which moves inversely with the price of a bond.

Other Determinants of Interest Rates

Another determinant of interest rates on 10-year Treasury notes (and all assets) is Federal Reserve interest-rate policy. Since the Fed can control short-term interest rates by setting the federal funds rate at which banks can borrow overnight, it also controls the rate at which an investor can borrow, using a string of short-term borrowing transactions, to finance the purchase and holding of a longer-term Treasury note.

It is especially interesting to see that the yield on 10-year Treasury notes has been flat to lower as US external deficits have risen. Another way of describing the rise in US external deficits is to suggest that the supply of dollars going into foreign exchange markets through the US current account deficit has increased to nearly $2 billion per day. For the US dollar to remain stable, foreign investors must purchase $2 billion a day. Purchases have probably fallen somewhat short of that figure over the past six months as the dollar has depreciated by about 10 percent.

Unique Appeal of US Government Bonds

US Treasury securities look even more attractive to foreign investors as a way to store wealth than they do to US domestic investors. Foreign official institutions that accumulate foreign exchange reserves need to store those accumulated reserves in a market that is highly liquid and safe. It may be necessary to buy or sell securities in multibillion dollar lots, and no other markets can accommodate, as well, transactions of such size that are simultaneously such a good store of value. The superiority of the Treasury market as a way to store wealth helps account for the low interest rates on Treasury securities.

There are other markets for government securities. Sovereign debt (the liabilities of governments) tends to represent a higher-quality credit than corporate debt does for the simple reason that sovereign debt in advanced industrial countries is backed by the government's power to tax to meet its liabilities. The catch has always been that governments may be tempted to levy an inflation tax and thereby depreciate the real value of their liabilities. Other governments are unable to collect taxes effectively and so are forced to use the inflation tax. But since the disastrous episode of the 1970s, when inflation and interest rates soared, governments and central banks that have a choice have learned that low and stable inflation contributes to higher growth by virtue of reducing the real cost of raising money in stable credit markets.

US government debt is a superior store of wealth that is in heavy demand globally.[2] It is a superior store of wealth because the United States government has a well-established tax system run by a notoriously efficient Internal Revenue Service able to raise the funds necessary to service the debts of the government, among other tasks. The "sovereign" portion of the attractiveness of US government debt is tied to the fact that the US is the world's preeminent military power, able to effect its goals globally with that power and able to finance the activities of its military by issuing debt. This has been amply demonstrated during the war in Iraq,[3] as the period of rising budget deficits tied to that war has produced no increase in US interest rates and no attendant increase in US inflation expectations. In fact, interest rates and inflation expectations have both declined over this period.

Alternative sovereign debt to US Treasury debt exists, but it is simply not as attractive. Euro-denominated debt is an amalgam of the liabilities of the many governments included in the European Monetary System. Outstanding euro debt may be euro-denominated liabilities of the governments of

Italy, France, or Germany—countries with different long-term reputations as stewards of stable purchasing power. Beyond that, most European governments shoulder retirement and health programs, the costs of which are far more onerous than even the costs being faced by similar US programs. Hence, the prospective borrowing needs of such governments and the temptation to pursue inflationary policies are perhaps more present in Europe than they are in the United States.

Looking Ahead

Alexander Hamilton, America's greatest Treasury secretary, observed during his effort to consolidate the debts of the new republic in 1781 that "a national debt, if it is not excessive, will be to us a national blessing."[4] Hamilton understood that sovereign governments perform a service by issuing large stocks of debt that pay predictable interest rates that, in turn, sustain stable purchasing power by virtue of stable prices. A national debt of $3.5 trillion, the current level, is not excessive for an $11 trillion economy like that of the United States.

The demand for US debt instruments will continue to rise worldwide. Investors in emerging markets—especially China where wealth is rising rapidly—are hungry for attractive ways to store wealth and are largely deprived of such outlets by controls on capital outflows. Chinese households that can only store wealth by earning 2.5 percent on deposits in an insolvent state banking system are forced to chase after back-alley investments through shady intermediaries raising money to fund highly risky real estate investments. They would be pleased to have the opportunity to own long-term claims on the US government paying a 4 percent rate of return. Indeed, the governments of many countries, including China, Japan, Korea, Taiwan, and other Asian nations, have found US Treasury securities to be a particularly attractive store of value and so have continued to buy them.

The appeal of US government liabilities as a store of value has contributed to the ease with which large US current account deficits are financed. It could be said that the US current account deficit has continued to rise because foreign governments and foreign investors will not permit it to fall. The United States exports superior claims on future goods or superior media for wealth storage, with US government securities among the best in this category. America's low national saving rate is as much a testimony to the attractiveness of US government liabilities as a store of value as it is a measure of US imprudence.

That said, conditions may change, and the terms on which foreigners are willing to finance a low US national saving rate may change. Indeed, if real returns on assets abroad were to rise, US real interest rates would rise, and the real return on US government securities would rise. The possibility that interest rates may rise in the future is another reason for the US government now to consider funding the transition to a sound Social Security system with long-term debt.

When all is said and done, it is the search for ways to store wealth that drives interest rates and not some hazy notion of unsustainable twin deficits. Markets clear every day. Today, everyone knows what the outlook is for US inflation, issuance of Treasury securities, and economic growth relative to the same variables in the rest of the world. It is somewhat ironic that the George W. Bush administration's plans to place its government programs for retirement and health care on an actuarially sound basis have been taken by critics as a reason for US interest rates to rise. Fortunately, based on the fundamentals of interest-rate determination, global markets know better.

Notes

1. Robert Rubin, a former banker at Goldman, Sachs & Co. in New York City, served as President Bill Clinton's secretary of the Treasury. Pete Peterson was an investment banker, and Bill Gross, founder of PIMCO, was an investor and fund manager.

2. See "Part II: Booms and Busts: A Journey Through Recent Economic History."

3. The Persian Gulf War (August 1990–February 1991), also known as Operation Desert Storm, was the outcome of the invasion of Kuwait by Iraq. A coalition of nations, led by the United States, joined together to oust Iraqi forces from Kuwait.

4. Alexander Hamilton (1755–1804), a Founding Father and delegate to the Constitutional Convention in 1987, served as the nation's first Treasury secretary from 1789 to 1795. All Things Hamilton, "National Debt and Credit Quotes," https://allthingshamilton.com/index.php/alexander-hamilton/alexander-hamilton-quotes/70-quotes/147-quotes-hamilton-and-debt.

4

INFLATION, DISINFLATION, AND DEFLATION

Worldwide Deflation?

SEPTEMBER 1992

Writing in 1992—with the country struggling to emerge from recession and in the middle of a consequential presidential election at the end of George H. W. Bush's presidency—Makin confronted what would be a persistent economic theme from the 1990s into today: consistently low inflation. A little more than a decade after the disastrous double-digit inflation of the Jimmy Carter years, Makin noted, "The major 'problem' facing the US economy and the world economy in 1992 is the simple fact that inflation has fallen further and faster than anyone intended or believed possible." In the intervening years, of course, inflation has never returned anywhere close to double digits, or even higher than 4 percent annually in the US—even in periods of strong economic growth. In this essay, Makin warned of the dangers of deflation and the decrease in prices and counseled that gradual disinflation, the lowering of the rate of price increases, is still the best policy.

The prolonged weakness of the US economy over the past three years, when annual growth has averaged just one-third of 1 percent, has given policymakers exactly what they said they wanted: lower inflation. By the broadest measure, the gross domestic product deflator,[1] inflation over the past year has been 2.4 percent, the lowest level since 1964, and it is heading lower.

36

The process of progressively falling inflation, called disinflation, is tricky. Like most virtuous achievements, lower inflation, while admirable, can turn into a disaster if it surprises too many people and goes too far too fast. Today's largely unanticipated disinflation after three decades of rising inflation shifts the burden of real losses from lenders to borrowers. As a nation of borrowers, the United States has experienced considerable pain as inflation has dropped from an expected average of about 5 percent to below 3 percent, while still heading lower. If disinflation becomes deflation, with prices actually falling, the pain will be magnified.

Everyone agreed that the double-digit inflation of the late 1970s and early 1980s had to be quelled before it led to ruinous inflation rates of 20 or 30 percent or higher, which would have wrecked the economy and eventually required a wrenching adjustment. By the mid-1980s, inflation had come down below 5 percent and seemed to be holding in a range between 4 and 5 percent.

The major "problem" facing the US economy and the world economy in 1992 is the simple fact that inflation has fallen further and faster than anyone intended or believed possible. The reasons for this unanticipated acceleration of global disinflation include the failure of policymakers and most companies, as well as households, to anticipate that US economic growth would remain very low while households and businesses are repairing their balance sheets in a disinflationary environment.

It is important for policymakers to remember that the best way out of the current disinflationary environment and the attendant risk of the disastrous self-reinforcing deflation is *not* to throw caution to the winds by returning to the inflation that has created so many problems over the past three decades while making disinflation necessary yet difficult to achieve. Gradual disinflation is still the best policy, but over the past year, the United States' inability to stimulate growth, coupled with Japan's and Germany's efforts to quell inflation, has pushed disinflation too close to deflation. If the line to deflation is crossed, the demand for cash jumps, while everyone sells goods to raise cash. Deflation begets more deflation, and the demand for goods collapses along with the output and employment.

The Japanese and German-European economies face more difficult problems. In Japan the collapse of asset prices and property values, long denied as a serious problem by the Japanese government, has proceeded too rapidly. In Europe, the problem is not Germany's fight against inflation but the stubborn insistence by other European countries that their currency should remain pegged to the deutsche mark, while the Germans fight inflation after the extraordinary shock of unification.

A worldwide depression requires a highly improbable combination of policy mistakes in all the major economies. Over the past several years, policymakers in the United States, Japan, and Germany have been preoccupied with their own problems. The feeble attempt to reduce US budget deficits in October 1990 came at exactly the wrong time, as the United States was slipping into a recession. Although the deficit-reduction measures were relatively small, amounting to about $40 billion per year, they were pro-cyclical in that they accentuated the weakness of the US economy. A $40 billion a year fiscal drag on the economy when in fact a $100 billion a year fiscal stimulus is called for constitutes a serious policy error. Had the right form of fiscal stimulus—tax changes to stimulate saving and investment—been applied late in 1990, economic growth conceivably would have been strong enough to create a lower 1992 budget deficit than the $325 billion that will occur. Ever since the sharp slowdown that followed the US fiscal policy mistake in the fall of 1990, the US economy has been unable to generate a self-sustaining recovery, largely because the needed balance-sheet adjustments have been underway.

Perhaps the biggest problem is that each major economic area—the United States, Germany and Europe, and Japan—has been operating under the assumption that recovery elsewhere would cushion its slowdown. One hears European forecasters constantly suggest a resumption of growth in 1993 contingent on higher growth in the United States and Japan. One hears the same predictions in the United States about Japan and Europe, while Japanese forecasters look forward to a resumption of export growth thanks to a resumption of US and European economic growth.

Notes

1. The gross domestic product deflator measures the changes in prices for the goods and services produced by a country over a specific period of time.

Should We Fear the Fear of Inflation?

APRIL 1996

Makin in 1996 looked at economic conditions around the world and saw the dangers of central banks "fearing inflation pressure where none exists." He highlighted instead the problem of hitting the zero-low bound and avoiding deflation. It did not take much longer than a decade for every major central bank to, in fact, face that problem. Within the next couple years, some big economies would indeed be in crisis, and Japan continued to struggle in the middle of its lost decade.

The fear of inflation is imparting a deflationary bias to the global economy that could result in a worldwide recession within a year. The extreme caution of the world's major central banks, not to mention jittery global bond markets, in the face of what they see as incipient inflationary pressure, is quite understandable when viewed in the context of the nearly disastrous inflation surges of the 1970s: From 1970 to 1975, Japan's inflation rate averaged 11.4 percent; Germany's, 6.1 percent; America's, 6.7 percent; and Britain's, 13 percent. By 1980, America's inflation rate had reached 13.5 percent, while the rate for Japan was still 7.8 percent and the rate for the United Kingdom a near catastrophic 18 percent.

But just as complacency about inflation is a necessary and often sufficient condition for it to accelerate, as it did in the 1970s, so too a fear of inflation pressure where none exists is a necessary and sufficient condition for disinflation to become deflation, as it has in Japan in the 1990s.

Accompanying what eventually may come to be seen, with the benefit of hindsight, as a dangerous deflationary bias to monetary and fiscal policy will be low growth, rising burdens of debt accumulated when inflation was expected to rise or at least hold steady, and persistently falling interest rates. The disinflationary process can and will continue until short-term interest rates controlled by central banks are driven virtually to zero while direct demand stimulation with large doses of fiscal stimulus is required, in addition to the low interest rates simply to arrest the chronic slowing of the economy.

How Low Should Inflation Go?

OCTOBER 1996

See if this sounds familiar: Several years into a long expansion, the economy continues to grow faster than expected, with unemployment persistently low. Yet inflation also clocks in lower than expected. That could describe the late 2010s— but it is also the situation Makin found in 1996 when he wrote, "Inflation rates are extraordinarily low by the standards of the past two decades." That economic landscape put the Federal Reserve in an "uncomfortable situation," Makin said, likening it to a "fire department in a town where there have not been any fires for several years." He laid out a plan and argued against a "passive approach to inflation control," lest the Fed set rates too low and create a bubble. The piece shows Makin noting concern about inflation and deflation even in an expansionary period.

In 1981 polls, more than 70 percent of Americans called inflation America's most important problem. The public's obsession with inflation continued as Ronald Reagan began his first term as president, even after inflation dropped below 10 percent, ending a two-year surge into double digits. By 1983, the concern over inflation had collapsed; only about 10 percent of Americans considered inflation the nation's top problem, even though actual inflation was running close to 5 percent. Today, with inflation below 3 percent for several years, virtually no one views inflation as the nation's number one problem, and few regard it as a serious problem. Some businessmen and economists suggest that pushing inflation still lower could damage the economy.

With concern about inflation in the United States either nonexistent or deemed hostile to further downward pressure on inflation, and with inflation rates in many other countries running even below US rates, the Federal Reserve Bank of Kansas City convened its annual conference of central bankers at Jackson Hole, Wyoming, on the eve of Labor Day weekend to consider the goal of achieving price stability. By the midpoint of the conference, clearly the real topic under consideration was: Having achieved price stability, what do we do now?

With inflation in double digits, the urgency of avoiding runaway inflation with the attendant disruption to households and businesses is well-
known. Everyone realizes that normal economic decision-making is badly
distorted with inflation at 10 percent and heading higher. Ample evidence
documents the widespread view that double-digit inflation is accompanied
by lower-than-average growth rates. A high degree of volatility in relative
prices lowers growth rates and makes rational economic decisions difficult.
Investors seeking a safe place to store purchasing power in an inflationary environment may turn to less productive forms of investment, which
penalizes the growth rate. With taxes levied on current dollar amounts, the
economic costs intrinsic in the collection of taxes are magnified. Further,
government revenues tend to surge along with inflation, providing Congress and state legislatures with extra revenues, which are usually spent
rather than employed to reduce taxes or accumulated deficits.

The United States is not alone in confronting the opposite side of the
problem of accelerating inflation. Global disinflation has been the rule for
several years. As a result, inflation rates are extraordinarily low by the standards of the past two decades. As measured by the consumer price index,
inflation rates in virtually all industrial countries are in the 0–3 percent
range considered safe by most central bankers, with some rates actually
below that range.

Against this backdrop of global disinflation, widespread hesitancy about
the appropriate next step for monetary policy in most countries is unsur-
prising. In the United States and elsewhere, the decision is complicated
by the tendency of the consumer price index to produce a measure of
inflation somewhat above actual inflation. It is difficult to measure quality
improvements that lower real prices and difficult to incorporate rational
consumer behavior.[1]

The ever-present upward bias in official measures of inflation, varying
from country to country, is relevant to policy when actual inflation rates
approach targets of 3 percent or less. At that time, attempting to push
inflation down further risks an episode of deflation, such as appeared in
Japan, which most policymakers wish to avoid. Once present, deflationary momentum can be difficult to break, as Japanese policymakers have
discovered over the past year. Deflation can create transitional unemployment problems if there is widespread reluctance to reduce wages. Further,

if deflation continues long enough and accelerates, a central bank cannot stimulate the economy by lowering real interest rates. Since real interest rates are nominal or market interest rates minus inflation, an inflation rate of –2.0 percent means that a low official interest rate of 0.5 percent, like that in Japan, actually results in a 2.5 percent real interest rate, a level that may be higher than desired in a deflationary environment.

The Federal Reserve's Dilemma

With inflation in the comfort zone, below 3 percent, and an economic recovery more than halfway through its sixth year, the Federal Reserve finds itself in an uncomfortable situation. The economy is growing at a year-over-year rate close to 3 percent—well above the central bank's assessment of long-run growth potential—and the unemployment rate is approaching 5.0 percent, or half a percentage below the Fed's last estimate of the minimum noninflationary unemployment rate. As the unemployment rate has moved steadily down, wage pressure has begun to pick up.

The upward pressure on wages has not yet produced an acceleration in inflation as measured by either the producer or the consumer price index.

Goods inflation is actually slowing quite dramatically, but the picture is exactly the opposite for services. Services inflation has accelerated moderately to a 3.5 percent annualized rate over the past three months. The faster inflation rate for services is consistent with the idea that global competition is holding down the inflation rate for goods. Typically, services are not internationally traded. It may be cheaper to have dry cleaning done in Canada exclusive of transportation costs, but a trip to Toronto to realize the "savings" is hardly worthwhile.

With no general concern that inflation is a problem and no convincing evidence in goods markets that inflation is accelerating, even if the Fed is convinced that inflation is about to pick up, how can the system take the early anti-inflation measures needed to preempt the emergence of inflation pressure? If the Fed cites rising wages as the reason for tightening monetary policy by raising short-term interest rates, it appears to be against higher wages for working Americans. Nor can the Fed complain about a low unemployment rate, even though such a rate has typically signaled higher inflation in the future. These conflicts with a preemptive approach to avoiding inflation are accentuated in a presidential election year.

If the Fed tightens preemptively, it runs two risks. First, by seeming to be against higher wages and fuller employment, the Federal Reserve runs the risk of losing significant political support, which eventually could translate into congressional efforts to rein in the Fed's independence. Second, as is always possible, if the Fed's forecast is wrong and the economy is already slowing down on its own, then the slowdown in the economy, and with it higher unemployment and slower growth, will be attributed to premature Fed tightening. Even if the system does tighten policy and thereby avoids inflation, this counterfactual "success" will not be observable, and therefore the Fed will get no credit for heading off inflation. The Federal Reserve's inflation-fighting risk-reward trade-off is skewed against it.

The Federal Reserve is currently a fire department in a town where there have not been any fires for several years. People begin to ask if they really need a fire department, and they are annoyed by the fire department's efforts at fire prevention. The firemen begin to wish for a few fires, not for their own sake but for the sake of making people realize that a fire department is a necessary and useful institution. Probably in this supply-side recovery, where inflation is unusually quiescent and where the level of inflation has actually reached a target range long sought by the Fed, the Fed must await the appearance of obvious and significant inflationary pressures before taking decisive action to raise short-term interest rates and thereby quell those inflationary pressures.

But there are well-known problems associated with the passive approach to inflation control. First, by the time inflation pressure actually shows up in goods prices, having begun with cost pressures from wages and prices of services, inflation momentum has become well-established. Producers do not raise prices unless they think consumers will pay higher prices. Consumers do not pay higher prices today unless they expect prices to rise still more. In short, actual inflation means that upward inflation momentum is already present. If the Fed begins to control inflation after it is already underway, the "price" of slowing inflation pressures may be an interest-rate increase of 2 or 3 percentage points instead of the preemptive increase of less than 1 percentage point that can slow inflation pressure before significant inflation momentum builds.

The second problem with delayed attention to inflation pressure is that, in effect, the Federal Reserve is holding interest rates artificially low. A combination of low interest rates, continued growth of earnings, and ample liquidity fuels higher and higher prices in financial markets, especially in stock markets.

The worst outcome from the Fed standpoint is a financial market bubble and a sharp acceleration of inflation pressure, both caused by delayed tightening. The financial market bubble, by increasing the feeling of well-being and the wealth of consumers, increases the probability that prices will begin to rise more rapidly as demand rises more rapidly than supply.[2]

The Fed is playing a dangerous game by delaying a response to the inflation pressure being foretold by tightening labor markets. Perhaps the Federal Reserve will try to minimize the risks by opting for a modest pre-emptive tightening.

Risks to the International Economy

The global disinflationary pressure that has emerged over the past several years complicates the monetary policy problem facing the Fed.

If US growth slows down toward the end of 1996, the fourth-quarter pace of official dollar buying may exceed even the first quarter's $50 billion–plus pace. The result will be a much-needed reduction in global deflationary pressure, thanks to what may seem a paradoxically stronger dollar as US growth slows down. The alternative, a slowing US economy and a weaker US dollar, would wreck plans for European monetary union in 1999 and would push Japan back into recession.

Perhaps the need outside the United States for more reflation pressure, combined with a need inside the United States for a gentle tap on the monetary brakes, will be a happy coincidence. Unfortunately, no such need was publicly acknowledged at the Jackson Hole gathering of central bankers. Maybe, as they think back on their discussions in Wyoming, they will realize what an attractive opportunity they have to rebalance the global economy.

Notes

1. Economists have different ways to measure inflation, none of them perfect. The consumer price index is the main measure, but economists also examine other data, including the producer price index and the gross domestic product deflator, to receive a fuller picture.

2. Although writing in 1996, Makin foresaw the "financial market bubble" that would lead to the tech crash just a few years later.

—w—

Confronting the Great Recession

MARCH 2009

Writing during the 2008–09 financial crisis, Makin laid out how central banks should respond, pointing out, "The most compelling message to emerge from the experiences in post-bubble economies centers on the need to avoid deflation and intensifying deflation expectations." Rather than risk deflation, Makin wrote, the Fed needed to take a clear stand indicating its preference for higher rates of inflation—which would help the world avoid the experiences of the Great Depression and Japan's lost decade. "Most of the lessons from past crises," he wrote, "arise from painful demonstrations of what not to do in a crisis." He also placed the world's economy in 2009 in historical context, finding that the interconnectedness of the world through trade and technology had created a circumstance in which "there is no place to hide in the global economic financial system."

As the global financial and economic crisis has grown increasingly dire—the deterioration just since the November US election is breathtaking—market participants and policymakers alike have looked to three past crisis models as part of an intensifying search for ways out of the current crisis. First, the Great Depression of the 1930s is being examined ever more closely for possible lessons now that commentators have moved past an understandable reluctance to mention that experience as relevant to today's situation. Second, the Scandinavian financial crisis of the early 1990s,[1] which included a proactive move toward bank nationalization by the Swedish government, is also widely discussed. Finally, many allusions have been made to the disquieting parallels between today's US experience and that of Japan during its "lost decade" (1991–2001) of recession and deflation, especially after 1998.

Most of the lessons from past crises arise from painful demonstrations of what not to do in a crisis. The most compelling message to emerge from the experiences in post-bubble economies centers on the need to avoid deflation and intensifying deflation expectations. Those are two necessary conditions for recovery. It is disconcerting that an anti-deflation message has not yet been transmitted clearly by central banks as the weakness in the global economy has worsened sharply over the past several months and demand has collapsed relative even to rapidly falling output. The awkward but compelling conclusion from post-bubble periods is this: It is better to risk a period of higher inflation than it is to risk an episode of self-reinforcing deflation.

Lessons: Encouraging and Disquieting

A careful examination of each of these crisis episodes is at once informative and disquieting in terms of possible lessons about causes and cures for the current global panic. The Scandinavian and Japanese crises resulted from the bursting of asset bubbles, which rendered banking systems dysfunctional. However, they were not nearly as difficult to manage as the current global financial and economic crisis insofar as they were not as broad in scope. In contrast, the Great Depression engulfed Western Europe and America but, again, was somewhat more contained insofar as it did not include, to nearly the degree that today's crisis does, the emerging markets of Latin America, Eastern Europe, and Asia. Asia here includes, of course, what has been a newly industrialized, super-growth engine: China. Indeed, even in the current crisis, the emerging markets group was, until only a few months ago, thought to be "de-linked" from the intensifying problems of the industrial world that are tied to the collapse of housing values and the resultant collapse of consumption and bank balance sheets.

But now, in 2009, there is no place to hide in the global economic financial system. The current crisis may not yet be as intense as the Great Depression (output and prices have not fallen by a third as they did in the early 1930s in the United States), but the crisis is more widespread and may well, because of its ubiquity, rapidly intensify. Beyond that, in this crisis, asset prices have already fallen by enough to erase more than a third of global wealth. US home prices have dropped by at least a cumulative 25 percent and appear headed to descend 20 percent further. Major US equity markets have dropped by more than 50 percent. Arguably, these huge wealth losses are more damaging to the global economy than the sharp drop in output and goods prices that occurred during the early years of the Great Depression. Sharp wealth losses prolong and intensify the increases in desired saving that depress demand growth and intensify pressure for more deflation.

Lessons from Sweden and Japan

Despite their relatively narrow scope in the global system, the Swedish and Japanese crises are worth examining for the lessons they provide to those attempting to contain the current crisis. Sweden's approach to its financial crisis was transparent, preemptive, and systematic. Sweden began its program with a "bank support guarantee" approved by its parliament, the Riksdag, in December 1992 after a year of sharp economic contraction and sharply falling bank shares. All but the shareholders of banks were protected, no upper limit on state support was set, and the efforts by the Swedes were advertised globally. The absence of an upper limit placed the Swedish state in the position of guaranteeing the solvency of the banks that it was going to either keep in operation or stabilize through interim nationalization.

The Swedish effort laudably emphasized openness regarding the extent of the problems the banks faced. Rather than allowing banks to defer recognition of market losses, steps were taken to report all expected losses and assign realistic values to real estate and other assets with the help of a valuation board.

The Swedish effort recognized that bank capital losses needed to be covered before banks could move forward as viable entities. State support of the banks during the crisis was undertaken to avoid the forced sale of assets.

Sweden arguably faced a more manageable situation, in terms of its scope, than the present one. But the key elements of its government's policy—transparency, proactiveness, and systematic application—are the opposite of the approach taken, so far, by American policymakers to the current crisis. "Opaque," "ad hoc," and "unsystematic" accurately describe the response thus far to the crisis that emerged openly in August 2007. This was typified by the unfortunate February 10 presentation of a financial rescue package by Treasury Secretary Timothy Geithner. That said, the same criticism applies as well to all the G7 countries, whose governments have spent much of the past 18 months first denying that a crisis existed and then promulgating ad hoc responses that have been insufficient to contain it.

It would be misleading to claim that Sweden's program for dealing with its banks constituted, by itself, a solution to Sweden's economic and financial crisis. As a relatively small, open economy, Sweden could reflate and stimulate demand for its output aggressively by allowing its currency to float. The resulting rapid depreciation of the krona against the deutsche mark by 30 percent, paired with the establishment of a viable Swedish banking system, formed a policy combination sufficient to reignite Swedish growth and move most of its banks into private hands.

Sweden's status as a small, open economy—not one engulfed in a global crisis of the scale we are seeing in 2009—enabled it to undertake the reflationary, sharp, and sudden currency depreciation that helped return the country to growth.

Japan's experience during its "lost decade," and more recently during the current crisis, provides powerful evidence of the dangers of allowing deflation to emerge and persist. Japanese officials exacerbated their country's woes by exaggerating the scale of fiscal policy packages designed to stimulate the economy while also failing to acknowledge and address the reality of a dysfunctional banking system.

Japan languished in recession until the world economic recovery after 2002 because it failed to recognize the extreme dangers arising from a by-product of persistent deflation and negative nominal gross domestic product (GDP) growth.

Negative year-over-year nominal GDP growth is virtually unknown in the postwar period outside Japan, save for two brief episodes in the United States during 1954 and 1958 that were tied to external factors. Persistently negative nominal GDP growth tied to a global economic slowdown and intensifying deflation is a phenomenon not seen globally since the Great Depression. In Japan, year-over-year nominal GDP growth fell to –2 percent during 1998 and remained negative for more than two years after the poorly timed 1997 consumption tax increase, the Asian crisis, and poor implementation of stimulus and financial rescue packages.

With the benefit of hindsight, it is probably fair to say that Japan did everything wrong in dealing with a post-bubble financial and economic collapse. Poorly designed fiscal stimulus packages with inflated numbers attached; opaque, reactive, and haphazard measures to try to restore a functional banking system; and a failure, proactively, to address an emerging deflation all doomed Japan for more than a decade of low growth and massive wealth loss. For its part, the Bank of Japan eventually cut interest rates to zero by 2001, but it did so only reluctantly, with announcements couched in promises that the minute prices started to rise again, it would abruptly reverse the low rates and easier liquidity conditions.

The Importance of Avoiding Deflation

The lessons derived from the post-bubble crises during the Great Depression and later in Sweden and Japan are many, but perhaps the most important one is the demonstrable need for a reflationary shock to end deflationary expectations and ensure positive, nominal GDP growth. The fundamental reason that a reflationary shock is needed in a post-bubble period is tied to the need to reduce the real burden of debt. As bubbles inflate, households and firms assume more and more debt with interest rates fixed largely in nominal terms.

Because the United States is not on a gold standard, it does not have the option to devalue the dollar against gold and thereby provide a sharp reflationary thrust to US and global recovery efforts. The devaluation of any major currency today simply exports deflationary pressure to other currency areas where, say, a weaker dollar means a stronger local currency.

There is a clear lesson from the post-bubble experiences during the past 75 years. Central banks must clearly articulate policy measures that will arrest deflation and the attendant disastrous collapse in nominal GDP. Deflation is an unstable process because as prices fall and nominal GDP shrinks, the real burden of debts rises, financial institutions' viability is severely impaired or destroyed, consumption and investment collapse, employment falls, and another round of further deflation continues the cycle.

To put it simply, it is a more attractive policy alternative to risk some inflation than to allow deflation to intensify. The Federal Reserve has begun to indicate its concern about deflation by suggesting that it wishes to avoid an inflation rate that is below that consistent with stable growth of output. That is a step in the right direction, but it is not explicit enough. Central banks need to articulate clearly their determination to assure that next year's price level will be higher than this year's. That way, the anticipated real burden of debt does not rise, and households do not reduce consumption even more in anticipation of continued falling prices.

The most important lesson about targeting a higher price level and the policy implications that arise therefrom comes from Japan's experience. Throughout a period of persistent deflation, wealth destruction, and negative growth, the Bank of Japan was never willing to articulate a target of above-normal inflation to mitigate the real burden of debt and quell behavior tied to a broadening expectation of falling prices.

The European Central Bank continues to express its concern about incipient inflation and will probably do so until actual deflation engulfs Europe and creates a quagmire even worse than the one that is already emerging. The European currency system will not survive a period of persistent deflation.

Leadership on the reflationary front will have to be exercised by the US Federal Reserve. The Fed needs to announce clearly its intention to prevent deflation by declaring a future price-level target that implies an inflation rate averaging between 2 and 3 percent per year until the real burden of debt and the attendant contractionary behavior in the economy begin to atrophy.

The rule that applies to financial rescues—be transparent, proactive, and systematic—also applies to central bank policy when it comes to arresting a move toward highly damaging deflation.

Notes

1. The Scandinavian financial crisis of the early 1990s was triggered by a burst housing bubble, widespread unemployment, and the near-collapse of the banking system.

5

FISCAL POLICY

Fiscal Orthodoxy and the Risk of Depression

NOVEMBER 1992

Just before the 1992 presidential election, Makin pondered how policymakers should react to the then-weak economy. Both President George H. W. Bush and challenger Bill Clinton had proposed budgets that drew on what Makin called "fiscal orthodoxy"—a mistaken belief that combating budget deficits is always wise policy, regardless of whether economic growth and inflation are rising or falling. In a time of economic stagnation, Makin said, such policies would be "self-defeating" and result in economic catastrophe. The "lethal combination of monetary mismanagement and fiscal orthodoxy" would be akin to the policy errors of the 1930s. "Apparently," he wrote, "two generations is more than a sufficient period to forget important economic principles." Both major parties seem unconcerned about deficits nowadays. But at the time, Makin used the circumstances as a chance to explain important fiscal lessons, and he foresaw the policy error in Clinton's 1993 tax increases that aimed to lower the deficit but did nothing for economic growth.

Both inflation and economic growth have been consistently lower than forecast in industrial countries in recent months. One reason is that forecasters have failed to appreciate how accelerating, unanticipated disinflation magnifies debt burdens, which in turn suppress consumer spending and economic growth. But a far more important reason is that, as the major industrial economies have grown weaker, their governments have weakened them further by moving toward tighter fiscal policy instead of stimulating tax cuts. Fiscal orthodoxy—the notion that reducing budget deficits is always a good idea, even when both economic growth and inflation are falling more rapidly than expected—is remarkably strong two generations after John Maynard Keynes' *The General Theory of Employment, Interest, and Money* warned against the dangers of just such orthodoxy.[1]

Dangers of Orthodoxy

The basic lesson of Keynes' *The General Theory* was that government deficits and surpluses should be used "countercyclically" to smooth out slowdowns and booms in the private economy. This lesson was perverted by policymakers in the 1960s and 1970s who invoked Keynes' academic prestige for the very different purpose of stimulating economic growth through constant, government-induced increases in demand. Steady overstimulation eventually produced accelerating inflation in the 1970s—which many laymen and policymakers, and even some economists, took as an invalidation of Keynesian economics.

The error has now come full circle: The link between Keynesianism and accelerating inflation, now presumed to be the lesson of a generation of practical experience, has left today's policymakers strongly inclined to follow deflationary fiscal policies in an era of accelerating disinflation. If these policies are pursued aggressively, they will cause a global depression. But a realization of the error and a resuscitation of the genuine message of *The General Theory* could prevent such a depression.

An important test of the strength of fiscal orthodoxy will follow Bill Clinton's likely election as president of the United States on November 3. The problem facing the new American president is a difficult one. In the aftermath of the collapse of the European Exchange Rate Mechanism,[2] the "weak" governments that were forced to devalue have attempted to restore their "strength" by pledging additional fiscal stringency. Nowhere is this tendency more pronounced than in England. John Major and Norman Lamont, who have driven their economy into depression by pegging sterling to the deutsche mark at an overvalued exchange rate, now promise to compound the error by pushing for bigger cuts in government spending when they should be pushing for tax cuts.[3]

The British are not alone. Italian, Spanish, and Scandinavian governments are also pressing for tighter fiscal policies. Tighter fiscal policy might be appropriate only in Germany, but it seems unattainable there. Meanwhile, the determination of the French to continue a fixed parity with the deutsche mark has forced them to tighten fiscal policy, just as a stronger franc has further reduced the prospect for growth because of a bleaker outlook for growing exports.

Even in Japan, fiscal orthodoxy holds sway in a way that probably will prolong its economic slowdown.

A broad trend at work in the industrial world today accounts for the steady downward revision in forecasts for growth. De facto monetary stringency in heavily indebted economies like the United States, where the Federal Reserve has been unable to induce money growth, and conscious monetary stringency in Europe, where many currencies have been pegged at overvalued levels relative to the deutsche mark, have caused economies to slow and budget deficits to swell as tax revenues have fallen with incomes.

So far, the response of most governments has been to propose still tighter fiscal policies to deal with the shortfall in revenues. If those policies are put into effect, while monetary stringency continues, economic growth and tax revenues will fall further, and deficits will rise even further. If this self-defeating process is continually repeated, the world economy will fall victim to the lethal combination of monetary mismanagement and fiscal orthodoxy in the 1990s just as it did during the 1930s. Apparently, two generations is more than a sufficient period to forget important economic principles.

Budget Proposals

Both George H. W. Bush and Bill Clinton have put forward budget proposals of strong fiscal orthodoxy. The Bush proposal tries to stimulate the economy, without increasing budget deficits, by cutting taxes and spending. The Clinton proposal tries to stimulate the economy, without significantly raising the budget deficit, by raising taxes and spending. Of the two, the Bush approach would probably be marginally better, because of its modest reduction in the deadweight loss from tax collections. But what is really needed is an immediate tax cut to stimulate investment and spending.

The Outlook for Clinton's Fiscal Policy

When President Clinton contemplates the economic outlook in the United States, he will face a basic choice on fiscal policy. Some of his advisers, in the fiscal orthodoxy camp, who might include Paul Volcker as secretary of the Treasury, would point out the necessity of instituting a long-term program of deficit reduction. To do so will require spending-growth caps on popular Social Security and government health programs, which have remained untouched in all the deficit-reduction battles over the past 10 years. To contemplate such cuts, the Democrats, who will by then control Congress and the presidency, will demand tax increases, initially labeled as higher taxes on the rich, which ultimately will result in higher taxes on everybody in the upper half of the income spectrum.

Immediate implementation of such fiscal orthodoxy, leaving the negative fiscal drag already present in the fiscal year (FY) 1993 budget and increasing the drag for budgets from FY1994 forward, would probably continue the 1–1.5 percent growth path, which cannot generate job growth. Needless to say, the new president would not have fulfilled his mandate to "get the economy moving again." Reinforcement of the view that Democrats cannot manage the economy could preordain the election of a Republican president in 1996.

With a Democratic Congress, a new Democratic president has a better chance of threading the fiscal labyrinth than President Bush had. Despite the tendency of American financial markets to anticipate a fiscal stimulus package—as US long-term interest rates have risen modestly over the past several weeks—the outcome of the battle between the fiscal liberals and the orthodox fiscal camp is far from certain. And the path of the US economy over the next year is also difficult to discern until the new administration's fiscal policy is settled.

Federal Reserve Policy

By not easing in the face of weak economic numbers, Alan Greenspan and his colleagues have acknowledged that fiscal stimulus may be necessary to get the US economy moving. That possibility suggests that the Fed should hold short-term interest rates exactly where they are. Then, if the Clinton administration proposes fiscal stimulus, the prospect of a faster-growing United States against the prospect of a further slowdown in European growth will create a stronger dollar. A stronger dollar will indicate and accentuate the attraction for capital to flow to the United States, where economic recovery is in prospect, and out of Europe, where economic slowdown is exacerbated by tight fiscal policy.

If the US fiscal stimulus package is well designed, say, to include investment tax credits to stimulate investment spending along with credible measures to reduce the budget deficit after 1994, the dollar rally could rival the one of 1982–84. With the US dollar currently undervalued by approximately 25 percent, even a move back to normal valuation suggested by calculations of purchasing power parity would imply a sharp appreciation of the dollar as a surge of capital inflows to the United States seeks the investment opportunities emerging in the world's only growing industrial economy.

Under ideal circumstances, and provided that the Fed maintains its monetary policy, a well-designed program of fiscal stimulus could result in a flatter US yield curve, even with the lower long-term US rates that the Fed has vainly sought by pushing down short-term rates. At the least, a flatter US yield curve might induce US banks to return to the business of making loans—and end the business of borrowing money in the overnight market and then lending only to the federal government for a riskless 200-basis-point spread.

The next several months will be fascinating ones for global economic trends. The strength of fiscal orthodoxy will be played off against the fear of an accelerating global economic slowdown. The outlook for the global economy remains highly uncertain.

Notes

1. An English macro-economist, John Maynard Keynes wrote *The General Theory of Employment, Interest, and Money* in 1936. Among other things, the book addressed the role of government policy in ending recessions. John Maynard Keynes, *The General Theory of Employment, Interest, and Money* (London: Palgrave Macmillan, 1936).

2. The European Exchange Rate Mechanism suffered when Britain left it in 1992, but it remained in place until 1999, when it was replaced by a new mechanism to ease governments into the euro.

3. John Major, a Conservative, served as British prime minister from 1990 to 1997. Norman Lamont, also a Conservative, served under him as chancellor of the exchequer from 1990 to 1993.

—⁊⁊⁊—

The Mythical Benefits of Debt Reduction

SEPTEMBER 2000

By the end of the 1990s, the US had experienced a prolonged economic boom. Pro-growth fiscal policies and the emergence of technology as an economic force had led to higher economic growth—and in turn, budget surpluses. This posed a different problem from earlier years: what to do with all the money.

Makin, writing in late 2000, took the occasion to clarify the cause and effect between lower deficits and growth: "It is higher growth that has led to lower debt and deficit levels, not lower debt and deficit levels that have led to higher growth." At the time, projections of future government surpluses were leading some pundits to propose paying off the national debt—which Makin called a "preposterous idea." He correctly foresaw increased government spending, and he expanded on the reasons for this advice: "Fiscal policy supports the economy best when government revenues are collected in a way least harmful to the economy and are allocated efficiently among essential government programs."

Contrary to widespread claims, there is no theoretical or empirical support for the enduring notion that either lower budget deficits or surpluses that lead to government debt reduction benefit the economy. Deficit and debt reduction require higher taxes or lower government spending than would prevail under rising or stable deficits. Neither measure, especially not higher taxes, is stimulative, in either theory or practice.

In fact, lower taxes, especially lower tax rates that encourage more investment and work effort, are far more stimulative and less inflationary than higher government spending. Lower tax rates increase the supply of goods and services available at any price level, an upward shift in aggregate supply. Demand may also increase as faster growth and less taxation per dollar of (higher) income drive up after-tax incomes, but the increase in aggregate supply will hold inflation in check. In contrast, higher government spending increases demand for goods and services with no impact on the economy's capacity to produce them and therefore is unambiguously inflationary. Consequently, it is fiscal stimulus in the form of higher government spending, not lower tax rates, that may require an offset from tighter monetary policy to avoid inflation.

Historically, large deficits and attendant increases in national debt have been tied to the conduct of wars. Presumably, feelings of vulnerability with respect to the inability to finance another war prompt urgent drives to reduce debt in the aftermath of war. America's Revolutionary War gave rise to a large debt, nearly $75 million, which was 42 percent of estimated national product at the time, not very high by current standards. More problematically, the interest burden consumed more than half of the meager federal revenues, whereas today interest on the national debt consumes about 11 percent of federal revenue. Still, Alexander Hamilton took the view that consolidating the debt and servicing it in a reliable and timely manner would enhance America's standing as a worthy creditor, turning debt from a liability into an asset. Hamilton also, no doubt, recognized at the time the value of a benchmark asset, an interest-bearing liability guaranteed by the government's ability to levy taxes to ensure payment of interest on the debt.

The current notion that the $4.2 trillion in prospective surpluses over the next decade ought to be devoted largely to eliminating the national debt of about $3.5 trillion is a preposterous idea. Paying off the national debt would leave global financial markets with no benchmark risk-free asset in the form of US government securities. High-quality liabilities of the US government confer benefits on both the private sector and the government, enabling the government to borrow when necessary at low cost. If the US government were to absent itself from the credit markets, it would hamper its ability to smoothly resume borrowing, should the need arise.

Debt Paydown and Taxes

The biggest downside to simply paying down the debt over the next decade arises from the need for taxes and tax rates to be higher than they would otherwise be if we aimed just to stabilize the ratio of debt to gross domestic product (GDP) between 30 and 35 percent—about one-half of the average for industrial countries. Critics respond by asserting that the remarkable prosperity of the 1990s—a period of deficit and debt reduction—outstripped the economic performance of the 1980s, when tax cuts and spending growth initially led to higher deficits. This claim is factually untrue and represents a major confusion of cause and effect. Higher growth led to lower debt and deficit levels; lower debt and deficit levels did not lead to higher growth.

First, consider the record. When President Ronald Reagan took office in 1981 and cut taxes on investment while the Federal Reserve pursued policies that cut inflation rapidly, the deficit rose from 2.6 percent of GDP in 1981 to a peak of 6 percent in 1983, then eased to around 5 percent through 1986. The fact is that much of the rise in the deficit was due to a rapid slowdown in inflation rather than to tax cuts or higher spending growth. But still, despite the much bemoaned higher deficits of the Reagan years, the economy grew at an average annual rate of 4.5 percent during the five years following 1982, while the Reagan administration's stimulative fiscal policies were producing an increase in deficits. The 4.5 percent growth rate for 1982 through 1987 was a full percentage point above the average growth rate of 3.5 percent over the four decades since 1959.

President Bill Clinton took office in 1993 and effected deficit-reduction measures, largely through higher taxes. The deficit as a share of GDP went from 3.9 percent to a surplus of about 1 percent over the five years following the enactment of the reduction measures. The surplus has continued to rise and probably will reach close to 2 percent of GDP in 2000.

During the five years following the 1993 measures, which followed on deficit-reduction measures enacted in 1990 under President George H. W. Bush, US economic growth averaged 3.8 percent, still above the average of 3.5 percent for the period since 1959, but below the 4.5 percent enjoyed during the period of fiscal stimulus and higher deficits in the Reagan years.

Productivity Surges

A full assessment of the determinants of growth is, of course, a complex process. Some of the faster growth during the 1980s was undoubtedly due to the elimination of the dangerously high and unstable inflation rates of 1973 through 1981. The higher growth rate of the 1990s, which did not appear until after 1995, was due largely to a surge in capital spending on new technology and an associated increase in productivity growth from a 1 percent average during the 20 years before 1995 to about 2.75 percent in the years after 1995. That extra rise in productivity has helped extend America's noninflationary expansion to a record of nine and a half years (and counting). No one links the post-1995 surge in productivity growth to the higher tax rates enacted in 1993.

The truth is that, in the 1980s, stimulative fiscal policy, especially lower tax rates coupled with monetary policy acting to reduce and stabilize inflation, pushed up growth. The higher growth generated the revenue to bring budget deficits down sharply and stabilize the ratio of debt to GDP.

Tax Cut Feedback

The lessons of history and basic economic theory suggest that the promise of the benefits of further federal debt reduction will not materialize, especially if tax rates are held at current high levels to achieve that goal. Beyond that, if surpluses persist, the risk is that they will be spent, adding to demand in an overheating economy, thereby requiring an offset of tighter money from the Federal Reserve. Or worse, in the highly unlikely event that the debt did disappear, the federal government would have to start using its extra revenue to invest the public's tax payments. Those favoring debt paydown are advocating a move toward paying taxes to the federal government so it can decide how to invest our money, a perverse turnaround given the widespread desire for more control over retirement funds.

But signs are already emerging that debt paydown is going to slow rapidly. Government spending has begun to accelerate, with the growth of discretionary federal outlays over the next fiscal year now set at 6.4 percent, more than triple the average growth rate of the past decade. Former Congressional Budget Office Director Robert Reischauer has warned that if the Congress just lets discretionary spending keep up with inflation over the next decade, then over $1 trillion of the prospective $4 trillion surplus will disappear.

Fiscal policy supports the economy best when government revenues are collected in a way least harmful to the economy and are allocated efficiently among essential government programs. The surge in economic growth and government revenues over the past five years provides an opportunity for the federal government to invest in sustained growth, both of the economy and government revenues, by reducing tax rates. That strategy will leave intact far more of the $4 trillion in federal surpluses projected over the next decade than would offering up the siren call of the benefits of debt reduction and then spending more of the taxpayers' money when those benefits fail to materialize.

—◆—

Myths About Budget Deficits

FEBRUARY 2010

By 2010, the worst of the Great Recession had ended. But policymakers faced important choices about how to get the economy growing again. In the background were concerns about budget deficits.

Makin found some of those concerns misplaced. He believed that raising taxes to tame budget deficits coming out of a severe recession was a "bad idea," and he also predicted that Barack Obama policies on health care and unemployment benefits would slow the economic recovery. At the time, Makin tended to counsel policymakers not to obsess too much about high deficits and debt.

February always brings with it the president's proposals for taxing and spending in the coming fiscal year. The president's budget proposals are accompanied by congressional and administration estimates of the path that deficits and government debt are expected to take in coming years. Last year, those projections, especially a three-year string of actual and projected deficits over a trillion dollars from 2009 through 2011, excited widespread comment and hand-wringing about runaway deficits and their allegedly damaging effects in the form of lower growth, higher inflation, and higher interest rates.

Nobody is happy about a sharp increase in government deficits and debt, which typically results from the extraordinary demands on government spending during a war or an economic crisis, such as the crisis that unfolded after the housing bubble burst in 2007. The financial crisis that followed the collapse of Lehman Brothers in September 2008 was particularly acute, and it elicited an unusually large increase in government spending to contain it.

In a sense, a spike in government budget deficits and debt is akin to an aggressive medical intervention, like chemotherapy to contain the spread of cancer. The process is unpleasant, and the prognosis somewhat uncertain. But ultimately, the outcome depends on measures undertaken to help a patient regain and sustain strength after the damage caused by aggressive treatment.

Returning to the sphere of economic policy, proposals to boost marginal tax rates at a time of elevated budget deficits are a bad idea. Higher rates will only compound the drag on the economy tied to other burdens associated with larger budget deficits. Alternatively, increased congressional pressure on the Federal Reserve to accommodate additional debt financing can be harmful if the result is a rise in anticipated inflation. In short, problems associated with a rapid buildup of deficits and debt should not be compounded by ill-advised, ad hoc policies.

The most reliable way to reduce government budget deficits is to reduce government spending. The alternative—raising taxes—has an ambiguous impact since higher tax rates tend to slow growth and, thereby, reduce the tax base. Alternatively, boosting inflation to boost the nominal tax base while reducing the real value of government debt is counterproductive given the resource misallocation and the rise in interest rates on outstanding debt that accompany higher inflation.

The most frequently cited negative by-products of higher government deficits and debt include a rise in interest rates, higher inflation, and lower growth. In addition, a rise in US budget deficits seems to occasion substantially more global outcry than a rise in budget deficits elsewhere, say in Europe or Japan.

The remorse and potentially bad policy proposals prompted by bigger budget deficits should be tempered by the fact that the collapse of the housing bubble and the attendant global financial crisis that followed required more government borrowing and spending to avoid an even more severe economic downturn than the one that has occurred. During the second half of 2009, for example, US fiscal stimulus probably added about 2 percentage points to growth, along with 2 percentage points added because of a normal cessation of an inventory sell-off. Given that actual growth averaged about 3 percent during that period, would it have been better to allow the –1 percent growth that probably would have resulted without the fiscal stimulus, which included over $700 billion aimed at staunching the financial meltdown that followed the Lehman Brothers crisis?

Some may argue that it would have been better to do nothing and simply allow the system to work through the aftermath of the housing bubble on its own, but, given the economy's underlying weakness and the modest recovery that has occurred (albeit with the aid of substantial support from fiscal and monetary policy), the damage from the "do nothing" approach could have been substantially greater than the considerable damage actually suffered. In any case, the measures have been undertaken, and we face these questions: What are the likely consequences of the measures, and what policies are appropriate now?

Global Rise of Deficits and Debt

Global increases in deficits and debt have been sharp in 2009 and 2010. Fiscal deterioration in the United States has been sharper than global fiscal deterioration, although the decline started from a sounder fiscal base than that of other industrial countries. US fiscal challenges, in the form of higher deficits, are projected to have peaked in 2009, although the challenges over the next two fiscal years may be substantial. Deficits will remain elevated, and the ratio of debt to gross domestic product (GDP) will continue to rise.

Impact of Deficits on Interest Rates

It is important to examine what the empirical evidence indicates regarding the likely impact of higher deficits and debt on future interest rates at a time when the economy may have recovered. Fortunately, the evidence strongly suggests that much of the impact may have occurred already, provided that the US fiscal picture does not deteriorate substantially from here.

Empirical studies of the impact of higher deficits and debt on interest rates have been plagued by a fundamental problem in the past. Straightforward regression studies, even those that control for other variables, such as expected or actual inflation, typically suffer from what is called cycle bias. The cycle bias results in a finding that larger government deficits and associated increases in debt actually result in lower interest rates. This paradoxical result occurs because, in the United States, nonfederal government debt (currently about $27 trillion) is nearly four times as large as federal government debt (currently about $7.2 trillion). When the economy enters a recession, countercyclical fiscal policy boosts deficits and government debt while private debt falls. Given that the stock of private debt is so much larger than government debt, the drop in private borrowing in a recession overwhelms the impact of a rise in government deficits on total borrowing.

The Right Way to Manage Deficits

For reasons that may or may not constitute a sound policy response to the trauma of a housing bubble collapse and a financial crisis, higher government spending—along with weaker growth—has sharply elevated deficits and debt worldwide. The rise in government debt in the United States, while starting from a lower base than elsewhere, has been sharper and has brought US debt to a point in which substantial further fiscal deterioration could trigger the problems—higher inflation and lower growth—shown over time and across countries to result from sharp increases in debt above a 90 percent debt-to-GDP ratio. A hopeful corollary, arising from empirical investigation of the impact of sharp debt increases on interest rates, is that substantial progress in reducing deficits, especially by containing government spending over the next several years, could actually help lower interest rates, given that the prospective increases in debt have already been reflected in those rates.

Currently, the outlook for containment of government spending is not particularly optimistic. Plans to increase spending on health care would probably add to estimated future deficits, as would enhanced measures to extend unemployment benefits and, thereby, slow the progress toward full employment. Taxes on pollution or carbon would likely produce a desirable reduction in pollution. Yet it might be better to reduce emissions by auctioning off permits to emit pollutants and using the proceeds of such permit sales to reduce the budget deficit. Whether the period during which the country is trying to recover from a deep recession is the best time to increase production costs is another matter that involves difficult trade-offs.

6

EXCHANGE RATES, MONETARY SYSTEMS, AND THE GOLD STANDARD

A Single Money for Europe?

JULY 1997

Turning his attention to the divergent economic paths of the US and Europe in the late 1990s, Makin examined the opportunities and perils of the pending European experiment with a single currency, the euro, which was scheduled to be introduced on January 1, 1999. Bound by the terms of the Maastricht Treaty[1] adopted in 1992 and taking cues from Germany's "inflation-obsessed" Bundesbank, much of Europe was steadfastly refusing to ease up on the money supply to fight unemployment. As a result, European economies were stagnating as the US was growing, and popular discontent led to the election of a socialist government in France. That dynamic prompted Makin to warn that Europeans risked achieving "monetary union without rationalizing the generous program of social benefits or establishing fiscal discipline" through political union and thus undermining its long-term viability—critiques that still resonate today.

Europe has been moving toward a single money for almost two decades. The single money, the euro, is scheduled to become legal tender on January 1, 1999. European policymakers have been pursuing tight monetary and fiscal policies since the start of the US recovery early in 1991. The result has been economic stagnation and rising unemployment, save for the United Kingdom, Spain, and Italy, which broke away in September 1992 from the rigid Exchange Rate Mechanism (ERM) that is the predecessor

66

of the single money. The stagnation has been particularly acute in France, but even Germany, Europe's traditional economic powerhouse, has not escaped rising unemployment and widespread departures of new plant locations by its leading corporations. Still, monetary union will probably occur on schedule.

Threats to Monetary Union

Confidence in a smooth path to European monetary union was shaken early in June when the Socialists in France scored a surprise election victory over the center-right coalition of French President Jacques Chirac. The French election result was a clear protest against the tight fiscal and monetary policies in place to ensure French compliance with the budgetary and inflation criteria for monetary union. In light of the French electorate's protest against high unemployment and persistent economic stagnation, the question now is: Will European leaders allow softer fiscal and monetary criteria in the preliminary steps toward the new European money, or will they delay—in effect, terminate—the progress toward monetary union?

The answer, if monetary union is a political goal as European leaders say it is, is clear: soften stringent fiscal and monetary policies and begin to combat high and rising unemployment in Europe. With Europe's large unused capacity, the initial effects on European inflation, which is already low, will hardly be noticeable. The "easing" option to combat rising unemployment evokes concern from Germany—and especially from Germany's central bank, the Bundesbank—that such easier policies would ultimately be inflationary. The conventional wisdom fed to American observers of the European scene, largely through London, is that most Germans remain deeply attached to the views and policies of the inflation-obsessed Bundesbank. Given Germany's subpar economic performance, with unemployment at the highest level in 25 years, belief that Germans are highly satisfied with these stringent budgetary and monetary policies of the Bundesbank and the German government suggests that an obsessive fear of inflation has made Germans somehow indifferent to employment and economic growth.

While it is true that Germans prefer low inflation and German history has provided ample evidence of the damage of high and runaway inflation, it is not clear that all Germans applaud the Bundesbank's stringent policies. Indeed, many Germans consider that a positive aspect of monetary union in Europe, aside from the usual benefits of a broader currency area, will be to rid Germany of what they see as the Bundesbank's overly tight monetary policies. The breakaway from the straitjacket of the European ERM in September 1992 by the United Kingdom, Spain, and Italy has led to far superior economic performance in those countries, with moderating inflation. Some Germans surely must wonder if such an option is not available to them if they could only escape the strictures of Bundesbank monetary policy.

The move toward monetary union includes a new European Central Bank (ECB) scheduled to begin operation on January 1, 1999. The new ECB would include representation from all the member countries of the European monetary union and, in effect, offer considerable dilution of the Bundesbank's power.

The actual desires of Germans regarding European monetary union and the implied future course of economic policy in Germany will be able to find expression in a series of German elections during 1998 that culminate with the election contest for chancellor in October. Germany's Chancellor Helmut Kohl has clearly identified himself with achieving monetary union, although, like most politicians, he has had to reassure those concerned about inflationary threats that the new European institutions, and in particular the ECB, will be as vigilant about guarding against inflation as the Bundesbank. The fact that the French electorate has clearly signaled a desire for more accommodative policies, coupled with a need to keep the German and French currencies rigidly fixed before and after currency union, complicates Kohl's task of convincing some skeptical Germans that the move toward European monetary union is anything other than a way to reduce the Bundesbank's power. By supporting the move toward monetary union and the inevitable relaxation of monetary stringency it entails, Kohl is betting that the majority of Germans, including far more than those vainly searching for employment, desire some relief from the Bundesbank's severe policies.

The Goal of Monetary Union

Stepping back from the immediate events surrounding the movement in Europe toward a single money, we should find it useful to observe that more than 25 years ago, European leaders conceived of monetary union as a means to political union. The usual course to a single money, however, is political union first, in a geographical area over which a single federal government enforces broadly uniform rules of commerce and manages tax and spending policies, before a common money is introduced. Europe is undertaking an unusual experiment by initiating monetary union before full political union. The stated aim is political, to use monetary union to increase political cohesion in Europe and avoid the possibility of war. German Chancellor Helmut Kohl puts it more bluntly: It is a matter of "war and peace in the 21st century."[2] Some Germans born after World War II may fail to see the logic of Kohl's reasoning.

While the goal of European monetary union is a noble political one that probably will be achieved, awkward economic realities are causing some difficulties as we move closer to January 1, 1999. On that date, Europe's moneys are scheduled to be irrevocably frozen together, and the new currency of all Europe, the euro, is to become legal tender, while the ECB takes over the management of European monetary policy.

A leftward shift in European politics has been superimposed on the late stages of the move toward monetary union. The French election, which brought Lionel Jospin to power early in June, ushering in a Socialist-Communist coalition government under Jospin that must cohabit with the center-right presidency of Chirac, is one example. The election of Tony Blair in the United Kingdom, whose participation in the European monetary union is as yet undecided, brings in a Labour government after 18 years of conservative Tory leadership.

However, Blair and Jospin represent very different political movements. Blair's election in the UK represents a successful shift of a traditional left-wing party toward the center, pursuing enlightened, market-oriented economic policies. French Prime Minister Jospin represents, in contrast, old-style left-wing policies that include raising the minimum wage, shortening work hours, and attempting to use the economic system to make transfers from capital to labor.

Jospin is probably an accidental prime minister, the result of gross political miscalculation by President Chirac. When Chirac decided to call an election to consolidate his position for the final move toward monetary union, he essentially announced to the French people that continuing to maintain a center-right majority in the Parliament would ensure two more years of the stringent monetary and fiscal policies that have caused France to suffer considerably over the past decade. To its credit, the French electorate said *non*.

Still, Jospin and the French Socialists have a strong commitment to monetary union, with much of the heavy lifting along the path to monetary union having been done by French President François Mitterrand, himself a prominent Socialist. Further, Jospin has, since his election, reiterated the commitment to European monetary union. In effect, France and Germany have simulated monetary union for most of the 1990s by maintaining a rigid parity between the franc and the deutsche mark, with an interruption in September 1992 when European currencies were permitted to deviate more from their central parities to accommodate the strains associated with the departure of the United Kingdom, Spain, and Italy from the ERM.[3] The system of rigid parities in Europe has provided an uncomfortable preview of the shape of Europe's economies if the new ECB follows policies as strict as those of the Bundesbank.

US economic performance provides a useful benchmark against which to judge that of core Europe. Between 1992 and the end of 1996, French employment actually fell by 12 percent. Some have suggested that this drop is due exclusively to inflexible labor markets, which can be adjusted to provide more employment in France. The political success of French Socialists, however, who have protested specifically the movement toward more flexibility in labor markets, has diminished that likelihood. Beyond that, capital investment in France has languished, with investment flows in France late in 1996 at about 7 percent below levels in 1992.

Even Germany has not escaped the economic costs of the stringent policies pursued over the past half decade. In late 1996, German employment was 6 percent below its 1992 level, while German investment was still 2 percent below its level in 1992.

By contrast, between 1992 and 1996, US employment rose by 13 percent, while US investment rose by 45 percent. For Italy, Spain, and the United

Kingdom, countries that departed from the ERM in 1992, performance is closer to that of France and Germany, with Spain and the United Kingdom experiencing only about 2 percent increases in employment, while Italian employment has actually fallen about 7 percent. In Spain and Italy, investment is still 3 to 4 percent below its 1992 level, while in the United Kingdom, investment has risen by a moderate 8 percent.

Conflict over Standards

The move toward monetary union in Europe has presented its leaders with a classic struggle between means and ends. By setting monetary and fiscal standards to be met by the first group of members included in the first round of membership of the European monetary union, Europe's leaders hoped they would be able to impose the discipline necessary to pare back budget deficits and ensure that a unified Europe is a noninflationary Europe. They are now struggling with the reality that as the date for currency union draws closer, the economic cost of having maintained stringent policies is becoming more obvious and a greater political liability, as demonstrated by the election of Socialists in France.

The contrast between the substandard performance of European economies and the extraordinary performance of the US economy is also a problem for European leaders. Europe's major corporations are already abandoning operations in core Europe in favor of more cost-effective operations in Eastern Europe, emerging Asia, or North America. This move of course is adding to the unemployment problem in Europe and subtracting from the tax base necessary to maintain generous social benefits. The more innovative segments of Europe's business community have noticed the superior performance of American companies and banks and have responded.

The real question facing Europe in the final 18 months before the designation of the new euro as the legal tender of much of Europe is whether the strict interpretation of the Maastricht Treaty criteria will be relaxed to whatever degree is necessary to include most of Europe among the initial members of the union.

The fiscal criteria of the treaty will be relaxed simply because none of Europe's major countries, nor most of its minor countries for that matter, can meet the literal terms of the treaty. The only risk to achieving monetary union on time would be a protest from either the Bundesbank or the German public, uncomfortable with the lack of fiscal discipline and an attendant lack of monetary discipline under the new unified currency of Europe. Potential monetary union protesters in Germany, however, will have no specific target to shoot at until March 1998, when the European Monetary Institute, the predecessor to the ECB, renders its judgment on the countries that have made satisfactory progress toward the Maastricht Treaty criteria.

Between now and then, there will be plenty of arguing, especially between the French and the Germans, about the degree of fiscal stringency required to satisfy the treaty and symbolically about whether Italy should be included in the first round of membership. This period of wrangling will probably produce two results. First, most European currencies, including the deutsche mark, which will probably not exist in 18 months, will weaken against the US dollar. This will have the useful side effect of giving some boost to Europe through extra export sales, although the ability of relatively high-cost European firms to compete with American firms may limit that effect.

A second result of the pre-union wrangling will be some relaxation of the fiscal controls in Europe. The Europeans will thus have somewhat larger budget deficits as they enter monetary union in 1999. The Bundesbank will be unlikely to counter such moves with higher interest rates, although it may resist any further reduction in interest rates, even if weaker economic conditions should argue otherwise.

Conditions for Successful Union

Should the relaxation of fiscal stringency and a Bundesbank on hold encourage an economic recovery in Europe, a condition that would greatly enhance the chances for successful monetary union, there could be some effect on the economic fortunes of the United States. Of course, an economic recovery would increase US exports to Europe. A truly powerful European economic recovery, which I emphasize is not likely, would increase global demands on commodity markets and probably eliminate some of the unusually favorable conditions that are now allowing the US expansion to continue along a noninflationary course. A strong economic recovery in Europe would also mitigate and perhaps reverse the dollar's strength, a result that seems unlikely if European economic performance remains tepid during the journey toward monetary union along likely lines of stringent fiscal and monetary policies.

Whatever the ultimate outcome of the push for increased political union by way of monetary union, events in Europe bear careful watching. Successful achievement of monetary and political union would represent an additional post–Cold War bonus: The union could bring about an extended period of peace in which European nationalism could subside and economic growth could prevail.

The major risk is that Europeans will achieve monetary union without rationalizing the generous program of social benefits or establishing fiscal discipline. If Europe simply declares victory by freezing its exchange rates together, without making the needed structural changes in the economy, European monetary union will not survive for long without resorting to a highly counterproductive increase in trade protection. That outcome would constitute a tragic confusion of means and ends, with Europe bearing the major portion of the costs.

Notes

1. The Maastricht Treaty was the Treaty on European Union, signed in 1992 by the members of the European Community. It established the European Union, laid out areas of closer cooperation, and laid the foundation for establishing the euro as Europe's currency.

2. Alan Cowell, "Kohl Casts Europe's Economic Union as War and Peace Issue," *New York Times*, October 17, 1995, https://www.nytimes.com/1995/10/17/world/kohl-casts-europe-s-economic-union-as-war-and-peace-issue.html.

3. The European Exchange Rate Mechanism was established in 1979 by the European Economic Community to stabilize exchange rates in Europe before monetary integration.

The Dangerous Preference
for Fixed Exchange Rates

MARCH 1999

In this piece from March 1999, Makin surveyed the global financial picture and found several policy mistakes that had contributed to financial woes. Using historical and contemporary examples from around the world, he showed how the preference for fixed exchange rates bedeviled many emerging markets by creating excess capacity that eventually forced them to devalue their currencies. Although those policies tended to help developed countries by providing them with a cheap source of raw materials, Makin foresaw eventual troubles, too: "The easiest of times for the US economy are behind it," he wrote.

The current preoccupation of the G7 nations (excluding the United States) with pegging exchange rates among major currencies follows downright perversely on the heels of nearly two years of disastrous efforts to foist exchange-rate rigidity onto developing countries. Fortunately, the refusal by America alone to join the drive toward repegging currencies is sufficient to stop it. One would think that the Japanese—who, intermittently, have made heavy use of exchange-rate depreciation to cushion the rising deflationary momentum on their unfortunate island—would be in favor of continued flexibility of exchange rates. But, disoriented and weakened by continued adherence to the old symbols of stability, hard money, and a stable currency, the Japanese can be counted on to side with the Europeans in pushing for exchange-rate pegs, as they did at the recent G7 meeting in Bonn.

Today, 20 years after the great battle against global inflation, most central banks and the International Monetary Fund have replaced the productive goal of avoiding inflation during an era of excess demand with the counterproductive goal of preventing currency devaluations during an era of excess supply. The prevalence of excess capacity (supply) has meant that the battle against currency devaluations has been lost in the developing countries of the world, with the list of losers extended from Thailand, Indonesia, and South Korea in 1997 to Russia in 1998 and Brazil in 1999.

With their devaluations, the developing countries have exported very harmful deflation to Japan, where it is already present; moderately harmful deflation to Europe, where it is about to appear; and helpful deflation to the United States, where it has served as a powerful tonic to extend dramatically an investment-led expansion. What happens over the next year in this excess-supply environment, which is so baffling to most policymakers, is crucial to avoiding a global financial meltdown. While central banks know how to end inflationary episodes by raising interest rates and slowing money growth, many are puzzled about how to end deflationary episodes. Witness the current struggle over deflation at the Bank of Japan, the rising tension with fiscal policy at the European Central Bank, and the queasiness attending a soaring US stock market and economy at the Federal Reserve.

Lies upon Lies

As the 20th century draws to a close, it seems that lying about exchange rate pledges has replaced lying about price stability as the fashion among central banks outside of America. The failure during the 1970s by G7 central banks, especially the US Federal Reserve, to keep their promises about price stability created an excess-demand, hot-potato scenario. Rising prices in industrial countries caused booms in emerging markets, especially Latin America, which pulled investment capital into those areas. The booms ended when the overheating got intolerable in the industrial countries (especially the United States), and the Federal Reserve called an end to the easy money scenario. Fed tightening, begun in 1979–80, eventually collapsed the emerging market boom in 1982 when Mexico declared itself unable to service its debts. There followed a major Latin American debt crisis associated with the battle to control inflation that, in turn, was necessitated by a failure of the Federal Reserve and other major central banks to keep their promises of stable prices.

Reacting to the clear costs of the inflationary environment during the late 1970s and early 1980s, the United States, Europe, and Japan persistently reaffirmed their commitment to price stability, and this spread abroad to the emerging markets. The late 1990s has seen the hot potato of excess supply replace the hot potato of excess demand in the 1980s. Under the excess-supply scenario, emerging markets pegged their currencies to the dollar, which was stabilized by the Fed's long and persistent anti-inflation efforts. Such pegging of the currencies of emerging markets allowed investors in these markets to use dollar interest rates, held unusually low by the Fed's anti-inflation efforts, to finance a myriad of investment projects. The unusually low cost of capital in the emerging markets created a chronic excess-supply (capacity) situation; consequently, the hard currency pegs to the dollar were no longer viable. One by one, the currencies of emerging market countries such as Brazil, Indonesia, Russia, South Korea, and Thailand have been devalued in an effort to redress the problems of large excess capacity.

The following description of Shanghai, another classic case of excess capacity problems, is typical:

> Shanghai's property sector is the most obvious case of excess capacity. Over two thousand high rises have been completed in the city in the 1990s. There are around five hundred under construction. Optimistic estimates project that it will take ten years or more to fill the existing buildings. If the property sector is cut back, Shanghai's economy will clearly slow down. The whole country has a similar problem. The manufacturing sector and the property sector account for about two-thirds of the total investment. If these two sectors have to invest less, can investment drive the economy?
>
> If investment and consumption won't lead the economy, it leaves only the external sector. East Asia is still crawling at the bottom. Europe is slower than last year. The U.S. probably peaked in Q4 1998. China will have to go for market share to achieve higher export growth, which means trouble for other East Asian economies.

This description of Shanghai's and China's economic problems and the need to export deflation was written in one of Morgan Stanley's daily reports by Andy Xie, a Morgan Stanley analyst based in Hong Kong. It is typical of the Asian economy's problems. Whereas in the 1970s excess-demand conditions in the developed G7 economies ultimately benefited the commodity-sensitive emerging markets, the process has been reversed in the 1990s. The promise by the central banks of the emerging markets to maintain a peg to the dollar put the cost of capital too low and created an excess-supply situation among emerging markets that has so far greatly benefited the developed economies of the G7. The export of the excess-supply conditions in the emerging markets has created a triple benefit for the financial markets and the economies of the developed world, especially the United States. The collapse of the economies of the emerging markets has lowered the prices of raw materials while creating a reflux of capital back to the safe haven of developed economies. The acute phase of the crisis in the emerging markets, the devaluation and default by Russia in August 1998, and the near failure of Long-Term Capital Management created enough turbulence in the advanced countries' financial sector to cause the Federal Reserve to ease sharply—cutting interest rates by 75 basis points in six weeks—and to accelerate money growth through the end of 1998.

Except in the United States, the global need is demand growth. As a result, monetary policy in the United States, accommodative as it has been, is oddly far more appropriate for areas such as Europe and Japan, where demand growth is inadequate, prices are falling, and unemployment is rising. Japan and Europe must now export deflation, with the United States as importer. But some problems in financial markets may arise in this process.

A New Race?

The easiest of times for the US economy are behind it. In 1997 and 1998, the US economy, with the wind at its back, was the fastest race car on the track when all the slow cars broke down and moved to the sidelines. The winner posted great lap times in the form of high growth rates in the gross domestic product and higher valuations of the earnings of US companies.

When the slower cars have been repaired and get back onto the track, the US economy, though the fastest in the world, must navigate through some traffic, such as a possible firming in raw materials prices, stable-to-rising interest rates, and a neutral Fed that might even consider tightening if any signs of wage pressure emerge. The problems in the emerging markets and Japan are by no means over. But events of the past month indicate that they have probably passed their most acute phase.

The next problem facing world financial markets and policymakers will be to make room for some of the slower economies to get back into the race. This allowance will require the US economy to throttle back; a stronger dollar is probably the ideal way to accomplish this move. A stronger dollar as the mirror image of weaker currencies elsewhere—which may be interpreted as the abandonment of promises to maintain fixed exchange rates—is not a bad thing.

If the world has learned anything in the past two years, it ought to be that promising stable currencies in a deflationary world characterized by excess capacity is a cruel hoax. Fighting for exchange-rate stability in a world of excess capacity is not the moral or practical equivalent of fighting inflation in a world of excess demand, as the International Monetary Fund, the European Central Bank, and the Bank of Japan seem to have supposed. Efforts to further the cause of a fixed exchange rate in a world of excess capacity are a mistaken carryover from the last global debt crisis in the 1980s, when promising price-level stability and hard currencies was the way out of the crisis.

It would be heartening to hear from the G7 some recognition of the distinction between the desirability of seeking price-level stability in a world of excess demand and the dangers of pursuing exchange-rate rigidity in a world of excess supply. Failing that, we shall have to rely on the markets and the Federal Reserve to do the job for them.

All That Glitters:
A Primer on the Gold Standard

OCTOBER 2012

In the aftermath of the financial crisis and continuing sluggishness in the world economy, some US politicians in 2012 began pining for the return of the gold standard to stabilize the economy and fight inflation. Makin took the occasion of the Republican proposal to study the issue to deliver a history lesson on tying currency to gold. He outlined why, with the extant monetary system of flexible exchange rates and the fact that the US was not a hegemonic economic power, reinstituting a gold standard like the one Britain and the United States used after 1925—or even the modified Bretton Woods system—would be impractical today.

The periodic debate around whether the United States should adopt a gold standard—a monetary system tied to the value of gold—has heated up again recently. Although some see such a system as a way to prevent inflation and excessive government debt accumulation, history has proved that it can lead to instability and sharp periods of inflation or deflation, as seen during the Great Depression and in the failure of the Bretton Woods[1] monetary policy system in the early 1970s. Serious consideration of a widespread return to a gold standard would be warranted only if the Federal Reserve's recent QE3+ quantitative easing measures and economic stability around the world lead to prolonged periods of high inflation and if a major world economic player—such as the United States or Great Britain—is willing and able to peg its currency to gold to provide a benchmark for price stability.

In August, discussion of the costs and benefits of a US return to the gold standard became popular when the 2012 Republican platform included a proposal for a commission to consider "the feasibility of a metallic basis for U.S. currency."[2] As the platform statement indicated, a gold commission appointed shortly after the election of President Ronald Reagan considered the feasibility of a gold standard and advised against such a move. Now, more than 30 years later, does a gold standard make sense for the

United States? The question takes on extra urgency now that the Federal Reserve has moved toward targeting higher inflation with QE3+.

The quick answer to this question is no if the aim is to unilaterally return the United States to a gold standard in today's world of floating exchange rates and the absence of any other currencies pegged to gold. That said, the gold standard issue still deserves serious consideration. The expectation is that at some point in the future there might be an effort to design a new international monetary system that includes a link to gold.

The Gold Standard and the Great Depression

The postwar gold exchange standard had its roots in the interwar period, specifically in the experience that followed Great Britain's return to a pegged gold exchange rate in 1925. Before World War I, the world had been largely on a gold standard. But the pressures of wartime finance after 1914 prompted most countries to cut the link to gold so that central banks could accommodate massive government borrowing associated with the expenses of the war. The break from gold resulted in substantial inflation after the war—especially in Germany, where, saddled with reparations it could not pay, the German government resorted to massive money printing that led to hyperinflation and a virtual destruction of the German currency.

The British link to gold had formed the heart of the prewar gold standard, and the British were eager to restore currency convertibility to gold to help stabilize their monetary system and the global monetary system. In 1925, Britain reestablished the prewar peg to gold by fixing the exchange rate between its currency and the dollar. The dollar price of gold was fixed at $20.67 an ounce, so a peg to the dollar amounted to a peg to a fixed sterling price of gold.

As it turned out, Britain's effort to return to gold at the prewar parity was a mistake. In effect, the peg overvalued sterling by setting the sterling price of gold below an equilibrium level. If a currency is overvalued as part of a gold standard, the country with the overvalued currency tends to run a balance of payments deficit that is settled by exporting gold to surplus countries. As British gold was exported, investors lost confidence in the sterling peg to gold, and capital outflows increased pressure on the country's dwindling gold stock. By 1931, Great Britain was forced to abandon the gold standard in the midst of an intensifying global depression.

In a volatile global environment, the dollar price of gold was too low, so speculators purchased gold from US banks. The loss of gold at the banks caused US depositors to convert their bank deposits into currency because they feared for the banks' safety.

The resulting negative cascade effect of a loss of currency and bank deposits caused the US money supply to shrink by a third between 1931 and 1933. The gold standard forced a monetary contraction at a time when the US economy was weak.

Finally, in January 1934, Congress passed the Gold Reserve Act, which nationalized the gold stock and prohibited the private ownership of gold. The price of gold was raised to $35 an ounce, resulting in a substantial devaluation of the dollar by over 40 percent. The sharp dollar devaluation helped encourage larger US exports of agricultural products and arrest the deflation that had set in after 1931 when the depletion of the Fed's gold stock had forced it to tighten monetary policy in a global depression.

The negative experience of Britain and the United States with a rigid gold standard after 1925 illustrates a basic problem tied to establishing a currency link to gold. If, as was the case with sterling in 1925, an excessively low currency price of gold leads to overvaluing of the currency, speculators will purchase gold for hoarding, expecting that the currency price of gold will have to be increased—that is, that the currency will have to be devalued against gold. But under the rules of the formal gold standard, a loss of official gold holdings requires a contraction of the money supply or some other restrictive monetary measure like higher interest rates, which causes wages, prices, and output to fall and unemployment to rise, especially if wages are somewhat sticky in a downward direction.

The fixed money price of gold implies a deflationary or contractionary tendency if it is set too low and leaves the government vulnerable to losses in its gold stock that in turn require a contraction of the money supply. Conversely, if the money price of gold is set too high—above a market equilibrium level—then gold flows to the government offering a higher price, and, under the rules of the gold standard, the central bank is forced to increase the money supply. A gold standard can be inflationary or deflationary.

Of course, the movements described here are self-correcting under a classical gold standard, when the majority of countries adhere to the standard.

In 1925, when Britain fixed the sterling price of gold, the world was on a gold standard in which every central bank ultimately had to tie the supply of money to the supply of gold in its coffers. The overvaluation of sterling created a balance of payment deficit and capital outflows, so the British gold stock fell. The reverse occurred in the United States as gold flowed in, but the United States did not let the money supply rise and push prices back up. Most of the adjustment burden fell on the United Kingdom, where wages and prices were forced even lower and an external deficit reduced the gold stock until Britain was forced to devalue sterling in 1931. If all countries do not link their money supply to their supply of gold, the gold standard breaks down.

A Modern Gold Exchange Standard: The Bretton Woods System

After World War II, with the US dollar peg to gold having remained fixed at $35 an ounce and the United States in a hegemonic position with most other nations, a monetary system was once again established based on a fixed exchange rate between the dollar and gold, the Bretton Woods system. Under the gold exchange standard, with gold pegged at $35 an ounce, other currencies were pegged to the dollar at a fixed price once they restored convertibility after the war, giving them a fixed value in terms of gold. As the world economy prospered, the need for international reserve assets rose, and other developed countries, particularly Europe and Japan, accumulated dollars transferred to them as the mirror image of their rising balance of payments surplus with the United States.

The resulting accommodation of US external deficits, which under the gold standard would have reduced the US money supply but under the gold exchange standard did not, eventually boosted US inflation to a level that meant that $35 an ounce as a gold price effectively overvalued the dollar. US trading partners began to convert dollars earned due to their balance of payment surpluses with the United States into gold, reducing US gold holdings.

With no link between the quantity of US money or US monetary policy and the country's physical stock of gold, US monetary policy was not constrained. The overvaluation of the dollar grew until, by 1971, then-President Richard M. Nixon had to either stop pegging the US dollar price of gold at $35 an ounce or let the gold flow out and sharply tighten US monetary policy. He chose to close the gold window, ending the convertibility of the dollar into gold for foreign governments, and the Bretton Woods system. The break of the dollar peg to gold set the stage for a rapid increase in the dollar price of gold, which was followed by a rapid increase in US inflation during the 1970s.

The end of the Bretton Woods system began a new monetary regime that makes it difficult to reinstitute a traditional gold standard. A combination of flexible exchange rates, permission for US citizens to own gold after 1974, and an absence of any link between the quantity of gold held by the central bank and the money supply has ushered in an entirely new system.

During the 1970s, sharp increases in the price of oil depressed US growth, acting as a tax on US consumers and producers. Efforts to maintain growth with accommodative monetary policy boosted US inflation and weakened the dollar against most other major currencies. With individuals able to own gold as an inflation hedge, the price of gold rose rapidly as US inflation intensified, and by 1979, it had reached over $800 per ounce. Higher US inflation before 1971 had effectively pushed the United States off of a gold link that obliged it to sell gold to foreign governments at $35 an ounce. By 1980, US inflation was running well above 10 percent per year, and interest rates on 30-year bonds had risen above 14 percent, reflecting fears of ever-rising US inflation.

Volcker Tames US Inflation

A return to a gold standard or a gold exchange standard was not a viable option for the United States in 1980. There was a gold market to set the price of gold, and any government effort to set it at a different level would mean the government would have to either acquire unlimited quantities of gold or sell unlimited quantities of gold to establish a new pegged price.

Instead, the United States went on a "Volcker standard." After he became Fed chairman in 1979, Paul Volcker simulated a tighter gold standard by sharply reducing money supply growth. The result was a sharp upward spike in interest rates as the Fed withdrew support from money markets and a collapse in US growth. Inflation fell rapidly, and by 1982, the US economy began a sustained recovery.

The Volcker standard did a good deal to restore the Fed's credibility and commitment to low and stable inflation. That commitment has been kept reasonably well over the past several decades, but it has been called into question given the tripling of the Fed's balance sheet in response to the 2008 financial crisis. Since then, the Fed has purchased over $2 trillion worth of government securities and mortgages. The result has been a sharp increase in the liquidity held in the US economy that many fear could not be withdrawn rapidly enough were prices to rise, causing a sharp reduction in the currently elevated demand for liquid assets on the part of households and firms.

That said, so far the rapid increase in the monetary base (cash and bank reserves), the result of the large increase in the Fed's balance sheet, has not been associated with any persistent rise in inflation or expected inflation. However, the Fed's September 13 introduction of QE3+ has increased the chance of higher US inflation because the Fed has signaled a willingness to tolerate higher inflation to reduce unemployment.

The Fed's sharply increased purchases of government securities have partially accommodated a sharp rise in the issuance of government debt and will continue to do so under QE3+.

How Would a Gold Standard Work Now?

We are in a world still struggling with the aftermath of a financial crisis, where Europe has entered a bitter recession, the United States is experiencing sluggish economic growth and persistent high unemployment, and Chinese growth is slowing. It would be difficult for the United States to unilaterally engineer a return to a gold standard. Such a gold standard in a modern era of huge international capital flows would require an international agreement to fix exchange rates, something that seems highly unlikely—not to mention undesirable—in today's world of volatile markets and weak demand, where most policymakers would prefer a weaker currency to help them shift a larger share of tepid global spending growth onto their own exports of goods and services.

Consider for a moment a thought experiment wherein the US government unilaterally decides to fix the dollar price of gold at a level that implies lower inflation. Under the rules of the gold standard, that would imply setting the dollar price of gold at a level below the current world market price. But that would not work. At such a level, private gold buyers would purchase their gold from the United States and experience a windfall gain. The US gold stock would fall, and the US money supply would fall as well, given a rigid gold standard rule. That kind of a deflationary shock would be disastrous in the current environment, where the Fed and other central banks have promised highly accommodative monetary policies aimed at increasing their holdings of government securities.

It may be that the current highly accommodative stance of the Fed and the European Central Bank will be highly inflationary. QE3+ has increased the chance of this outcome. That unhappy result would sharply erode confidence in fiat money. Support might grow for the development of a new international monetary system that includes a gold standard or some other mechanism to limit central banks' ability to arbitrarily adjust the money supply to accommodate large government borrowing.

But without a hegemonic financial power, like Britain before World War I and the US after World War II, that is willing and able to peg its currency to gold, it is difficult to see how a modern gold standard would evolve and function. The gold standards like those in place during the late 19th century can deliver relatively stable prices—and perhaps falling prices if the supply of gold does not rise rapidly enough. But the gold standard also delivers high volatility in real output and tends to be associated with more financial crises. Like it or not, the modern world has grown used to central banks that aim at price stability and full employment and provide an elastic currency in an effort to achieve higher growth while avoiding financial crises.

A unilateral American move toward a gold standard is not feasible at this time. That said, if a widespread episode of high inflation emerges in coming years, an international consensus may develop for a need to return to a more stable monetary system anchored to gold—a tall order in a world where no hegemonic country exists to peg its currency to gold and provide a benchmark for price stability for other countries.

Even the post–World War II Bretton Woods system broke down when the international reserve role of the dollar tied to its link to gold enabled the United States to run overly expansionary policies that eventually created inflation that eroded confidence in the dollar pegged to gold. The ease with which the US government brushed aside that link does not instill confidence in the durability of a new system that depends on a credible peg between gold and a major currency like the dollar.

Notes

1. The Bretton Woods system, adopted in 1944, established gold as the basis for the US dollar to which other currencies are pegged.

2. Republican National Committee, "We Believe in America: 2012 Republican Platform," American Presidency Project, August 27, 2012, https://www.presidency.ucsb.edu/documents/2012-republican-party-platform.

7

SAVINGS

Should Americans Save More?

MARCH 2005

In the mid-2000s, a lot of economic commentators were wringing hands about Americans' poor savings habits. In this piece from 2005, Makin examined that concern and observed that the relationship between savings and a country's economic health is complex. Looking at the experiences of other countries, such as China and Japan, he noted that high levels of savings don't always translate into economic growth because they can create overinvestment. Writing just a few years before the big housing crash that would lead to the Great Recession, Makin wondered if American overreliance on using housing as a form of savings would cause future problems. He said that the "search for return irrespective of risk results in too much asset acquisition, and when reality dawns, a sharp drop follows in the value of some assets. Such could easily be the fate of America's much-favored real estate."

Alarmists who call for American households to save more point to a steady drop in the conventionally measured US saving rate to about 1 percent at the end of 2004 and to a rise in household debt to a level well over 100 percent of personal disposable income. The current account deficit, our external deficit, measures national dissaving at close to 6 percent of gross domestic product (GDP). The federal government's budget deficit contributes about 4 percentage points to national dissaving, and it, too, is the subject of considerable hand-wringing by those who point to a need for higher US saving at both the household and national levels.

Government dissaving, better known as the budget deficit, has received adequate attention elsewhere. Suffice it to say that the federal budget deficit has probably peaked at around 4 percent of GDP, with no apparent damage having resulted in the form of higher interest rates, higher inflation, or slower growth—notwithstanding claims to the contrary emanating from the many critics of deficit spending. This essay will focus on household saving, the form it is taking, and whether households actually should increase their saving.

Saving is a good thing, but it is possible to overdo it. The uncritical acceptance of the notion that more saving is always better than less saving is a bad guide to individual behavior and a bad guide to public policy. Anyone who thinks that a nation whose people consistently work hard, save, and invest will be consistently better off than a nation whose people may work hard but save less need only compare the economies of Japan and the United States since 1990. Over the past 15 years, America's real net worth has risen by nearly 80 percent (about 4 percent per year), while Japan's wealth has actually dropped despite its much higher saving rate.

The form that saving takes is also important. Saving involves forgoing current consumption in return for the security of having accumulated assets or for the earnings on investment that is financed by saving. The very low level of American saving, measured as the difference between income and consumption, suggests that a rise in the value of housing is being viewed as saving by many US households. That may not be the best way to save, however. A consumption-based tax that taxes all saving only once, rather than twice as the current income tax system does, makes a lot of sense.

What Is Saving?

Saving is the difference between consumption per unit of time and the sum of income plus the change in accumulated wealth over the same unit of time. When a household or individual begins a working life with no accumulated wealth, then saving is simply nonconsumption, the portion of income that is set aside to accumulate wealth, perhaps for a rainy day (when no income is available) such as sickness, for retirement, or to provide for one's heirs. The bequest motive is strong, especially for those who began their working lives with no wealth, because appreciating or income-producing assets make it possible for one's offspring to consume current income while still accumulating wealth. The frequent gifts by parents to children of a home or a down payment on a home come to mind.

Alfred Marshall reminds us in his *Principles of Economics* that the habit of saving for the future is not a constant. Where no secure means to store wealth exists, or where income is at a subsistence level, there is likely to be virtually no saving. Marshall notes that the earliest forms of accumulated saving or wealth were probably hunting or fishing implements along with clothing or huts in the colder climates. These items all represented stored-up sources of future use or enjoyment much as durable goods, including automobiles and appliances, do today. More elaborate implements, huts, and clothing, together with perhaps growing herds of domestic animals, provided storage for future enjoyment and needs at the expense of maximum consumption as these items were being accumulated.

A necessary condition for saving is the realization by the prospective saver that provision of future wants can be stored. The more wealth one accumulates, the less rigid is the link between a variable and often uncertain stream of future income and future consumption. As wealth accumulates, provided the means exist to store it, the more it is possible to accumulate future wealth or enjoy a steady stream of future consumption independently of a future stream of income.

Saving Begets Saving

It is difficult to escape the notion that wealth accumulation is self-reinforcing, at least up to a point. As more wealth accumulates, the means to store it safely, which in the fullest sense entails a modern nation-state whose primary responsibility is self-defense, is more likely to appear and grow in strength. More wealth, in turn, enhances the accumulation of productive capital that enhances labor productivity and provides its owners with an attractive rate of return. The payment of interest on accumulated capital further smooths and enlarges the prospective stream of consumption that is possible for those who store wealth.

On all these points, 19th-century Britain provides a helpful example. The combination of a powerful empire and the Industrial Revolution created a stock of wealth owned by the propertied classes that transformed Britain. The consol, a long-term liability of the British government paying an average of about 3 percent, displaced land as Britain's primary asset. The owners of consols, Britain's prosperous merchant class, watched carefully the returns on their favorite asset, which rose upon the prospect of war, thereby depressing the value of existing consols, then fell when peace returned, thereby enhancing the value of consols acquired during the conflict. Of course, it was essential that the war not be lost, at least not disastrously so, and the British were consistently successful on that score for over a century, until after World War I, a disastrous conflict that eradicated many institutions of the 19th century, including much of the accumulated saving of the middle class.

Of course, mature wealthy nations are often tempted by the prospect of even higher prospective returns from investment in newer, more vigorous economies. During the 19th century, British investors were tempted to invest heavily in the United States in ventures including canals and railroads. While some British investments in the United States did well, the results were not uniformly positive. A wealthy nation, or at least a nation's wealthiest households, can save too much, at least judged after the fact, if they are tempted by high prospective rates of return that divert savings from lower, less risky ventures.

Too Much Saving in One Nation

The problems faced by modern China's growing class of the newly wealthy provide a reminder that limits do exist to the self-reinforcing aspect of wealth accumulation. Given the desire of many Chinese to build wealth rapidly, coupled with the rapid inflow of foreign capital, rapid income growth in China has boosted investment to a level reportedly above 40 percent of GDP. Such investment is probably above the level that can be absorbed profitably inside China. The result has been a helter-skelter rush to store wealth through questionable investments in unoccupied apartment complexes and often-empty high-rise office buildings, just to mention a few, instead of in the state-owned banking system, the insolvency of which is well-known. The flow of too much savings into China can produce overinvestment that drives the return on capital to zero or, after the fact, below zero. Savers beware.

Japan's negative experience after its high-growth period in the 1970s and 1980s reminds us that a high level of national saving can turn out to be oversaving. Japan's remarkable post–World War II recovery, a testimony to the national ethic of working, saving, and investing, was highly successful in the 1960s and 1970s as capital accumulated and earned an attractive rate of return. As the process continued, and Japan's prodigious national savings drove the accumulation of more and more capital inside Japan, the return on that capital began to fall.

By the end of the 1980s, Japan's high level of national saving spilled over into purchases of property until the Japan bulls proudly declared that the plot on which the emperor's palace sat in the middle of Tokyo was "worth more than California." Japanese savers, when on rare occasions they could extract money to invest outside of Japan, were so eager to diversify their holdings that they became legendary as over-payers for prime sites such as the famous Pebble Beach Golf Links in California. But broadly, Japan's trapped savers drove up the price of income streams from wealth, specifically the price of stocks and land, until the stock and property bubbles burst after the 1980s. Japan's property market has still not recovered, nor has its stock market. During the 1990s, Japan tried to engineer a recovery by having the public sector finance overinvestment in railways and public works projects, thereby driving the return to savers and investors even lower.

American Saving Experience

Turning to the experience of the United States as a saver and investor, some disquieting signs have arisen that there may be too much saving (not all of it American saving) chasing investment in US assets. The rapid run-up in high technology stocks from 1996 to 2000, followed by the March 2000 bursting of the tech-stock bubble, suggests, in retrospect, overinvestment in that sector. Overinvestment of course can only be fueled by what retrospectively comes to be known as oversaving. Those who lost money in the tech-stock bubble, after the fact, wished they had either invested elsewhere or simply consumed the funds that flowed into the tech sector.

Of course, for American savers there is an asset that provides a tax-sheltered way to enhance consumption while storing wealth. US residential real estate has surged in value by 44 percent, over 10 percent per year, since 2000. Even adjusting for inflation, the real gains in the value of US residential real estate between 2000 and 2004 are estimated at 38 percent. For purposes of comparison, the real gains during the late 1970s real estate boom between 1976 and 1980 totaled 26 percent.

Thinking about residential real estate as a store of value for US households suggests a number of insights about US saving behavior. The tax preferences for US residential real estate are well-known. Interest on mortgages up to $1 million is fully deductible from income tax. Capital gains on sales of residences are exempt from tax in amounts up to $500,000. So, too, are state and local real estate taxes, although the alternative minimum tax may be starting to atrophy this benefit. Still, the largest tax benefit lies with the fact that the consumption services from owning real estate and living in it, either as a primary residence or a vacation home, constitute a non-taxed form of consumption. These extraordinary tax preferences for residential real estate amount to $1 trillion in tax revenue losses over the next five years. Those funds could be used to finance a move toward a far more efficient consumption-based tax system wherein all forms of saving are treated the same—and more favorably— than under the current system.

One of the reasons that the conventionally measured US saving rate is so low, having dropped virtually to 1 percent from a still-low 4 percent in the late 1990s, lies with the fact that the consumption of housing services is subsidized, while increases in the value of owner-occupied real estate are not counted as conventional saving. Once again, after the bursting of the stock market bubble, Americans are saving by overinvesting in tax-preferred housing as a store of value. Unfortunately, housing does not add as much to labor productivity as more traditional capital does, so the rush of American saving into housing raises questions about the durability of America's decade-old rise in productivity growth from about 1 percent to about 2.5 percent annually.

Too Much Saving?

The discussion of the experience with saving and investment in advanced industrial countries suggests a crude criterion to use when answering how much saving is too much. The rough answer is that the appropriate level of savings is related to the return that can be earned on investments financed with those savings. For example, one of the reasons the US runs a large current account deficit financed by a heavy net flow of foreign investment into the United States lies with the perception that the real return on investment in US assets is higher than the real return on investment elsewhere. The Chinese government, which does not allow large-scale capital outflows by its citizens, is investing about $200 billion a year abroad, much of it in US Treasury securities on behalf of its population, which is generating more savings than can be profitably absorbed inside China.

The result is, of course, to accommodate US consumption, especially of owner-occupied real estate, given the ability of US households to increase their leveraging of purchases of real estate through low-interest, tax-advantaged mortgages. In effect, the Chinese government is helping subsidize more US saving in the form of an increase in the value of the stock of real estate in the United States, which in turn builds an ever-larger stream of untaxed benefits to US households while enabling them to store and enhance wealth.

The problem lies with the fact that real estate bubbles are only supported by the prospects that the next buyer of a property will pay even more than the last since real estate does not actually produce anything other than residential services for its owner. The value of those services shows up in a property's rental value, and, ominously, rental returns on properties in the stronger real estate markets in the United States are extraordinarily low, as is often the case in the late stages of a real estate bubble. The suggestion that too much saving worldwide is chasing investments with returns that are too low is permeating world markets. Unsurprisingly, in a world of aging societies that are growing wealthier, the search for ways to store wealth and thereby generate future streams of income for retirement is intensifying.

Rising House Prices Not the Best Way to Save

The definition of savings as the difference between consumption per unit of time and the sum of income plus the change in accumulated wealth over the same unit of time reminds us that the simple, conventional notion of saving, not spending out of current income, is inadequate and misleading. If the substantial rise in house prices over the past four years is counted as saving, Americans are saving enough, although they are accumulating wealth in a highly illiquid and potentially risky way. Who wants to sell their home to cushion consumption if income falls? It is not like taking money out of the bank.

In a society that is aging and growing wealthier, the price of income streams from wealth can rise rapidly. In those circumstances, it is not surprising to see asset managers ignoring risks to earn a higher rate of return. Eventually, this search for return irrespective of risk results in too much asset acquisition, and when reality dawns, a sharp drop follows in the value of some assets. Such could easily be the fate of America's much-favored real estate. A gradual transition to a consumption-based tax system that favors all forms of saving, not just housing, would accomplish the dual goal of encouraging more US saving in all forms while reducing the risk of disruptive real estate bubbles.

PART II

BOOMS AND BUSTS: A JOURNEY THROUGH RECENT ECONOMIC HISTORY

8

THE GOLDEN AGE

Is This the Golden Age?

MAY 1995

Writing in mid-1995, Makin surveyed the economic scene—moderate inflation, stock and bond rallies, and low deficits attributable to a confluence of economic events, including policymakers' decisions. While acknowledging there is still economic trouble in other parts of the world, notably Japan, which threatens to harm the US economy, he turned to the prevailing conventional speculation over whether the US would ease into a downturn—a soft landing—or encounter one that is more abrupt—a hard landing.

Makin offered a third possibility that the US economy is, over the long run, in a golden age. He went on to clarify that a golden age or a golden-age recovery is characterized by high levels of investment, often associated with "a major technological breakthrough that, when widely adopted, increases the return on investment." Makin concluded that if it is a golden age and policymakers conduct policies aimed at managing a soft landing, the economy could continue "to outperform expectations and equity prices [could] continue to rise," thereby convincing investors of the possibility of "eternal prosperity." Citing 1929 in the United States and 1989 in Japan, Makin hinted of trouble ahead, possibly in the form of a stock market bubble. Indeed, defying expectations, the economy would continue booming for most of the rest of the decade.

Despite the consternation about the collapse of the dollar against the deutsche mark and the yen, 1995 has so far emerged as a golden age for the US economy and financial markets. Growth has slowed obligingly to a sustainable pace of around 2.5 percent, down from the 5.1 percent growth rate at the end of 1994. Inflation has remained moderate. Even more noticeable, stock and bond markets have rallied powerfully, with stock prices on average up more than 10 percent since the beginning of 1995 and interest rates between 1 and 1.5 percentage points lower than they were in late 1994.

Positive Economic Factors

The good news for US financial markets is more than just a moderation of growth to a sustainable level with steady inflation. Combined federal, state, and local government deficits are at their lowest levels in years, requiring only about $120 billion a year, or about 1.5 percent of the gross domestic product, to finance. The supply of equities—based on data available through the end of 1994—is actually falling at a rate of about $100 billion per year. America's corporations are generating so much cash that they can afford to finance a high level of capital acquisition while buying back outstanding stock.

The recent takeover bid for Chrysler Corporation underscored the healthy liquidity situation of large US corporations and investors. Chrysler's earnings have risen so rapidly relative to its capital outlays that the firm has accumulated a large pool of about $7.5 billion in cash. According to Chrysler management, the amount was to see the corporation through the coming slowdown of the US economy. If, however, that slowdown is not close at hand, then Chrysler becomes an attractive takeover candidate for financial engineers, who could reconfigure Chrysler to take advantage of an unusually long economic recovery.

Just as surprising as the remarkable performance of US financial markets over the past several months is the aid to the market from an increasingly accommodative policy stance of the world's three leading central banks. The Federal Reserve has stopped raising interest rates while providing ample liquidity for the US banking system, which in turn has been making loans available to American households and corporations.

More surprisingly, the Fed's steady policy stance, even in the face of a sharply weaker dollar against other major currencies, has forced an end to the disinflation policies of Germany's Bundesbank, which cut interest rates by 0.5 percent at the end of March. More significantly, Fed policy has forced the Bank of Japan (BOJ), which has been risking a dangerous accelerating deflation, to cut interest rates by 75 basis points on April 14.

Dangerous Instability from the BOJ

The BOJ's policy of supporting the dollar with dollar purchases approaching $15 billion per month creates a dangerously unstable potential disturbance to the golden-age scenario. The BOJ has been purchasing US government securities, mostly two-year and five-year notes, with the dollars it has acquired while trying to stem the yen's rise. This extra buying, especially given the light supply pressure, has tended to depress US interest rates further, with two-year yields down to a level of just 42 basis points above the federal funds rate. That narrow spread usually portends a further Fed easing, a move that does not seem likely right now.

The unstable aspect of the BOJ's dollar support policy, resulting in lower US interest rates, is its tendency to push the dollar still lower by reducing the attraction of dollar assets and stimulating US spending; such activity in turn raises the US external deficit. The unstable sequence—weaker dollar, more BOJ dollar and US note buying, lower US interest rates, weaker dollar, and so on—has become quite clearly defined.

The BOJ could stop buying US Treasury notes with the dollars it accumulates and instead buy gold or could simply hold the dollars in cash to break the unstable dollar support cycle. The resulting higher US interest rates would help support the dollar. But then a higher US inflation rate or a stronger US economy could accentuate upward pressure on US interest rates and force a rapid inversion of the US yield curve and a quick return to the hard-landing scenario. The deflationary pressure already evident in Japan and Germany would be accentuated, the outlook for global exporters would worsen, and fragile emerging markets could collapse further. We could be looking at a dark age instead of a golden age.

A Golden Recovery?

Barring the emergence of a dark age, the more parochial argument about the path of the US economy continues. That debate has been conducted in terms of the hard-landing scenario versus the soft-landing scenario. The hard-landing scenario, which marks the end of a typical demand-led recovery with a sharply inverted yield curve and a weak stock market, has been decisively rejected by markets in favor of the soft-landing scenario, whereby the economy drifts down to a sustainable growth path of about 2.5 percent and inflation pressures remain in check. How much of the apparent soft-landing scenario is really tied to the BOJ's dollar policy and the US fixed-income support policy remains to be seen.

Despite the risks of a near-term dark age, a possibility far more intriguing than the choice between a hard landing and a soft landing is beginning to emerge from a closer examination of market behavior. Underlying the likely oscillation of analysts' views from hard landing to soft landing and back again is the possibility that the US economy is, over the long run, in a golden age.

An economy in a golden age grows for a longer time at a higher rate with lower inflation than anyone expects from typical historical experience. A golden-age recovery is supply-led rather than demand-led. A rise in the real return on investment causes increased capital formation with an attendant increase in aggregate supply that outstrips the rise in aggregate demand. Underlying price pressures are held well below pressures that usually emerge during a sustained economic expansion.

Historically, golden-age recoveries have been called investment-led recoveries because they are characterized by unusually high levels of investment. The reason for the high level of investment is often a major technological breakthrough that, when widely adopted, increases the return on investment. The improved accuracy and timeliness of information flows associated with the rapid development of computers may be related to the jump in the productivity of capital. But whatever the cause, there is strong evidence that the real return on investment is unusually high during the current business cycle expansion.

More specifically, on the supply side, the trough of the recovery may have fallen in March 1991, while on the demand side the trough actually came two years later, in March 1993. That timing would give the supply side a distinct lead over the demand side so that the economy would look like, and for most purposes would be indistinguishable from, one in a golden age, at least until demand growth catches up with supply growth. In a golden age, closure of the demand-supply gap would come much later than expected.

Misstating the trough on demand growth in this recovery is like marveling at the performance of a 40-year-old athlete who is really only 20 years old. Miscalculating by two years the spring 1993 birthday of the recovery of demand growth would produce large surprises for investors who think they are looking at a tired five-year-old supply-constrained expansion when really a three-year-old demand expansion has been superimposed on a five-year-old supply expansion.

Many years of economic data and the benefit of hindsight will be necessary to discover whether this recovery is a golden age or just one with a misidentified birth date. But for the next two years, the difference really does not matter. Either a golden age or a recovery that began in March 1993 instead of March 1991 will produce extraordinary behavior in the financial markets. We shall call both versions of the alternative to the hard-landing/soft-landing scenario a golden age.

Differentiating Between a Soft Landing and a Golden Age

How can we distinguish between a soft landing and a golden age? In a soft landing, stocks are supported largely by lower interest rates instead of higher earnings: Defensive stocks, which perform well in a weak economic environment, improve relative to cyclical stocks, which perform better in a strong economic environment. In the bond market, the yield curve should flatten, and real yields may fall as the economy comes in for a soft landing and may even anticipate rate cuts by the Federal Reserve. In the currency market, the dollar should be weaker because of a prospective fall in real interest rates, lower growth, and moderating increases in asset prices. In the commodity markets, raw materials prices should fall relative to finished goods prices, while precious metals prices should be weak relative to both.

The contrast between a soft landing and a golden age would become clear from the different behavior of financial and commodity markets. In a golden age, earnings continue to rise for a longer time than expected in a soft landing. As markets begin to sense extended earnings growth, cyclical stocks should begin to outperform defensive stocks. The higher level of interest in Chrysler shares and other cyclical companies over the past month hints at this possibility.

If a soft-landing scenario gives way to a golden age, bond yields may actually rise, largely because of higher expected real returns on alternative investments rather than a sharp rise in expected inflation. The composition of inflation is important in trying to identify a golden age. Prices of raw materials ought to rise relative to prices of finished goods, as suppliers bid aggressively for inputs while productivity gains moderate the pass-through of cost pressures. Prices of precious metals ought to fall relative to raw materials prices because, while the demand for raw materials to produce more goods is rising, high real interest rates increase the opportunity cost of holding precious metals, as does the lower-than-expected inflation that accompanies a golden-age recovery.

Currency markets would provide one of the most dramatic clues to the emergence of a golden age. In a true golden-age recovery, the dollar would strengthen for two reasons. First, the current account deficit should fall as superior US productivity growth encourages higher exports and lower imports. Second, while a falling current account deficit would reduce the supply of dollars to global financial markets, sharp increases in equity prices that would accompany the golden-age scenario of higher earnings of US companies would begin to attract a high level of foreign capital inflows from countries without the golden-age scenario. Neither Germany with its tepid demand-led recovery nor Japan with its deflationary weakness looks anything like a country in a golden age.

Leading to a Hard Landing

Should the soft landing give way to a hard landing instead of a golden age, the differences would be readily apparent from the prices of financial assets and commodities. In a hard landing, stock prices would fall, with cyclicals hardest hit as expected earnings collapsed and interest rates rose. In fixed-income markets, short-term rates would rise rapidly until the federal funds rate was pushed up to a level 1 or 2 percentage points above rising bond yields. The dollar would weaken or strengthen depending on the pace of Fed tightening relative to the pace at which the hard-landing scenario emerged.

Commodity prices would provide one of the most useful clues of the emergence of a hard landing over a golden-age scenario. Prices of precious metals would rise relative to prices of raw materials. The hard landing would bring on a rapid increase in expected inflation, while the sharp slowdown engineered by the Fed would cause the demand for raw materials to collapse.

Eternal Prosperity?

Without the benefit of hindsight, neither a hard landing nor a soft landing nor a golden age will emerge with shining clarity. Rather, we will probably continue to oscillate between the hard-landing and the soft-landing scenarios while, if the golden age remains the underlying reality, investors in US equities will continue to be pleasantly surprised, and dollar bears will be in for a rude shock.

Decisive evidence of a golden age is unfortunately not only retrospective but painful. As the economy, driven by the reality of a golden age, continues to outperform expectations and equity prices continue to rise, the public becomes convinced of eternal prosperity. (That conviction emerged in 1929 in the United States and in 1989 in Japan.) The stock market bubble—inadvertently fed by a central bank that believes it is performing well by keeping inflation moderate although prices actually ought to be *falling* in a supply-led recovery—begins to expand so rapidly that the increase in wealth from that bubble causes demand to run away. Demand growth quickly comes to dominate supply growth, and the central bank is forced to collapse the bubble to avoid runaway inflation.

In short, once the golden age gives rise to the myth of eternal prosperity and eternally rising stock prices, that age will be over. But because few analysts are even thinking about a golden age now, but rather are preoccupied with the hard-landing/soft-landing dichotomy, a golden age, if one is underlying this recovery, probably has several years to run.

—ᴍ—

Is the Golden Age Over?

MAY 1996

A year later, Makin revisited his golden-age theme—checking in on the country's economic conditions. He found that despite the hand-wringing of economists of the time about recent weaker economic numbers, his thesis that America is in for prolonged expansion was holding up nicely. Still, he pointed out that no golden age lasts forever—and that it often collapses when people come to believe prosperity is eternal and irreversible. As he presciently says, "In 1996, we are still in the pre-bubble stage of the golden age."

Writing just a year ago in the *Economic Outlook*, I raised the possibility that the US economy had entered a golden age: a time when growth stays close to a comfortable (sustainable) rate of 2.0–2.5 percent and inflation remains subdued, giving no hint that the economy is overheating and thereby no reason for the Federal Reserve to push up interest rates to halt unsustainably rapid growth. Since February, higher interest rates, higher energy and grain prices, and a stagnant stock market have appeared to alter this happy picture. Still, the golden-age scenario remains intact.

Economic Expansion

Underlying the golden age is an economic expansion led by unusually strong investment that produces a supply-side recovery: an economic expansion in which supply grows faster than demand so that price pressures are contained. The long period of investment growth results in sustained output growth, higher corporate profits, and a large increase in prices on the stock market. Eventually, as happened during the 1920s, a sustained rise in profits leads to a stock market bubble that pushes up wealth and demand so rapidly that the central bank eventually is forced to raise interest rates and collapse the bubble to avoid runaway inflation. But in 1996 we are still in the pre-bubble stage of the golden age.

With interest rates having risen by more than a full percentage point during the past two months and stock prices first stagnating and then actually falling by more than 3 percent during the week after Easter, the question naturally arises as to whether the golden age has come to a premature end. If the stock market does not go up from here, it will certainly be possible to say that the golden age never reached full flower but rather the economic expansion that began five years ago in the spring of 1991 simply ended because of the strains brought on by demand-growth pressures on capacity that pushed the Fed to raise interest rates in the face of rising inflation pressures.

Any phenomenon as unusual as a golden age will certainly encounter periods when its existence is seriously called into question. As I wrote a year ago,

> Without the benefit of hindsight, neither a hard landing nor a soft landing nor a golden age will emerge with shining clarity. Rather, we will probably continue to oscillate between the hard-landing and the soft-landing scenarios while, if the golden age remains the underlying reality, investors in US equities will continue to be pleasantly surprised, and dollar bears will be in for a rude shock.

The golden age is the exception and not the rule. Markets in the spring of 1996 are pricing the usual outcome, which has the economy running out of capacity, pushing up interest rates, and possibly ending the rapid growth of profits that has supported the stock market.

However, I am prepared to stick with the golden-age scenario.

Still Sustained Growth?

No single interpretation of the path of the US economy survives un-jostled from quarter to quarter. Repeating again last year's observation: "Without the benefit of hindsight, neither a hard landing nor a soft landing nor a golden age will emerge with shining clarity." In the spring of 1996, a combination of higher real interest rates, a stronger dollar, and higher prices for commodities that serve as inputs for production has not shaken our conviction that we still may see a period of sustained growth over the next several years that will come, with hindsight, to be viewed as a golden age. If this scenario comes to pass, the US stock market will exceed the 6,000 level we predicted for 1995.[1] And if that happens, the real danger will lie in the resulting conviction that the golden age will continue forever. It will not.

Notes

1. Indeed, the Dow closed at 6,463.94 on December 6, 1996, the day after Federal Reserve Chairman Alan Greenspan's "irrational exuberance" speech at AEI.

What Ends the Party?

JUNE 1998

By the middle of 1998, the eighth year of the "extraordinary" investment-led recovery, economic signs in the US were still looking strong as investment growth was "quickening," validating Makin's 1995 speculation that the country was experiencing a golden economic age. Growth was strong yet inflation was low, which made policymakers uneasy.

But as the US economy was shining, Asian economies were in crisis, leading Makin to consider how the era of US prosperity might end. Makin pondered that the onset of the Asian crisis in 1997 had not "mark[ed] the end of America's investment-led recovery" as he had thought it would, remarking that "investment-led recoveries do not end well." He emphasized that they needn't end badly, as they did after the 1929 crash in America and the 1989 crash in Japan, if central banks properly manage the economy. Because it is impossible to know if high inflation or an end to capital formation would end this investment-led recovery, he admonishes, "The first rule of economic policy is (or ought to be): When the behavior of the economy being managed cannot be understood or predicted, do nothing."

The American economy roared into spring 1998 with yet another wave of unexpectedly good news. The economy grew at more than 4 percent during the first quarter, the sixth consecutive quarter exceeding predicted growth, while inflation, measured by the broadly based deflator for the gross domestic product (GDP), fell below 1 percent for the first time since 1964. The idea that the Federal Reserve, prompted by expectations of mounting inflation pressures, might tighten at its May meeting vanished almost instantly with the release of the stellar first-quarter figures.

The dream combination of above-consensus growth and below-consensus inflation has left financial markets and policymakers strangely uneasy. Although much more improvement in the United States is hard to imagine and Europe is also getting better, conditions are worsening in Asia. Something must give.

The party for the American golden age can end in two ways. In the first way—the way that demand-led recoveries usually end—the economy overheats, and inflation pressure forces the Fed to tighten to fulfill its mandate to maintain stable prices. Alternatively, overinvestment puts too much capacity in place (as it has in much of Asia), investment and earnings collapse, and lower spending slows the economy.

Overheating as the end to expansion is far more familiar and much easier for a central bank to manage. Surely there are days when Chairman Alan Greenspan and the members of the Federal Open Market Committee, constantly baffled by spectacular, inflation-free economic growth that defies the forecast of the Fed's staff and most economists, fervently wish for the familiar inflation pressure, which enables them to apply the monetary brakes with a comfortable feeling of confidence. Nothing makes central bankers feel more certain that they are doing their jobs than taking away the proverbial punch bowl when the party starts to get out of hand.

Central banks have more difficulty in managing the end of an investment-led recovery. Clearly, the US recovery is investment-led. Business fixed investment has accelerated since 1983 and has outstripped increases relative to its level at the trough in all but the long 1960s expansion. Even in that expansion, investment growth had been flat for a year by the eighth year of the recovery. But, in the eighth year of this extraordinary investment-led expansion, investment growth is still quickening.

Surge in US Investment

It was tempting to believe, as I did, that the onset of the Asian crisis would mark the end of America's investment-led recovery. Slower growth in Asia would constrain pricing power and compress earnings growth so that stock prices would fall, consumer exuberance would moderate, and the economy would even glide naturally into a soft landing without any action by the Fed. So far, based on first-quarter numbers, markets and the economy have proved that view wrong. After pausing in the fourth quarter when investment growth was flat, US business fixed investment rallied in the first quarter of 1998 to rise at an 18 percent annual rate, slightly above the rate of increase before the Asian crisis.

Clearly, in a selection process of American corporate leaders today, optimists are being promoted while pessimists are being dropped by the wayside.

The End of Investment-Led Recoveries

But investment-led recoveries do not end well. They need not end badly, but the two big investment-led recoveries of this century—the United States in the late 1920s and Japan in the late 1980s—did end so because of policy errors after sharp declines in equity prices.

The problem at the end of investment-led recoveries concerns the mixed messages to the central banks. Central banks cannot fulfill their usual mandate of controlling inflation—because inflation does not appear. Central banks are then left with the dilemma of deciding whether to target asset markets, which rise sharply in an environment of steady growth with no inflation. The Fed faces this exact dilemma today.

The bad endings to the American and Japanese investment-led expansions earlier in this century seem at first glance to have been caused by central banks' attempts to deflate asset bubbles. But the real problems were not the attempts to deflate asset bubbles, but rather mistaken policies after those attempts. In the 18 months before fall 1929, the Federal Reserve raised interest rates by nearly 300 basis points while inflation stood at zero. Once real short-term interest rates reached 6 percent, the stock market collapsed. The full-blown development of the Great Depression, however, required consistent and extraordinary bungling by the Fed after its initial effort to deflate the stock market. The money supply was allowed to collapse, and deflationary pressure thereby increased. Those mistakes need not be repeated and almost certainly would not be repeated in the United States.

The Bank of Japan (BOJ) at the end of the 1980s faced a trickier problem. Japan's investment-led recovery had produced a capital stock far too large for the Japanese economy. The BOJ tightened just as businesses were deciding that the capital stock was too large and were cutting back sharply on investment plans. The coincidence of the tighter monetary policy, which collapsed the asset bubble and hence slowed consumption, with the breakdown in the investment expansion threw the Japanese economy into a deep tailspin. The attendant damage to bank balance sheets was never repaired and has kept the economy struggling since 1990. With a trillion dollars of bad loans still on the balance sheets of Japan's banks, the economy remains weak, with deflation pressure increasing.

The Fed's Nightmare

The Fed's nightmare would be to encounter the same problem that the BOJ faced in 1989–90. If the Fed tightens to quell asset market exuberance, while a combination of chastened consumers and the Asian crisis renders the US capital stock too large in the view of most corporate managers, the US expansion will come to a sudden, wrenching stop.

No one knows whether higher inflation pressure or a sharp end to capital formation will end the current expansion. The route of inflation pressure is far more familiar, but the data simply do not support that outcome at this stage. As social scientists, economists need to be a bit more humble and should not trumpet either a new age or a "just you wait" inflation scenario.

The following mental experiment is useful, if chastening. Look at the growth data over the past 18 months and ask: Had you known these data in advance, what would have been your forecast of the inflation rate observable by this time? Most honest economists would have supposed a broad acceleration of prices; that has not occurred. Wage growth has accelerated, but the broadest measure of wage increase, including benefits—the employment cost index—is now climbing at a 3.3 percent annual rate, up only slightly from the 2.8 percent rate a year ago.

Central Banks and Passivity

The first rule of economic policy is (or ought to be): When the behavior of the economy being managed cannot be understood or predicted, do nothing. Arguably, the Fed faces this situation in spring 1998; it has been appropriately passive. In contrast, the BOJ faces a clear need to reflate; it has been inappropriately passive. And the Bundesbank faces extinction in just half a year; it, too, has been passive.

Beyond this simple first rule, the Fed must address the painful reality that investment-led recoveries rob it of the option to be preemptive. The inflation numbers will not provide the familiar traction at the end of demand-led recoveries. While eschewing any significant tightening, the Fed must bear in mind the powerful deflationary pressure in Asia. Japan, with its $4 trillion GDP, and China, with its $1 trillion GDP, together account for 80 percent of Asian GDP and nearly a fifth of world GDP. Prices are falling at a 2 percent annual rate in both countries and are likely to dip lower as the distress intensifies in China, Northeast Asia, and the countries of the Association of Southeast Asian Nations.

Asia's investment recovery has already ended, with a tremendous stock of excess capacity still in place. The continued existence of excess capacity accounts for the reemergence this spring of a more serious phase of the Asian economic crisis. (See the next section.) The first phase, in fall 1997, consisted of a sudden collapse of financial markets. Now the problems are tied to real economic weakness, as producers cannot generate sufficient cash flow to service their large debts, many still denominated in hard currencies.

A Reflationary Stance for Japan

The corollary of the passive stance of the Federal Reserve and probably the Bundesbank and the European Central Bank is a desperate need for an active reflationary stance by the BOJ. Japan could announce its strong commitment to reflation by publicly authorizing the BOJ to purchase Japanese government bonds in huge amounts sufficient to inject a liquidity surge into Japan's businesses and households. Such measures are not only essential for the health of the Japanese economy but also necessary to contain rising deflationary pressures throughout Asia.

The focus of the American and Japanese governments on the dollar-yen exchange rate must end. If, after a large injection of liquidity to push up demand, the Japanese economy is starting to recover with the dollar-yen exchange rate at 160 rather than continuing to languish with the exchange rate at 120, Japanese, Asian, and global economies will be far better off.

The Japanese Finance Ministry's insistence on effectively pegging the exchange rate renders the BOJ's new "independence" meaningless. With a pegged exchange rate, a central bank must set the money supply at whatever level is necessary to validate that exchange rate. In Japan's case, that level has choked off recovery and has contributed to intensifying deflation.

The recent G8 summit in Birmingham ended with bland statements about fighting international crime and helping poor countries. Entirely missing was any mention of the most important need for today's world economy: a call for aggressive reflationary measures in Asia, beginning in Japan.

9

THE ASIAN CRISIS

The Benefits of Devaluation in a Deflationary World

SEPTEMBER 1998

The Asian financial crisis that began to unfold in the summer of 1997 stemmed from deflation and excess capacity, which was confusing to many observers who were far more accustomed to the challenges of inflation. Failure especially by Russian and Asian policymakers to grasp the implications of deflation, Makin explained, had serious economic consequences that could be alleviated in part by currency devaluations.

In this essay from 1998, Makin observed that the failure of Indonesia, Russia, South Korea, and Thailand to devalue their currencies beginning in July 1997 had disastrous consequences for their economies. Makin attempted to set the record straight and explain why currency devaluation—which has a "bad reputation"—and currency weakness in a deflationary world could be a plus: It can result in desirable reflation while "shifting . . . demand from countries with an excess supply to those with excess demand."

There is a compelling need for the International Monetary Fund (IMF), finance ministers, central bankers, market analysts, and headline writers to learn the difference between the dangers of currency devaluation in an *inflationary* world and the benefits of currency devaluation in a *deflationary* world. Policymakers, far more accustomed to an inflationary world than to today's deflationary world, have failed to make the distinction.

That failure has cost Asia and now Russia dearly. Some market analysts and newspapers continue to create dangerous and unnecessary confusion about the cause of falling stock markets worldwide. Headlines are trumpeting the view that global equity markets are falling because of currency weakness. This makes no sense and seriously muddles cause and effect.

We must understand why currency devaluation has a bad reputation and yet how it can play a constructive role. In a far more typical inflationary world of excess demand, currency devaluation is perilous and often counterproductive. A sudden devaluation—like that by the British in 1967—raises the cost of foreign goods and shifts demand onto a domestic capacity that may already be overstrained. Unless a tight monetary policy accompanies currency devaluation in a world of excess demand, the shift in demand induced by a weaker currency away from foreign producers and onto domestic producers will only push up prices even faster without reducing an external imbalance. Thus, the IMF insists on a tight monetary policy after a devaluation. A tight fiscal policy may also be required to keep the government sector from absorbing resources that are slated to produce more exports for the demand increased by devaluation.

Deflation, Devaluation, and Demand

In the less typical world of deflation that characterizes Asia, including Japan, and an increasing share of the global economy, devaluation can be more constructive. Once again, devaluation shifts demand onto domestic producers and away from foreign producers. But, with excess capacity, there is no need for a tighter monetary or fiscal policy. Pursuing such policies may be destabilizing if they reduce aggregate demand for domestic output more than a devaluation raises it. Devaluation in a region of chronic excess capacity such as Asia might do just that. And so the initial application of restrictive IMF programs in Indonesia, Russia, South Korea, and Thailand during the summer of 1988 produced deflationary results. With no attendant fall in currency values, the tight monetary and fiscal policies merely increased excess supply.

Given *global* excess capacity, devaluation is a zero-sum game: It shifts demand onto devalued currency countries and away from stable (revalued after others devalue) currency countries. Yet, in a world like today's with strong demand growth still present in the United States and some countries of Europe, devaluations in Asia can be and have been helpful in preventing overheating in the stronger economies. Naturally, if the excess supply and deflationary pressure in one part of the world like Asia get too large, a global excess supply through large currency revaluations may result in the rest of the world. The risk of this outcome has risen significantly with Japan's decisive movement into the excess supply camp since 1997. Japan, accounting for about one-fifth of world output, brings the share of deflationary Asia in world production to about one-third.

The beneficial shifting of demand from countries with an excess supply to those with excess demand has been reflected in equity markets. The Asian crisis and plummeting currencies have been a great plus for US and European equity markets. Between October 27, 1997—the day of the 7 percent one-day equity market sell-off, when market pundits began to notice that Asian economic problems could hurt earnings growth—and July 17, 1998, the recent peak in Western equity markets, the US stock market rose by 35 percent, while European equity markets, led by Germany's DAX index rise of 65 percent, surged even more. These climbing equity markets mirrored the constructive transfer of demand away from overheating economies and onto stagnating economies, encouraged by the devaluation of the currencies of stagnating economies.

The Currency Peg

Still, in light of this positive relationship between weak Asian currencies and strong Western stock markets, newspapers are attributing the early August drop in global equity markets to a decline of the yen and possible devaluations of the Chinese yuan, not to mention the weakness of the Russian ruble. But Asia is simply in a deflationary spiral, and the currency weakness there is a symptom of the failure to address the problem, not a cause of weak stock markets in the West. The obsession with pegged exchange rates as a solution to problems in emerging markets and Asia has been costly. Ever since Thailand resisted devaluation with higher interest rates in June 1997, a parade of countries, including Indonesia, South Korea, and now Russia, has followed the same disastrous path.

The recent $22.6 billion IMF package of relief for Russia was aimed at pegging the currency and giving the Russians time to design revenue collection to pay for their bloated government expenditures. But most Russians and foreigners wanted to abandon rubles—around $50 billion worth—and the fresh infusion of dollars from the IMF package only prompted them to move more rapidly. Simultaneously, a lack of confidence in the Russian government to collect taxes and cut expenditures led to the rapid sales of Russian stocks and bonds. With Russian assets and the ruble collapsing, the Russian government on August 17 declared that the ruble would be allowed to float 30–40 percent above the existing range. In effect, the Russian government defaulted on its short-term ruble-denominated obligations and imposed restrictions on currency transactions.

As the Russian situation, along with developments all over Asia, has clearly demonstrated, there are no neat and clean solutions to the serious problems confronting Asia and the emerging markets. Pretending that holding currencies stable will somehow make the problems go away has been a disastrous error, akin to treating symptoms instead of causes.

Is Stability the Issue?

Under most circumstances, currency stability is a desirable goal, especially for developing countries. A stable currency tends to attract capital inflows, which thereby lower the cost of capital and enhance capital formation and growth. Unfortunately, the basic problem in Asia has been too much capital formation, resulting in huge excess capacity and requisite price cutting by countries attempting to minimize the losses associated with persistent excess capacity.

South Korea is a prime example. It has virtually eliminated imports while pressing for maximum exports. Because the country has more than enough capacity to satisfy any domestic needs, South Korea is desperately attempting to use that capacity by selling more into global markets. But Korean sales of products like rolled steel at any price put extreme pressure on other producers in China and elsewhere. Hence, markets begin to expect defensive devaluations in countries like China. The Chinese resist any notion that they might devalue and back it up with intervention and, as in Hong Kong, higher interest rates. As the higher interest rates put further downward pressure on local real estate and stock prices, headlines scream the negative results in financial markets.

The realization of the extraordinary weakness of Japan's economy and its banking system—encumbered with $1 trillion worth of bad loans and unable to perform normal banking functions—has intensified the Asian crisis over the past several months. Japan is 60 percent of the Asian gross domestic product; with domestic demand collapsing, the weaker currency is merely a sign of the market's assessment that the Japanese must sell more products outside Japan to avoid an even weaker equity market.

Somewhat ironically, the solution to Asia's problems will probably involve a still more debilitated yen and possibly more debilitated Chinese and Hong Kong currencies. The Japanese need desperately to reflate by aggressively printing money to a point where Japanese consumers will believe that prices will actually rise over the coming year and therefore reward them for spending more money now rather than hoarding. A large, reflationary increase in the Japanese money supply will shove the yen down until higher spending helps the economy recover. A lower yen will put downward pressure on the Chinese and Hong Kong currencies.

Continuing Misunderstandings

The weaker currency scenario is preferable to the alternative approach. Like the rest of Asia, the last thing Japan needs is more of the wrong kind of investment. In Japan's case, the wrong investment has been the objective of more than 70 trillion yen of public works expenditures over the past five years, much of it added to excess capacity in the public sector, just as Japan's investment boom in the 1980s produced excess capacity in the private sector. Surely, Japan's elaborate system of bridges to barely populated islands and its paved streambeds are not contributing to economic strength in Japan or the rest of Asia.

The confusion over Asia's unusual excess capacity problem—more investment is not always best—and the impact on exchange rates has been aggravated by a careless financial press, one day suggesting that a falling yen was preferable to the alternative and the next intimating that the decline of the yen was pushing global markets down. If a falling yen can help prevent a Japanese meltdown (which it can do), then a falling yen should not be identified as the cause of falling global markets.

The misunderstandings about exchange rates and their relationship to the deflationary environment in Asia probably stem from a misinterpretation of the role of currency devaluations of the 1930s. The Great Depression is often associated with the competitive devaluations or "beggar thy neighbor policies" followed by countries desperately attempting to increase their market share in a deflationary world of shrinking markets. But, then as now, falling exchange rates were a symptom, not a cause, of the excess supply problems that plagued many countries. Britain's arbitrary decision to return to the gold standard in 1925 at a sterling price of gold that severely overvalued the currency triggered a deflationary cycle that spread to the United States and the rest of Europe and culminated in the Great Depression. The British were not solely to blame for the Great Depression, but other countries' attempts to maintain their pegs to sterling and gold contributed to the deflationary environment.

Once markets began to sense the desperate problems of excess capacity in much of Europe and eventually the United States, currencies fell largely because of the need to increase demand. When global excess capacity exists, no fall in exchange rates, which only reallocate demand from one country to another, can eliminate the deflation problem. Hence, the 1930s saw a number of currency devaluations associated with chronic excess capacity as more and more countries joined the quest to attract shrinking global aggregate demand to their increasingly idle production facilities.

Today we seem to assume that if we do not allow the symptoms of excess supply (weak currencies) to emerge in Asia and Russia, somehow the problem of excess capacity will go away. It will not go away and can be remedied only by ratcheting up demand while limiting new additions to excess capacity. That is why support for a stable exchange rate that cuts the cost of capital and thereby helps increase investment and growth is counterproductive in the current excess supply situation in Asia.

The last thing Asia needs is more investment. What it needs instead is more demand for the products that past investments in capacity can produce. Hence, monetary stimulus—printing money, not just ramming interest rates down—is preferable to fiscal stimulus, which often is complicated by either passive measures such as tax cuts or pork-barrel measures such as the ridiculous construction projects the Japanese government pursued over the past seven to eight years.

Today's confused headline writers in the financial press should be writing that the decline of the yen and weak financial markets are all symptoms of a desperate need for monetary stimulation in Asia. Currency weakness in a deflationary world can be a plus since it defines reflation. The sooner we get over the mistaken notion of trying to divide a group of symptoms such as falling currencies and stock prices (all caused by global excess supply) into cause and effect categories, the sooner we will have a better understanding of the problems in Asia and global financial markets.

Some guidance from the US Treasury along these lines would certainly be helpful and preferable to engineering more packages like July's disastrous $22 billion IMF package for Russia. Asia needs to reflate. Robert Rubin and Alan Greenspan should stand up and say so before deflation reaches America and Europe.

—◊—

Interference with Free Markets Causes Global Crisis

OCTOBER 1998

As the fallout of the Asian crisis spread to Brazil and threatened to spread to China and Hong Kong, Makin replied to commentators who blamed the troubles on free markets and unfettered capital flows. Pointing out that the crisis was because of "failure to diagnose the global excess capacity problem, resulting from mistaken policies designed for the largely inflationary postwar period," Makin wrote that the International Monetary Fund's (IMF) bailout of Mexico in 1995 exacerbated the problem by creating "a massive problem of moral hazard that turbocharged additional flows of private capital into

Asia, Russia, and Latin America," despite a lack of progress enacting market reforms. He decried the IMF's discrediting of "free markets and unfettered global capital flows" and wrote, "It is a great irony of the desperate situation in today's financial markets that a failure of IMF programs administered by IMF bureaucrats unaccountable to markets is taken as a sign of market failure." The only way to counter the rising threat of deflation to the industrial world, he argued, is to pursue aggressive monetary easing and avoid further compromising the flow of global capital.

Some of the great ironies and tragedies of a global financial crisis, such as the current one, are the misperceptions created by governments attempting to avoid responsibility. Along with currency devaluation, the free market and the unfettered flow of capital across national borders are being vilified as the causes of this disaster. Such blame is absurd and dangerous for two reasons. First, it leads to government actions that worsen the crisis. Second, it leaves in place false impressions that make more likely the reemergence of another tragedy like the one unfolding today in Asia, Russia, and perhaps Latin America.

Real Reasons for the Crisis

The causes of this crisis can be traced to sources distinctly inconsistent with free markets and unfettered global capital flows in both directions. The International Monetary Fund (IMF) must shoulder much of the blame for discrediting free markets and unfettered global capital flows. That institution, along with the US Treasury, engineered an extravagant bailout for Mexico after it had followed distinctly nonmarket policies leading up to the 1994 Mexican presidential election. The Mexican bailout and the self-congratulation by the IMF and the US Treasury in 1995 created a massive problem of moral hazard that turbocharged additional flows of private capital into Asia, Russia, and Latin America. Those capital flows contributed to the creation of massive excess capacity alongside grossly unrealistic expectations about the return on investments.

A continuing and rapidly deteriorating problem of excess capacity in Japan has accentuated the tragedy building in Asia from the overinvestment that followed the Mexican bailout. This problem results from distinctly non-free-market policies and the impediment of global capital flows. For many years, Japan fostered policies that virtually forced domestic consumers to save their money and invest inside Japan. The ensuing massive buildup of excess capacity and overinvestment in the stock market led to a crash in 1990. Since then, Japan has failed to recover because of heavy government intervention in all areas of the economy.

The Japanese government's solution to its problems was to engineer a 70 trillion yen program of overinvestment in the public sector while covering up critical problems in the banking system. As a result, the Japanese economy has languished. The problem in the banking sector has become so severe that no amount of fiscal or monetary stimulus has been able to stem the rapid deterioration of the Japanese economy. This appalling collection of policies, which are the exact opposite of the free-market principles being decried in today's deteriorating global environment, has created an economic disaster in Japan exactly when the rest of Asia needed an economic miracle.

Recent disastrous economic statistics, totally contrary to the Japanese government's unrealistic and virtually untruthful past representations of the Japanese economy, show a virtual collapse of private investment and consumption that will not soon be arrested. This problem feeds back to the acute problems faced by other Asian nations that have been desperately trying to restrict domestic demand and increase output as mandated by the traditional strictures imposed by the IMF. But the ability to increase output is severely reduced by the collapse of domestic and total demand in Japan and other Asian nations.

The global economy has entered an ugly "shrinking pie" phase: Increasingly desperate emerging economies can benefit only at the expense of other emerging economies. The most dramatic example came in August with Russia's decision to not only devalue its currency but also default on many of its debts. Russia's unilateral default horrified the global financial community because it forced institutions to write down to zero the value of their Russian holdings. This distinctly differs from the situation in the 1980s; although Latin American debtors then failed to service their debts, they avoided declaring defaults so that financial institutions could carry the loans at book value or 100 cents on the dollar.

Today the loans to emerging markets are securitized and traded in open financial markets; a dramatic fall in their value must be reflected promptly in the balance sheets of banks, mutual funds, hedge funds, and other investors. The losses associated with the Russian default alone are huge, probably totaling $100 billion so far.

The IMF Failure

The IMF's performance over the Russian package was disgraceful. The IMF rushed to assemble a $22 billion package for Russia, supposedly conditional on the Russians suddenly discovering how to collect taxes to replace the $5–$6 billion per month that they had been borrowing from the global financial markets. When the initial $5 billion tranche from the IMF was dispensed to Russia after July 13, Russian oligarchs, anxious to convert rubles into hard currency, immediately consumed it. The Russians then expected to receive more funds from the IMF by threatening devaluation and default. Even the IMF saw that further funds would simply be consumed by the same clique moving funds out of Russia, and the Russians unilaterally devalued and defaulted.

The Russian episode is *hardly* an example of free-market operation and free and unfettered flows of capital. The IMF essentially expropriated resources provided by industrial countries and irresponsibly allocated those funds to a country that had absolutely no hope of meeting the conditions allegedly attached to the IMF program. Russian technocrats such as Anatoly Chubais openly chortled to the Russian press that they had "conned" the IMF and its chief negotiator, Stanley Fischer.

The Russian episode, not to mention the IMF performance in Indonesia, South Korea, and Thailand, reflects the actions of people who face no accountability for their performance. If the IMF managing director and deputy managing director had been managing funds in the private sector in the same way, they would have long ago been bankrupt and forced out of business.

It is a great irony of the desperate situation in today's financial markets that a failure of IMF programs administered by IMF bureaucrats unaccountable to markets is taken as a sign of market failure. Quite the contrary, these actions are a sign of the necessity to let markets work in allocating scarce capital globally. That private markets have chosen to piggyback on the IMF's irresponsible actions is more an indictment of the IMF's irresponsible actions than it is of private institutions, which certainly carry their share of the blame for overinvestment in emerging markets over the past half decade.

The balance sheets of those private financial institutions and the compensation of their decision makers, however, will this year suggest strict accountability for the excesses of the past several years.

Almost incredibly, now that Brazil has joined the crisis-a-month club, the IMF is working feverishly to assemble a package for that country. The rationale is the same. The spreading international contagion must be stopped in Brazil. An election is underway in Brazil, and the IMF and Washington favor the leading candidate, Fernando Henrique Cardoso. Therefore, Brazil's dwindling foreign exchange reserves should be shored up by the IMF to help ensure the reelection of a supposedly market-oriented leader.

The IMF is again setting itself up to vilify free markets. The reelection effort by Brazil's President Cardoso has been a classic process of cynical expedience. After a brief "heroic" stand against the outflows arising from the sharp stock market correction in October 1987, the Cardoso government has abandoned much of its promised fiscal discipline. The public-sector borrowing has increased to about 7 percent of gross domestic product (GDP), from 4.5 percent just a year earlier. The current account deficit has risen sharply as well, from about 3 percent of GDP in 1996 to about 4.5 percent in 1998. This deficit reminds us that Brazil needs to borrow nearly $3 billion per month in global capital markets.

The Brink of Japanese Deflation?

Japan is even less likely to contribute to global reflation—quite the contrary. Japan is slipping into a dangerous deflationary environment. The deflationary impulse in Japan is so intense that although the Bank of Japan, while attempting to increase the money supply, announced September 9 a drop in its overnight lending rate to a mere 25 basis points, the stock market continued to fall. Even long-term interest rates—the lowest such rates in recorded history—have fallen to about 70 basis points.

Simultaneously, as financial markets in Japan have registered an incipient depression, the yen has strengthened. This movement is not a sign of Japanese economic recovery. Rather, the strengthening of the yen and the sharp drop in the Nikkei signal that Japan is reentering a liquidity crisis, this one more intense than the crisis of the summer of 1995, when the yen spiked to 80 yen per dollar while the stock market fell. The yen's strength simply reflects the accelerated repatriation of funds back into Japan by financial institutions desperate to obtain liquidity before publishing September 30 balance sheet statements.

The stronger yen hurts Japan's only contributor to growth: its export sector. This damage, in turn, pushes stocks down further and requires more repatriation. If this dangerous deflationary spiral accelerates, Japan will enter an even more intense financial crisis with a wave of bank failures and a further collapse in the stock market. Given this dangerous backdrop, although Japan should be anxiously pushing for global reflation, it remains passive, mired in domestic political struggles over the effort to rescue one moribund bank, the Long-Term Credit Bank.

Global Reflation?

The rapid succession of crisis-a-month events in the global economy—from Japan in June to Russia in July and August to Brazil in September, with continuing concerns about Hong Kong and China always in the background—carries a clear message. The failure to diagnose the global excess capacity problem, resulting from mistaken policies designed for the largely inflationary postwar period, has led to a global financial crisis. These concerns have engendered the suggestion, eagerly fostered by a troubled President Bill Clinton in a September 14 address to the Council on Foreign Relations, that the G7 nations must band together to contain the global financial crisis. While such an idea has appeal and some merit, its implementation is problematic. Clearly, the United States, Japan, and Germany would have to lead a credible policy of global reflation.

The president of the German Central Bank, Hans Tietmeyer, quickly rejected the idea of global reflation. He reacted promptly and specifically to President Clinton's suggestion by saying there was no need to adjust

European interest rates now. In fact, the Europeans remained preoccupied with the move toward currency union, which starts January 1, 1999.

The United States as Rescuer

With Germany and Japan clearly out of the picture as rescuers in the global deflation process, the task (as usual) falls clearly on the shoulders of the United States. The central actor in this play is Federal Reserve Chairman Alan Greenspan, who faces a dilemma. The American stock market remains unrealistically optimistic, in view of weaker prospective earnings of American companies. Chairman Greenspan fears that if he eases, the stock market will shoot back up to record highs, only to collapse even more sharply when the reality of weakened earnings begins to appear later this year.

This dilemma was vividly illustrated during the Fed chairman's September 16 testimony before the House Banking Committee hearings on the global financial crisis. Greenspan revealed that no global reflation effort was in play and seemed to imply that no immediate Fed ease was in the offing, barring a sharp US slowdown or, unsaid, a collapse in the US stock market. Whether the US stock market is prepared to collapse to induce the chairman to ease remains to be seen, but if the chairman refuses to ease, the market may collapse anyway.

While it is easy to understand Chairman Greenspan's wish to be prudent about the incipient inflationary pressures embodied in the low US unemployment rate and the steady upward trend in wages, the global situation should begin to outweigh these factors drastically this fall.

Whatever the timing, the global reflation effort will probably follow the pattern of two waves. As the currencies of the emerging markets, probably led by a devaluation in Brazil and in Hong Kong and China, collapse further, the deflationary wave sweeping toward the industrial world will intensify. While imperfect, the only response available to G7 policymakers will be a counter-wave of rapid and aggressive monetary easing that will merely minimize, not eliminate, the severe damage that seems set to be visited on the global economy. We can hope only that the attendant compromise of truly free and unfettered global capital flows does not make the outlook even worse.

What's Next?

FEBRUARY 1999

Surveying the global economy in early 1999 at a time of great financial stress, Makin continued to explore the role of unwise policy decisions in contributing to the continuation of the crisis. He examined the International Monetary Fund "bungling" in Asia, Brazil, and Russia, which not only harmed those economies but also contributed to what he said was an obvious stock market bubble in the US that was ripe to be popped.

Writing in February 1999, Makin correctly predicted the market collapse that would begin a little more than a year later. Using the example of Yahoo's exorbitant stock price relative to earnings, he found that a large correction was inevitable. Makin believed "the US stock market bubble is the last prop for global demand growth," fueled by an accommodative Federal Reserve policy that would force it to stop lowering interest rates, thereby bursting the bubble. The downfall of the overheated tech sector would be a dominant financial story for the following few years.

The most remarkable aspect of the global financial crisis—gradually being correctly recognized as a symptom of global excess capacity—is the degree to which it has played out exactly according to script. The 1995 Mexican bailout encouraged a late surge of capital flows to Asia on top of the considerable previous flows (especially from Japan). That surge became unsustainable in mid-1997 as Japan's returning recession, coupled with the waning ability to service the dollar-borrowing surge, caused the crisis in Thailand. This phenomenon spread rapidly around Asia and, as the excess-capacity problems escalated, then on to commodity-sensitive economies with poor financial and fiscal underpinnings, such as Russia's.

Brazil as Victim

The latest victim of the global financial crisis is Brazil, which has succumbed to the inevitable need to devalue in a deflationary world, notwithstanding the odd preference for fixed currencies at the International Monetary Fund (IMF) and the US Treasury. Brazil was victimized by the IMF's $41 billion relief package, which provided it with a rapid infusion of cash in exchange for a promise of economic suicide. The Brazilians were asked to reduce their budget deficit by 3 percentage points of the gross domestic product (GDP) for each of the next three years. This condition so damaged economic prospects that convincing people to keep money in Brazil required interest rates of 40 or 50 percent and higher. Extraordinarily tight fiscal and monetary policy resulted, followed by a sharp and disastrous recession. As Brazilians desperately tried to move their funds out of the country in the face of considerable browbeating from the government, Brazil's currency reserves began to leak away.

The Brazilian capitulation on its pledge to maintain a currency peg to the dollar was classic. Strong denials that the currency would be devalued, describing such a move as unthinkable, were followed by ever-rising pressure on Brazil's IMF-augmented, yet dwindling foreign exchange reserves while the Brazilian private sector desperately tried to protect its assets from a devaluation that surely had to come. When the pressure became too great, the Brazilians relented and allowed the currency to fall, initially by about 8 percent. The insufficient drop gave the markets nasty indigestion. Three days later, when the currency was allowed to float, it settled about 25 percent below its original parity—almost exactly where most commentators had put an equilibrium exchange rate for Brazil.

Once the devaluation occurred, Treasury and IMF officials murmured that it was probably the best thing for Brazil, as indeed it was. More to the point, it would have been far better for the Brazilians not to tie their currency to the US dollar through the currency peg and thereby suffer the additional pain of two or three months of a total collapse of economic activity driven by the extraordinarily tight monetary policy necessary to validate an invalid currency peg.

Of course, the Brazilian devaluation is dangerous for American and European banks and their affiliates in Latin America, whose exposure is not captured in the official Bank of International Settlements statistics. Loans to Latin America equal about 17 percent of US bank capital and 23 percent of European bank capital, according to Goldman Sachs. That relationship explains the importance of Brazil not devaluing.

The Stock Price Fantasy

The other unfortunate by-product of the November 17, 1998, Brazilian rescue package was the Federal Reserve's last in a series of three quick interest rate cuts of 25 basis points. By underwriting an unsustainable Brazilian package, the Fed gave the green light to US financial markets to inflate the existing bubble in the technology sector even higher.

The US stock market now willingly prices internet firms at extraordinarily high and dangerous levels. Yahoo is a company that offers an internet search engine, with sales of about $300 million a year. Its 1999 earnings are expected to be 74 cents per share. The company's share price reached $450 per share, or 608 times estimated 1999 earnings, in mid-January, giving it a market capitalization of $45 billion, larger than the capitalized market value of firms such as Boeing, Anheuser-Busch, Monsanto, Colgate Palmolive, and Seagram's.

But, say market watchers, Yahoo's earnings growth justifies the high price. Not so. Even given its predicted 60 percent annual rate of earnings growth over the next five years, 608 times earnings is more than three times the level justified by the most generous valuation. A company whose earnings grow at 60 percent annually for five years, to be sold at the end of a five-year holding period, is today worth the discounted present value of its earnings stream over the next five years plus the discounted present value of the sale price of the stock in five years.

Some assumption about the price-earnings multiple five years from now must be made to determine the future sale price of the stock. A high average of 30 times earnings, above the current level of 27, is generous. A discount rate of 10 percent is about right for a volatile earnings stream like Yahoo's. These assumptions yield a price multiple of 196 on current earnings of 74 cents, or about $145 per share—just 31 percent of the recent Yahoo high of $450 per share. To justify $450 per share, one would have to assume a price-earnings multiple on Yahoo of 94 five years from now, nearly five times the long-run average price-earnings multiples for all stocks.

These extraordinary assumptions justifying $450 per share for a share of stock currently earning 74 cents per share—even granting the ambitious forecast of 60 percent earnings growth—may be among the reasons that Yahoo was priced far more conservatively, at about $100 per share, before the fall round of Fed easing. Some of these valuation issues, not to mention the implausibility of the 60 percent earnings growth forecast, may have pushed the company's shares down to a mere $287 per share by January 20.

Extraordinary valuations aside, a sensible rationale exists for the relative pricing in today's equity markets. The manufacturing sector (read the tradable goods sector), which must compete in a world of massive excess capacity, is struggling. The stocks that are doing especially well in the US market are those such as Yahoo and Microsoft, which promise firms an ability to cut costs and save on labor. In a world where the sales pie is shrinking, profits growth can be maintained only by producing the same amount at less cost. The technology offered by many high-priced-stock companies provides just that possibility while adding the chance of cutting labor costs. Regardless, the price is still way too high for internet stocks like Yahoo and some others.

It is not the relative price action in the stock market that is surprising, but the absolute level of equity prices. The Yahoo example is not an extreme in the technology sector. Even the market as a whole—like the S&P 500 index with a price-earnings multiple of 27—continues to forecast a level of earnings growth that simply cannot exist in a world where prices are either rising less rapidly (disinflation) or falling outright (deflation).

The usual pattern of a last-minute fall in earnings estimates has developed for fourth-quarter earnings. Between November 27 and January 15, analysts' estimates of earnings growth for the S&P 500 stocks sagged from a +1.4 percent to a –3.1 percent. The forecast for the level of earnings during the fourth quarter of 1999, however, remained unaltered; hence the implied year-over-year earnings growth between the fourth quarter of 1998 and the fourth quarter of 1999 has risen to 29 percent, far above a credible level. Even optimists are expecting only 8 percent earnings growth this year; zero growth is entirely possible.

Given a crisis of global excess capacity, US corporate earnings are no exception. Earnings growth has slowed, but the stock market has continued to go up because the stock price multiple attached to lower earnings has simply risen.

Probably some of the multiple increase is simply because the longer the US expansion continues (at 95 months it exceeds the record 93-month expansion of the 1960s), the further into the future analysts are willing to extrapolate positive earnings streams for US corporations. A longer stream of earnings discounted at a lower interest rate does suggest a higher earnings multiple in the stock price but does not fully explain the sharp run-up in technology share prices, with earnings multiples far above levels justified even by implausibly rapid earnings growth over extended periods.

If the currency contagion—forced devaluation by country after country—has played out exactly as expected by producing downward pressure on commodity prices and profits of traded-goods companies globally, an obvious question remains: How long can the equity markets of the G7 countries, especially the United States, continue to hold their value or rise further and thereby defy the predictions implied by the growing global excess capacity?

Actually, the process that will lead to a sharp drop in the US equity market, probably by 30–50 percent, is underway. Export growth, or the traded-goods sector, in all G7 countries is slowing rapidly, as are the outlooks for the manufacturing sector in those countries.

The Downward Cycle

The US stock market bubble is the last prop for global demand growth. That bubble has been fueled by a highly accommodative Fed, which in turn has been made more accommodative by the very global crisis that is depressing the prospects for future earnings growth. This circularity has recurred in deflationary crises of global excess capacity. The excess capacity itself results from heavy investment flows from banks and financial institutions in advanced industrial countries to the developing world. These flows create excess capacity, which renders the financial system of the advanced countries vulnerable to defaults and financial crises in the emerging countries of the world. As the symptoms of excess capacity and financial crisis begin to emerge and spread along with chronic currency devaluations, a crisis atmosphere emerges, and the investments of G7 financial institutions are threatened. While the limited shocks from the Southeast Asian crisis could be absorbed, the spread of the crisis to South Korea forced heavy intervention by the US Treasury and the Fed to accommodate borrowing needs.

Continued deflationary pressures, however, led to a crisis in Russia. Throughout this process, the IMF has exacerbated the problem by forcing countries to defend undefendable currency pegs and thus intensified the crisis when the currency peg collapses. The Russian fiasco might have been more containable if the Russians' response to the pressures from the ill-advised IMF package had been only a devaluation and not a default. The Russian default set off alarm bells in the legal sector of a global system that has considerable leeway to ignore un-serviced debts so long as a government has not explicitly defaulted on those debts. The Russians, much to the dismay and consternation of the IMF and the US Treasury, not to mention the large banks, decided unilaterally to break the rules and default on their debts.

The US equity investors who are pushing technology stocks to astronomical levels can thank IMF bungling and the resultant crises in Asia, Brazil, and Russia for the latest run-up in the US stock market. The Russian panic and the virtual default by Long-Term Capital Management[1] forced the Federal Reserve to ease interest rates by 75 basis points in just six weeks. The last ease, immediately after the Brazilian package, rightly or wrongly underscored the message that the Fed stands ready to cut interest rates whenever an apparent crisis hits the markets.

This cycle—underlying excess capacity, deflationary pressure, an inability to finance external debts, a poorly designed IMF package, and finally a currency devaluation—fits Brazil perfectly just as it does the other countries in the sorry string of financial "crises." The problem is made worse by interventions of the US Treasury, the IMF, and more recently the Federal Reserve that, taken altogether, amount to an elaborate process of denial. The denial comes from helping countries defend exchange rate parities that are indefensible, as if maintaining a currency parity will somehow make the chronic problem of excess capacity and deflationary pressure go away. It has not, and it will not.

What this process has done is put the Federal Reserve in an impossible position. If, after all the bungling and the resultant panic in financial markets, the Fed fails to ease, it will be blamed for precipitating a systemic global financial crisis. If, conversely, it does ease, the Federal Reserve will contribute, as it has done mightily since last September, to the continued inflation of a US equity market bubble. That bubble in turn adds hundreds of billions of dollars to the paper wealth of US households, which in turn causes spending growth to accelerate to an unsustainable level above income growth.

Ultimately, the central bank must stop validating absurd equity prices. It may follow the US and Japanese examples when the equity bubbles were more domestically generated and raise interest rates. Today, the Fed has reached the point where it will probably have to burst the equity bubble simply by not lowering interest rates any further because continuing problems in the global economy would require further Fed easings to sustain the US equity bubble.

The Japanese Trap and China's Problem

The Japanese financial crisis has deepened. The world has begun to notice the Japanese government's $700 billion spending spree, undertaken while the economy and its government revenues were still weakening, that has turned Japan into a fiscal disaster. If the Japanese economy continues to founder, as seems likely, revenue growth will slow further (especially in Japan's deflationary environment) and push the budget deficit even higher.

China presents another problem for the Fed. The Chinese maintained artificially high growth rates of more than 7 percent during 1998, partly by lying about the numbers and partly by pressing ahead rapidly on government infrastructure investment projects equivalent to 30 percent of GDP. The Chinese government has directed state enterprises to continue to produce goods. Many of these are then dumped into inventory and add to incipient and actual deflationary pressure on global markets.

Unfortunately, China's accelerated spending on infrastructure is guided not by any market principles, but rather by the perception among the Chinese leadership about what projects are most urgently needed. Rapid execution of government investment projects without any market guidance has a bad history and often leads to useless projects. Japan has forged ahead in this area; the Chinese seem remarkably willing to follow that bad example. China's symptoms continue to be accelerating deflation and rising unemployment.

Looking Ahead

The answer to the question of what is next in this new year depends on the Fed's assessment of yet another in the series of predictable crises in financial markets as a harbinger of "systemic" risk and therefore justification for a further easing. There is a good chance that next time will be different and that the Fed will leave rates unchanged. The surge in the equity markets and the surge in consumer spending above sustainable levels during the fourth quarter after the Fed's recent easing exercise cannot have pleased the Federal Reserve. Financial markets will be disappointed if the current euphoria is predicated on yet another Fed easing in response to anything other than a recession in the United States. And a US recession would itself be a disappointment to financial markets.

Notes

1. Long-Term Capital Management was a Connecticut hedge fund that collapsed in 1998, endangering the global financial system. It was bailed out by 14 Wall Street banks at the urging of the president of the Federal Reserve Bank of New York.

10

THE PROSPEROUS '90S DRAW TO A CLOSE

The End of the Golden Age

APRIL 1999

Just as Makin was early in identifying the "golden age" of American prosperity in 1995, so too did he anticipate its end. In this essay from April 1999, Makin noted that despite a surging stock market and high consumer confidence, "the golden age is threatened." Americans were saving less and spending more, and inflation and interest rates looked to be on the rise.

Still, Makin took the occasion to remind readers that the disappearance of fast growth, low inflation, and high stock prices was no reason for pessimism. Rather, he wrote, it could signal "a transition to a more balanced global economy." He predicted a big drop in stocks, which materialized in the dot-com crash the next year when the Nasdaq peaked in March 2000. It wouldn't reach similar levels until about 15 years later.

In May 1995, I described a golden age for the American economy that included (1) an extended period of investment-led growth without inflation, (2) rising stock prices, and (3) a rising current account deficit with a strengthening dollar. Over the past four years, the golden-age scenario has been played out even more powerfully than I foresaw, especially in the stock market, which has enthusiastically priced an American golden age.

As widely recognized, the global financial crisis that emerged in Thailand in the spring of 1997 considerably boosted the American golden age. But the high level of investment that has served America's supply-side expansion so well was, in the end, a disaster for many emerging markets, because it created global excess capacity in basic industries on which smaller economies are heavily reliant. The overinvestment resulted primarily from an unsustainably low cost of capital to emerging markets whose currencies were unwisely pegged to the dollar. The dollar peg made borrowing in the local currencies of Asia and Latin America too cheap. The resulting excess capacity, in tandem with the existing massive excess capacity in Japan, made those currencies overvalued, and the currency pegs collapsed. The prices of raw materials dropped, capital flowed back to the American safe haven, and the Federal Reserve found it necessary to ease in the face of a perceived systemic crisis—all developments that helped Americans extend the domestic golden age into 1999.

Threats to the Golden Age

Now the golden age is threatened, although the stock market at record highs and the American economy with yet another burst of higher growth and lower inflation seems to be predicting its indefinite continuation. The acute phase of the crisis in emerging markets is over, thanks largely to the abandonment of the currency pegs that created deflationary overvaluations. This broad positive development will create some additional demand for raw materials—and for global savings—which had been lacking for nearly two years. These are negative supply-side developments for America's supply-side, investment-led expansion.

The most serious threat to America's golden age comes from Japan. There, the need for Japanese savings to fund massive fiscal deficits and bank recapitalization has escalated sharply, to a level of $400–$500 billion over the next year alone. Japan's net export of savings, about $110 billion a year, will shrink. Simultaneously, the American need to import savings is growing, as domestic saving has fallen virtually to zero, while the current account deficit (a measure of the need to import savings) is expected to approach $300 billion this year. Taken altogether, these elevated demands on global savings will produce higher interest rates.

That climb has already begun, with Japanese interest rates increasing from 0.8 percent last fall to an average of 2 percent so far in 1999 despite the Bank of Japan's offer of zero interest rates in the overnight market. American interest rates have gained a full percentage point since last fall despite the Fed's reduction of the overnight federal funds rate from 5 percent to 4.25 percent. Yield curves are steepening. In Japan this movement is springing from the increased real interest rates necessary to accommodate the huge fiscal deficits, while the upsurge in the United States comes from rising inflationary expectations. These expectations can be identified from a comparison between yields on inflation-indexed Treasuries (Treasury Inflation-Protected Security) and regular Treasury securities.

Continued negative pressures on the Japanese export of savings—first to fund large government borrowing and perhaps to fund rising private-sector demands on Japanese savings should the rising Japanese stock market be forecasting an eventual economic recovery in Japan—are significantly changing financial markets. The end to the acute phase of Japan's financial and economic crisis is also being foretold by rising interest rates and a stronger yen. These movements are profound challenges to America's financial markets insofar as they signal mounting demands on the savings of the world's largest exporter of such reserves, Japan.

On the American front, the threat to the golden age surfaces from some imbalances created by shock waves from the debt crisis of the emerging markets. The positive by-products for the American economy (especially the Fed easing)—created by fears of systemic risks emerging from the turbulence in the financial markets last year—have accelerated US demand growth. US consumption spending, which was expected to slow in the second half of the year, has held up well as it rose at an annual rate of nearly 4.5 percent and contributed nearly two-thirds of the powerful growth surge in the overall economy. Since consumption spending was running ahead of income growth, that spending was expected to slow, and with it the US economy, toward the end of 1998. This has not occurred, and, in fact, demand growth has quickened, with a resulting drop in savings.

With US demand growth sustained at a high level, the US manufacturing sector, which had been contracting in anticipation of slackening demand growth, has begun to expand again. As a robust stock market and an accommodative Fed with a rapidly expanding money supply have pushed up demand growth, the production side of the economy has responded with more output. Simultaneously, employment has grown modestly to an average payroll addition of 269,000 over the past three months, up slightly from the strong average level of 232,000 for the past 12 months.

Inflationary pressures in the United States have been held at bay by rapidly deteriorating global conditions over the past year. A mere stabilization of conditions in emerging markets, and by implication in commodity markets, will see year-over-year inflation rates begin to run up by the second half of 1999.

By the end of 1999, several models suggest, the cessation of commodity deflation and some modest reflation will mean that year-over-year US inflation rates of the consumer price index (CPI) will more than double the current 1.5 percent to more than 3 percent. Specifically, some models are calling for a 3.4 percent year-over-year CPI inflation rate by the end of this year. Given a 3 percent real yield, market yields on long-term government bonds would rise to about 6.5 percent, or nearly another full percentage point from current levels. Such a gain would not include a rise in real yields necessary to alleviate the global savings shortage that is developing from accelerated consumption in the US and climbing fiscal deficits in Japan.

Relief from Japan?

The Bank of Japan could provide some constructive relief for the global economy by setting and achieving a target for money growth or moderate inflation and could thereby help the Japanese economy recover and relieve the heavy burden on Japanese savings that results from burgeoning budget deficits. In early February, the Bank of Japan raised world hopes by announcing it would take additional steps to stimulate the Japanese economy. Unfortunately, those steps were primarily a force-feeding of the Japanese banking system with unneeded reserves (given the banks' continuing passive stance), as overnight interest rates dropped to zero. Consequently, Japanese banks have purchased short-term government securities largely with maturities of less than a year and pushed the yields on those maturities down to 0.15 percent. In short, Bank of Japan policy has focused more on lowering short-term interest rates in Japan than on helping the Japanese economy.

A recovery of the Japanese economy will require more than a force-fed increase in the supply of credit to Japanese banks, which so far have used that increase only to purchase Japanese securities. The demand for credit in Japan's private sector must rise also, and the banks must be recapitalized so they can resume their role as viable financial intermediaries.

Part of the difficulty encountered by the Bank of Japan may come from its total transformation almost a year ago. The Bank of Japan was granted additional independence, and an entire new governing board was put in place. Similarly, the US Federal Reserve achieved additional independence from the Treasury in the early 1950s with the Treasury Federal Reserve Accord—which no longer required the Federal Reserve to underwrite the financing of Treasury securities. Like any new institution, the Bank of Japan is moving cautiously on new initiatives and is tending to stick to the same paradigm for interest rate targeting as the institution followed during the postwar period.

During the mid-1950s, the Federal Reserve followed a method of targeting free reserves to stimulate or slow the economy. (Free reserves are essentially reserves in excess of required reserves. If the central bank engineers a low borrowing rate for the banks while leaving higher lending rates in the marketplace, banks desire less in free reserves and therefore expand their lending.) This is the policy the Bank of Japan is pursuing, but, so far, the only demand for credit in Japan is that of the government to finance large fiscal deficits.

A New Reality

The major obstacle to a continuation of the US golden age with rising stock prices and a growing US economy is a global shortage of savings at current interest rates, especially if Japan recovers. Even if the Japanese recovery falters again, huge government deficits will eat up savings. Meanwhile, American spending growth is shifting more from investment and capacity building into consumption, a less viable competitor for global savings than investment. Simultaneously, inflation expectations in the United States are rising and thereby push up longer-term interest rates and steepen the yield curve. Japan and other global suppliers of savings have been content to finance US current account deficits as a means to fund the rising investment in the United States, but they may be more reluctant to do so to back consumption growth.

Japan's absolute need to use its savings at home to fund rising fiscal deficits in a weakening economy or fund rebounding investment in a recovering economy makes it all the more likely that interest rates in Japan must rise to levels that will keep more savings in Japan. The Japanese seem to have resorted to a combination of exchange rate volatility, higher interest rates, and threats about the unsustainability of US equity prices to avoid higher capital outflows. Ultimately, higher interest rates and a rising stock market in Japan will do the job more constructively.

The global economy need not be such a gloomy place after the characteristics of the golden age—faster growth, lower inflation, and higher prices of favored stocks—have disappeared. Rather, we shall be witnessing a transition to a more balanced global economy. Emerging markets will continue as a diverse group of economies, among which investors will choose investment prospects more carefully. Japan will start to recover, as investors seek to identify the companies that are moving most rapidly to reduce production costs and jettison the old style of rigid operations tied to preferential regulation. Once the recovery gains momentum, the demand for credit will grow, as will Japan's closely watched money supply, though more as a symptom of economic recovery than as a cause. Other Asian economies, especially those that can contribute to lower-cost methods of production at home and in Japan, will grow.

In America, the end of the golden age will not mean all bad news. Investors will discover more than 40 or 50 companies worthy of consideration. The idea that stocks ought to rise at least 20–25 percent a year will disappear, and the legions of day traders holding to that belief as a ticket to retirement at age 30—or maybe 35—will return to their normal jobs.

The result will be a more balanced and sustainable growth path for the world economy. Golden ages are wonderful, but they can create the false impression that growth of the economy and earnings can go on forever based on only the remarkable performance of a smaller and smaller group of companies and national economies. We shall be lucky if a 20 or 30 percent drop in the US stock market sometime before the new millennium begins is all it takes to remind us of that reality.

The Myth of Clintonomics

DECEMBER 1999

Makin took the occasion of the closing of the decade to reflect on the causes of what he termed the "golden age." Although President Bill Clinton received much of the political credit for a booming American economy, the real roots of the era of prosperity were the policies of the Ronald Reagan and George H. W. Bush administrations to promote deregulation and free trade, remove threats to global instability, and cap spending. The Clinton contribution was to be "sufficiently ineffective" in derailing the momentum, Makin wrote. With the benefit of hindsight, Makin made his case, citing economic data from the early 1990s. And he made a prediction in December 1999 on when the prosperity would end that is eerily accurate: "My bet is that the day of reckoning will come next spring." The dot-com crash took place just three months later, in March 2000.

Economic "golden ages," periods of sustained noninflationary growth led by strong investment, emerge during peacetime when governments are less involved in resource allocation and inflation is low. The latter half of the 19th century was a golden age of golden ages, and the 1990s, too, have been a golden age for the US economy. The Ronald Reagan administration's policies—the end of the Cold War, deregulation, free trade, and falling inflation—reinforced by those of the George H. W. Bush administration—successfully quelling the threat to global peace from rogue states in the Gulf War and placing a durable cap on government spending growth with the 1990 budget agreement—contributed far more to the emergence of a golden age in the 1990s than did Clintonomics.

Clintonomics' main contribution was to do relatively little harm to the favorable economic environment it inherited. Efforts to create an expensive and unwieldy program of health care and the higher tax rates enacted during the 1993 budget agreement created burdens for the economy to overcome; fortunately, the Clinton health care program was defeated. Rising marginal tax rates have tied deficit reduction to a rising stock market rather than to smaller government. Those marginal tax rates will exacerbate the economic downturn that accompanies a falling stock market, since government revenues will fall more rapidly than usual during the next recession. A vanishing budget surplus and, possibly, a return to deficits will increase the sense of malaise that accompanies a recession and may extend its duration.[1] The shock of sudden budget deterioration will make it more difficult to move toward the lower and uniform tax rates that could be an important part of the next economic expansion.

There is a great irony about the economic and policy environment of the early 1990s. The environment helped set in place the conditions for the most powerful sustained economic expansion of the 20th century, and yet its most painful elements, coming as they did during 1991 and 1992, helped end the Bush presidency. The Clinton presidency needed only to be sufficiently ineffective during its first term as not to derail the powerful economic momentum that was created during the expansion of the 1980s and extended by the policy measures of the early 1990s.

Hard Decisions Late in the Bush Presidency

Nine years ago this fall, President Bush and his military and economic advisers were forced to engage in some heavy lifting. On the military front, they were laying the groundwork for a decisive victory in the Gulf War, which would establish America as a guarantor of global peace and help launch the US economy and its stock market on a trajectory that has created a prosperous and peaceful decade. On the economic front, budget negotiations were underway wherein the Bush team successfully designed the spending caps—successors to the Gramm-Rudman deficit reduction measures[2]— that held down the growth of government spending. The capped low rate of government spending growth in a decade of great wealth generation made possible the elimination of the budget deficit by 1997 and is set to create a trillion dollars in cumulative surpluses over the first decade of the new millennium.

The likely benefits of the conditions—low inflation, steady growth, and rising stock prices—that fostered the decade's generation of great wealth went unnoticed as recently as 1995. In that year, my characterization of the American expansion as a golden-age investment-led recovery that could continue for a long time without inflation was met with great skepticism, as were my "bold" calls for a Dow reaching 6,500.[3] In 1995, the Congressional Budget Office was estimating that, by 1999, the federal budget deficit would increase from just short of $200 billion to close to $300 billion—and would reach $500 billion by 2005.

The Bush-Created Golden Age Has Benefited Clinton

The slow start to the powerful US economic expansion of the 1990s was politically costly to Bush and his administration. In retrospect, it seems hard to understand how Clinton won the 1992 election, given the great military and economic contributions the Bush team put together in the midst of a recession in 1990. After the historic military victory of early 1991 and the solid record of economic accomplishment during the 1980s, Bush, with some logical if not political justification, seemed to believe that everyone would simply understand what extraordinary things he had accomplished in the dark days of late 1990. But the flush of military victory faded throughout 1991, and the economy, which was in the listless early stages of a golden age, displayed only hints of the powerful, investment-led recovery that later materialized.

During the critical years of 1991 and the first half of 1992, talk of a "jobless" recovery hurt Bush's bid for reelection. Fiscal policy, by virtue of the mandated and strict spending caps engineered by the Bush team in the budget agreement of late 1990, continued to be a drag on the economy. After the end of the Gulf War and the disappearance of any incipient oil crisis, inflation collapsed—falling by 3 percentage points from December 1990 to December 1991. By late 1990, the Federal Reserve realized a recession had started, and it cut rates to 4 percent, down from 7.75 percent in November 1990, in a series of 13 rapid 25- and 50-basis-point steps by the end of 1991. The Fed further cut rates to 3 percent in three more rapid steps by September 1992.

But because inflation was falling even faster than interest rates during 1991, the real federal funds rate actually rose by more than a full percentage point over the first eight months of the economic expansion that began in March 1991. Economic growth was slow to recover during 1991, and year-over-year growth did not turn positive until the end of the year.

Even though the economy grew at a 4 percent rate during the second quarter of election year 1992, that was not enough to give voters a foretaste of the remarkable economic performance that lay ahead. In the February 1992 *Economic Report of the President*, Bush expressed his disappointment clearly: "1991 was a challenging year for the American economy. Output was stagnant and unemployment rose."[4] For him politically, that was a leaden age.

Precursors of a Golden Age

The early part of the ultimately vigorous investment-led expansion of the 1990s was unusual in a number of other ways that turned out to be constructive for a long, sustainable expansion—and disastrous for an incumbent president trying to get reelected in November 1992.

Supply-side expansions like the one in the 1990s tend to start slowly. As cautious employers seek to conserve on labor, the unemployment rate may even rise initially before dropping to record lows (as it did in the 1990s). Simultaneously, a sharp drop in inflation, as seen in 1991, can catch the central bank by surprise, push up real interest rates, and further depress demand growth. The 1990s have been the first decade in more than 60 years in which disinflationary and deflationary surprises have prevailed globally. Japan is the most dramatic example, but there have been many others. The International Monetary Fund's restrictive policy prescriptions following the crisis of excess capacity in Asia exacerbated the deflationary problems and caused currencies to collapse even further, as countries such as Thailand, Indonesia, South Korea, and eventually Brazil desperately tried to export their deflation.

During the postwar era, policymakers became more attuned to demand-led expansions. These expansions usually begin with a sharp drop in the unemployment rate after a sharp easing of monetary policy. That easing pushes up consumer demand by creating a more dramatic, though less sustainable, demand-led recovery. Comparing the data from early in the current expansion with early data from previous expansions reveals the difference between the preconditions for a sustainable supply-side expansion and those associated with a more dramatic but less sustainable demand-growth expansion.

Gross domestic product (GDP) growth shows that the US economy was clearly expanding from March 1991. During the year ending in the second quarter of 1992, just after the March 1991 recession trough, the economy expanded at a respectable 3 percent annual rate, despite both a slight 0.1 percent drag from government spending and the sharp rise in real interest rates that accompanied the 1991 collapse in inflation.

For the Bush presidency, one of the most damaging aspects of the early stages of the 1990s recovery was the lack of employment growth—and the rise, in fact, of the unemployment rate. The unemployment rate stood at 6.8 percent in March 1991 when the recovery began. But slow demand growth and the tendency of producers to concentrate on increased investment spending sent the unemployment rate to 7.5 percent by the fall of 1992, when the election occurred. The term "jobless recovery" sounded a death knell for the Bush reelection bid. The creation of more output with fewer workers is viewed as a good sign today, with the unemployment rate approaching 4 percent. But in 1992, accompanied as it was by a surge in investment, the labor-conserving rise in productivity created the erroneous impression that the only beneficiaries of growth during a Republican administration were capital-intensive businesses; labor was left behind.

Thanks to the effective Bush budget caps, real government expenditures did not rise at all from the beginning of 1991 to the beginning of 1996. Government spending rose modestly with low inflation.

The US investment-led recovery has enabled the nation to benefit from the growth in world trade during the 1990s. During the first year of the expansion, when monetary and fiscal policies were acting to constrain demand growth, US exports rose by 10.6 percent, thereby helping cushion the drag from weak government spending and the moderate growth of investment and consumption. The rapid surge in import growth has helped cushion the US economy from cost pressures that might otherwise have intensified during a period of global growth. US producers have benefited from lower-cost imported components, while US consumers have benefited from access to lower-cost imported goods.

In sum, America's golden-age expansion in the 1990s has been characterized by remarkable stability, low inflation, and a strong (twice the average) contribution from investment. The outlook going forward is fundamentally bright, provided that the investment returns on the newly enlarged stock of capital can be sustained and will satisfy the high level of expectations that drove the investment boom.

What Comes Next?

Looking forward, we must ask what the outlook is for the remarkable American expansion. The answer to the question is as important for American businesses and workers as it is for the politicians who will vie for the presidency in the 2000 elections. Mixed economic data over the past year have caused markets to oscillate from a rosy vision of indefinitely sustainable growth, with no inflation, to sudden waves of fear about moderate signs of overheating. The consequent need for some Fed tightening could push interest rates to levels that might be dangerous for currently elevated stock prices. Usually, investment-led expansions end when the capital stock gets too large and the return on new investments falls sharply. Since the global economic rebound of 1999, however, the US expansion is facing the possibility that a rise in demand growth that outstrips sustainable (noninflationary) supply growth may jeopardize the expansion and, ultimately, the current level of equity prices.

Signs of excess demand growth have begun to appear in the United States. GDP growth measures the growth of output or supply, while final sales growth measures the growth of demand. Over the past three quarters, year-over-year growth rates of final sales have exceeded year-over-year growth rates of GDP by an average of about 0.5 percent. Simultaneously, another measure of excess demand growth, the current account deficit, has risen sharply, from below $20 billion per month to about $30 billion per month. The larger external deficit reflects the combination of a sharp drop in private savings in the United States, to a –4 percent of GDP, and its mitigation by a rise in public savings measured by government budget surpluses. Even so, government spending growth has begun to accelerate moderately again, to an average of about 3 percent over the past year. Only powerful revenue growth tied to a rising stock market and high levels of capital gains and rising incomes have kept the government surplus rising.

The stronger growth of global spending and a rising level of US demand in excess of supply have produced a steady, though moderate, acceleration of inflation pressures over the past year. Most broadly, year-over-year consumer price index inflation rose from 1.6 percent at the start of the year to 2.6 percent in September. That rise reflected a steady buildup of pipeline pressures in the producer-goods sector. During the three months ending in October, producer prices rose at an annual rate of 6.9 percent—up sharply from the year-over-year growth rate of 2.7 percent.

Clearly, the tension is rising in global markets over the sustainability of a noninflationary expansion in the United States, especially as US inflation and the current account deficit creep upward while US stock prices continue to move higher. Unfortunately for the presidential candidates, it is impossible to predict whether the rising imbalances that ultimately will end a sustainable US economic expansion will reach a critical level before or after next November's election. My bet is that the day of reckoning will come next spring.

Now that the Fed has taken back its 75 basis points of emergency easing, continued inflation pressure is likely to suggest to markets that more tightening is in order. A resulting sharp decline in the stock market and an inflationary drop in the dollar would take the bloom off Clintonomics and give Republican candidates a leg up in the elections. That would be payback for the unusually good luck Clinton enjoyed throughout his presidency, courtesy of Bush.

Notes

1. In fiscal years 1998 through 2001, the government had surpluses of $69.2, $125.5, $236.2, and $128.2 billion, respectively.

2. Gramm-Rudman was a deficit-control measure Congress passed in 1985 that provided for automatic spending cuts if congressional appropriations exceeded budgeted amounts.

3. The Dow closed above 6,500 at 6,547.79 for the first time on November 25, 1996.

4. *Economic Report of the President* (Washington, DC: US Government Printing Office, 1992), https://www.presidency.ucsb.edu/sites/default/files/books/presidential-documents-archive-guidebook/the-economic-report-of-the-president-truman-1947-obama-2017/1992.pdf.

The Present US Expansion Outshines the 1960s Expansion

FEBRUARY 2000

At the start of the new century, Makin stepped back to consider how the extended expansion of the 1990s compared with the long expansion of the 1960s. He found that the two eras were quite different—that the 1990s expansion extended for longer and was more robust at its peak. The 1990s showed "extraordinary staying power," as evidenced by the huge stock surge. Although economists in the 1960s boasted that they had learned to control the business cycle, the 1990s were "a tribute to the persistence of an unprecedented investment boom, containment of government involvement in the economy, and attendant absence of inflation pressures."

Makin highlighted the unprecedented accumulation of wealth in the 1990s, which was distinctly different from the 1960s. Some of this wealth accumulation he attributed to the stock market, but he wondered if "we are beginning to see the limits of the wealth-driven US expansion, with the wealth being generated in a narrow sector of global equity markets—the so-called IT sector" and speculated whether "capacity in the IT sector will far outstrip demand, and prices obtainable for the products of IT companies will fall rapidly—eventually bursting the bubble." At the time of his writing, however, he found that the economic health of most countries "is far better now than at any time in the past century."

January 2000, the first month of the new century, was a milestone in US business-cycle history. It brought to 106 months the longevity of the present expansion, which began in March 1991. That was only the second time in history that the American economy had expanded for 106 months—two months short of nine years—without a recession. More significant for the economic outlook now, it was the first time that the expansion reached such a length while showing virtually no signs of strain. That is a favorable omen—a sign that the expansion is likely to roll on for a while.

Other favorable signs to be adduced in this essay emerge from a comparison of the present expansion and that of February 1961 to December 1969. Especially encouraging is a comparison of the last three years of the 1960s expansion with the most recent three years of the current continuing expansion, because of the far greater generation of wealth during the latter period. Other differences favorable to the present outlook include a diminished role for fiscal policy in trying to fine-tune the economy by demand management, a surer grip of monetary policy on inflation, and the accumulated benefits of the deregulation—of communications, transportation, banking, and exchange rates—that began to unfold in the middle 1970s and ran right through the omnibus financial services overhaul legislation of 1999.

Before proceeding, a word about style: For the moment, we must call the present expansion the upswing of the 1990s, because that is when all of it but one month (so far) occurred. This is not meant to suggest that the current expansion has ended. Perhaps, in time, economists will refer to it as the expansion of 1991–200X or by another short title. That label is still to be revealed, as is the ultimate staying power of this upswing in the business cycle.

Two Impressive Expansions

The first five years of the expansion that began in February 1961 resembled the golden age of the current expansion. That golden age only emerged in 1995, four years after the expansion began. From 1961 through 1965, US private investment grew strongly, more rapidly than it did from 1991 through 1995. At the same time, inflation remained tame, holding in the 1–2 percent range. Real government spending rose at about 3 percent per year during the first four and a half years of the 1960s expansion—well above the zero growth rate of real government expansion during the comparable phase of the 1990s expansion, but moderate for its time.

The government still had the Cold War to contend with, underscored by the Cuban Missile Crisis during the fall of 1962. The anxious feelings that crisis engendered about the Soviet threat and the intensity of the Cold War stood in sharp contrast to the relaxation of global tensions associated with the fall of the Berlin Wall in 1989 and the collapse of the Soviet Union in 1991. In the early 1960s, the stage was set for intensive expansion of technology for use in defense against the Soviet threat and for symbolic "peaceful" applications, such as putting a man on the moon.

In contrast to the 1960s, the early 1990s experienced two benefits from technology. First, many advances, particularly those related to the efficient storage and manipulation of information, had existed for two decades but had yet to see effective application for cost reduction and other civilian uses. Second, information about technological advances could spread more rapidly and was less likely to be secreted by the defense effort, as such information had been during the Cold War.

The first half of the 1960s expansion was also characterized by extreme optimism about the government's ability to manage the economy. Activist, Keynesian demand-management policies applied during the Kennedy and Johnson administrations led many practitioners to declare by 1965 that governments had found a way to control business cycles. The business cycle, it was thought, was a thing of the past.

One of the casualties of this optimism—a serious casualty in light of the tumultuous inflation in the 1970s—was monetary policy. With inflation running between 1 and 2 percent and exchange rates fixed globally under the Bretton Woods system, many economists concluded that fiscal policy could manage the business cycle; monetary policy would play only a passive role with little significance for aggregate economic performance. Contrast that with the credit given to monetary management by Alan Greenspan and the Federal Reserve for the stability and length of the 1990s expansion. There was nothing like the US economy of the 1970s, with its high and volatile inflation and its disastrous consequences for emerging markets in the early 1980s, to underscore the importance of low and stable inflation.

The American stock market, with uncanny accuracy, marked the end of the healthy phase of the US economic expansion in the 1960s. The Dow Jones Industrial Average, the major index of the time, peaked on February 9, 1966, at 995, some 86 percent above the trough reached in June 1962. During its expansion phase in the 1960s, the Dow rose for three years and eight months at an average rate of 18.4 percent per year. Stocks struggled after their February 1966 peak, dropping 25 percent by August 1966 and then recovering nearly to their old highs by the end of 1968. But then they dropped even more sharply to a low of 631 in May 1970 as markets succumbed to rising inflation pressures and the uncertainties attendant upon the Vietnam War, with its implied upward pressure on government spending.

The February 1966 stock market peak marked an end to the wealth-generation phase of the American expansion during the 1960s. With an average annual rise of over 18 percent, the stock market had certainly outperformed the first five years of the 1990s expansion, which saw an average annual rise in the Dow of just over 11 percent per year. The extraordinary thing about the 1990s expansion, both in absolute terms and in comparison with the 1960s expansion, is its powerful acceleration after a modest performance during its initial five years. That acceleration, with little sign of strain yet to emerge in the form of slowing investment spending or rising inflation, has created a powerful "second wind" for the economy and the stock market's valuation of the economy. During just under four years from March 1996 to January 2000, stocks have risen by an incredible 152 percent, for an annual rate of 27.5 percent.

It is the extraordinary staying power of the 1990s expansion—signified by the sustained and accelerating rise in investment and attendant price stability and manifest in a powerful rise in equity prices—that distinguishes it from that of the 1960s. Indeed, one underestimates the power of the 1990s expansion if one suggests that by February 2000 it will have equaled the 1960s expansion in duration. As a wealth-generating expansion, the 1960s boom was over by February 1966, while at a comparable stage, the 1990s expansion was just entering a remarkable phase of wealth generation. The 1960s boom was extended only by the artificial stimulus provided by rising outlays for the Vietnam War and the Great Society. That expansion was demand driven, and it showed. Inflation jumped from just over 1 percent early in 1966 to nearly 4 percent in 1967 and thereafter continued to rise—reaching 7 percent late in 1969. By contrast, investment spending accelerated after 1995, and inflation fell.

The signs of demand expansion through faster government spending—in contrast to investment growth, which creates additional capacity—emerged clearly after 1965. Real government spending surged for three years, reaching annual growth rates as high as 11 percent. Taxes were increased, and tax rates remained at the extraordinarily high levels that prevailed in the 1960s. In the 1990s, real government spending growth began to rise modestly in 1997 and is increasing at about a 3 percent rate.

Extraordinary Creation of Wealth

The contrast between the 1960s and the 1990s is perhaps best captured by a comparison of wealth creation during each decade. Real net worth of households measured in 1996 dollars rose from $7.262 trillion in 1960 to $10.277 trillion in 1970, a rise of 41.5 percent. By 1990, real household net worth had reached $20.397 trillion. It rose to $34.107 trillion by the middle of 1999, for an increase of 67 percent.

Much of that extraordinary generation of wealth has come during the three years since December 1996, when Chairman Greenspan raised the possibility of "irrational exuberance" in stock markets. The past three years have shown that the exuberance was not so much irrational as it was a tribute to the persistence of an unprecedented investment boom, containment of government involvement in the economy, and attendant absence of inflation pressures.

Foreign Investment and Trade

Problems confronting the US external sector emerged during the 1960s that, in some ways, presaged the experience of the late 1990s but in some ways were different. Remember that during the 1960s the global economy was on a fixed exchange rate system with the US dollar pegged to gold at $35 an ounce. In that system, the United States acted as a supplier of world liquidity.

Because exchange rates were fixed, the jump in US inflation during the late 1960s put inflationary pressure on other industrial countries. The European countries were especially displeased by the inflationary pressure imposed on them from the United States, and in 1969 West Germany unilaterally revalued its currency upward. The resumption of US inflationary pressure in 1971 and the reluctance to absorb that pressure finally led to an end of the Bretton Woods system; the US dollar was cut loose from gold, and other currencies were free to float. The US inflationary pressure of the mid-1960s had created a considerable overvaluation of the dollar, and the dollar depreciated against most other major currencies after it was set free in the fall of 1971.

In 2000, the situation facing the US external accounts is superficially similar but actually quite different from that of the late 1960s. As US wealth has risen rapidly, private savings as a share of gross domestic product (GDP) have dropped to -4.5 percent. Simultaneously, the current account deficit has expanded to a level about 1.5 percent below the private saving gap. That reflects a government surplus of 1.5 percent of GDP. In effect, in 2000, foreign savers are financing an excess of US private investment over private saving. That is because foreign investors continue to be attracted to the opportunities in the large, rising, and liquid US equity markets.

Complaints from foreign governments about the US current account deficit in the 1990s were less valid than those in the late 1960s. At that time, foreign governments were forced, in effect, to finance the US public-sector deficit and follow more inflationary policies than they wished to by virtue of the fixed exchange rate regime. During the 1990s and into 2000, foreign private sectors have been financing a surplus of US private investment over private saving without being compelled to do so. Indeed, in some cases where a lack of private-sector capital outflows would imply an appreciating currency against the US dollar (such is the case in Japan), the central bank is providing the capital outflows necessary to fund the US current account deficit. In sum, the United States is supplying the world with needed demand growth in 2000 and is consequently pulling the rest of the world toward growth instead of pushing the world toward inflation as America did during the late 1960s.

The US economic expansion over the past three years and the huge creation of wealth that has accompanied the expansion have been a great source of strength for the rest of the world economy. That was especially true during the Asian and global financial crises of 1997–98, which reflected considerable excess capacity in emerging markets. Thanks to the continued vigorous and noninflationary growth of the US economy and its requirements for inputs, the sharp depreciation of currencies of emerging markets against the dollar that occurred in 1997 and early 1998 helped reignite demand growth for the products of those countries and led to a sharp recovery in most emerging markets in 1999.

A Key Question

As wealth creation continues to fuel demand growth in excess of output growth, Chairman Greenspan has indicated that the Fed will continue to push interest rates up until demand growth slows to a more sustainable pace below the extraordinary late 1999 rate of more than 5 percent. A key question facing the global economy today is whether the interest rate necessary to slow the demand growth of the US economy is above or below the interest rate that will collapse share prices or, more likely, will collapse the less vigorous financial markets of some emerging economies.

A comparison of the expansion of the 1990s with that of the 1960s is at once heartening and troubling. It is heartening to find that the 1990s expansion, founded as it is on a continued rise in private-sector investment in productive technologies and not on higher government spending and false hopes that government fiscal policy can end the business cycle, is far healthier than the 1960s expansion. The remarkable increase in private wealth by more than 67 percent during the 1990s, which far outstrips the 41.5 percent increase during the 1960s, is testimony to the greater vigor of the 1990s expansion and to its more formidable and sustainable foundations. But, because the 1960s boom was a traditional demand-driven (rather than investment-supply-driven) expansion, eventually ended by obvious pressures of demand on prices, wages, and the external sector, the central bank's role in ending the 1960s expansion was easy to define. Take away the punch bowl, and slow down the inflation.

In the 1990s, the appropriate role of the central bank is far more difficult to determine. As Chairman Greenspan hinted during his January 13 address to the Economic Club of New York, the limits to this expansion will be set by the available supply of labor and perhaps by the available supply of world savings to finance the continued rapid growth of investment in the US economy. While the upside possibilities in this expansion are far greater than they were in the 1960s, the chance for a mistake by policymakers in this unprecedented economic environment is also greater. No one, including the prescient Fed chairman, can predict when the investment boom will begin to sour, as expected productivity increases fail to materialize and profits disappoint just as labor costs start to rise, thereby depressing expected future profits.

Perhaps, as we enter the year 2000, we are beginning to see the limits of the wealth-driven US expansion, with the wealth being generated in a narrow sector of global equity markets—the so-called IT sector. As noted earlier, the market capitalization of the IT sector has risen by $1.4 trillion in the past three months. That increase represents, in constant dollars, half of the US wealth increase generated during the entire decade of the 1960s. The power of IT companies to raise capital has brought forward the logical possibility that those companies should simply absorb all capital that markets have to offer and turn around and buy all other companies. A possible manifestation of this process is the acquisition by America Online (AOL), a company with modest earnings, of Time Warner, a company with substantial earnings. Before the proposed merger, AOL's revenues were one-sixth of Time Warner's, but its stock market capitalization was twice that of Time Warner.

The fact that investors are so excited about the prospects of IT companies, irrespective of their current earnings, that they are prepared to bid those firms' stocks to levels where they constitute a virtual currency with which to acquire companies that actually have high current earnings may mean that we are reaching the limit of a process whereby, in the extreme, IT companies would absorb all investable funds. Well before we reach that point, capacity in the IT sector will far outstrip demand, and prices obtainable for the products of IT companies will fall rapidly—eventually bursting the bubble.

Whatever the ultimate outcome, the 1990s was a far more exhilarating and successful decade than the 1960s. In the 1990s, economic performance and wealth creation were far superior, driven by private-sector investment and a reduced role for government and government policy. While the future may bring significant volatility in financial markets, the real economic health of the US economy—and by virtue of its example, the real economic health of most economies in the world—is far better now than at any time in the past century.

11

BUBBLE TROUBLE:
THE TECH BUBBLE

Central Bankers and Stock Markets

JANUARY 1997

In December 1996, at the Annual Dinner and Francis Boyer Lecture of the American Enterprise Institute, Fed Chairman Alan Greenspan asked, "How do we know when irrational exuberance has unduly escalated asset values, which then become subject to unexpected and prolonged contractions?"[1] The Nasdaq[2] was nearly three times higher than it was 10 years earlier, reflecting a remarkable rate of growth, and concerns about a stock market bubble were growing. Greenspan's comments sent financial markets into a brief uproar, but the question lingered.

Makin, who attended the speech, took the occasion to reflect on the connection between monetary policy and equity markets. While he attributed some of the dustup to "overeager wire service writers aiming at catchy one-line headlines," Makin noted that there did seem to be some nervousness about the state of the economy and "the likelihood that the unusually favorable underlying conditions will not persist for much longer"—which he assessed in typically thorough fashion, finding that it seems not to be in danger of overheating.

Central bankers have always worried about the relationship between financial markets and the "real" economy that produces the goods and services of everyday life. The concern is often focused on equity (stock) markets, but lately central bankers and an occasional finance ministry official have seen fit to comment on the appropriateness of exchange rates.

The Effects of Exuberance

Seldom do we hear about overly exuberant bond markets and the corollary that interest rates are too low, presumably because a rising bond market is a vote of confidence in central bank policy. A rising stock market is more a vote of confidence in the ability of private firms to continue to deliver solid earnings growth while producing more goods at stable prices so that the central bank will not have to raise interest rates to control rising inflation.

In his recent Francis Boyer Lecture, delivered on December 5 at the American Enterprise Institute, Federal Reserve Chairman Alan Greenspan presented a comprehensive overview of American monetary policy since the founding of the Republic. No such speech would have been complete without addressing the crucial issue of the relationship between financial markets and the real economy. Greenspan wondered aloud how we can know when investors' "irrational exuberance" pushes stock prices too high, citing the example of the Japanese equity market "bubble" that burst after December 1989. The Fed chairman also observed that the central bank need not support a rapidly falling equity market, provided that it does not hurt the real economy; Greenspan pointed to the 1987 US stock market crash as one that was not followed by a recession. He omitted any reference to the prolonged recession and ensuing deflation that followed the collapse of the Japanese stock market at the end of 1989 and the US equity market collapse of 1929.

For those who attended the dinner at which Greenspan delivered his now-famous comments about the possible "irrational exuberance" of equity markets, the inescapable conclusion was that if such an observation, perfectly reasonable in the context of a lengthy discussion of American monetary policy, could cause the gyrations in financial markets that were observed in the hours following his speech, then financial markets must be nervous. Beyond that, there is the issue of what Greenspan said and the characterization placed on what he said by overeager wire service writers aiming at catchy one-line headlines to attract the attention of traders. Some even went so far as to suggest to a nervous Japanese market, open at the time of the speech, that the chairman had hinted at raising interest rates. That was totally untrue, and anyone with any sense would know that the chairman of the world's largest central bank would not give any hints about the future path of interest rates in a public discussion.

Market Behavior

Another, and probably more useful, way to describe the behavior of equity markets early in December 1996 is to point out that they fell by 2–3 percent after having risen by more than 20 percent in the previous year. Specifically, between December 1 and December 8, the S&P 500 fell by 2.3 percent after having risen by 20 percent in the previous year. During that same week, the French stock market fell by 3.2 percent after having risen by 20 percent over the previous year, the German stock market fell by 1.9 percent after having risen by 23 percent, and the struggling Japanese stock market fell by 3.5 percent after having risen by 5 percent.

Beyond the effect of normal year-end position-squaring, many observers have failed to note that the US stock market has fallen in December because interest rates have risen. Since Election Day, November 5, most of the up and down movement in stock market indexes such as the S&P 500 has been accounted for by falling interest rates in November and rising interest rates in December.

Avoiding an Overheated Economy

The biggest risk to the US stock market is an overheating US economy. We saw this in the summer of 1996, when the second quarter's 4.7 percent growth rate, along with strong employment and wage numbers, caused interest rates to rise and the stock market to fall by about 7 percent. Since then, however, the economy has obligingly slowed.

It is difficult to escape the conclusion that the US stock market has gone up because the factors that determine stock prices—prospective earnings, interest rates, and the durability of the expansion—have all been favorable. When the risk of overheating that emerged in the past summer was removed and interest rates fell, the stock market began to rise. It paused as the election approached, with hopes for a continuation of a status quo Republican

Congress and Democratic presidency. When that wish was granted and data continued to suggest that the economy was slowing to a sustainable pace with benign inflation data, the S&P 500 stock market index rose by about 8 percent during November. Since then, checked by Greenspan's reminder and usual year-end position-squaring, the stock market has dropped by 3 percent, driven down by a December rise in US interest rates.

Consistency in the Market

Actually, the stock market has performed with maddening consistency. The current rise in the stock market, measured by the more comprehensive S&P 500 average, has continued for six years and one month, since October 1990. The average annual increase has been far more moderate than the run-up during the 1920s, at 12.3 percent per year. True, the increase in the past year of 19.7 percent through the week ending December 8 is 60 percent above the average annual increase, but that rise is down smartly from the 34 percent increase during 1995.

The American stock market has performed unusually well because the underlying conditions have been unusually favorable. More than six years into an economic recovery, profits growth has stood up well while interest rates have failed to rise because an increase in inflation has yet to signal significant pressure on productive capacity. One of the reasons for an absence in significant pressure on productive capacity has been the solid growth of investment. Instead of showing signs of overheating, the US economy continues to show signs of slowing due largely to a slowdown in the growth of consumption spending.

Equity markets are unworried by signs of excess supply because the central bank can always remedy a shortage of demand growth. Real, inflation-adjusted short-term interest rates in the United States are about average, based on the record of the past 10 years, or slightly above average, if one believes in an upward bias in the measure of the consumer price index. If demand growth continues to slow, inventories will build, employment growth will slow further, and the Fed will need to cut interest rates to help boost demand growth. With the cut in interest rates will come improved earnings expectations and a higher stock market. Before such conditions emerge, disappointing earnings reports may appear during the first half of 1997 as a by-product of a slowdown in spending. That news would cause the stock market to fall until the Fed undertook measures to correct the situation by cutting interest rates and creating the expectation of a resumption in spending growth.

Corrections and Discomfort

This discussion is not meant to be a forecast but rather an indication of the reasonableness of current equity prices based on an unusually benign set of underlying conditions. If the opposite scenario—overheating and upward pressure on prices—emerged, interest rates would rise, and the stock market, fearing a Fed tightening, would fall. How far it fell would depend on how much interest rates rose and how far earnings were expected to fall as the Fed tightened.

A sustained increase in the S&P average of over 12 percent per year for more than six years is unusual. But so, too, are the underlying conditions in terms of sustained earnings growth, absence of inflationary pressure, and a nice balance between supply and demand growth, which few have expected to persist. The nervousness in the equity markets, particularly in the United States, is due not so much to the absolute rate of increase of equity prices on average as it is to the likelihood that the unusually favorable underlying conditions will not persist for much longer. This situation suggests a powerful belief in the tendency of economic conditions to revert to the mean.

Ultimately, this is true, but the difficulty arises in defining a mean over a certain period. Based on 50 years of history, US inflation rates of 2 percent are not unusual. Based on history since the inflationary episodes of the 1970s and 1980s, those same rates are unusual. A noninflationary expansion persisting over six years in the late 20th century for a mature industrial economy is an unusual experience. It has occurred, however, and it has been reflected in a run-up in equity prices that is unusual absolutely but not relative to the favorable underlying conditions.

Many analysts talk about a healthy correction to the stock market. Perhaps, but higher interest rates or lower expected earnings growth would not necessarily be healthy. The scenario that most professional equity managers seem to equate with a healthy correction is a slowdown in the economy that produces earnings disappointments and some sell-off in equity prices. That kind of a correction can be remedied by monetary policy and reduced interest rates. Since this is well-known by professional portfolio managers, a large drop in the stock market driven by reduced flows into mutual funds would require frightening less sophisticated household investors into selling shares and pushing prices down to levels that represent better value based on the yardsticks professional investors use. In view of the desire to create better value for fund managers anticipating continued inflows of investable funds from households, warnings from "top market strategists" of market corrections are not surprising.

A kind of intrinsic conflict emerges when an equity market rises to levels that seem high based on the laws of probability governing the conditions that underlie the determination of equity prices. Wealthy investors, primarily concerned with the preservation of their wealth, become uncomfortable about a perceived absence of good value in the equity markets based on historical standards. But the people driving US equity markets today are, by contrast, wealth builders. Middle-aged households desirous of building wealth to finance the education of their children and their own retirements are being increasingly drawn to participation in the equity market. A stock market that has risen by over 12 percent per year for the past six years, by 35 percent in 1995, and by 20 percent in 1996 presents a tempting opportunity.

Continuing Surprises

With all the focus on equity markets, few investors have noticed a logical corollary of Greenspan's concern about the level of US equity markets coupled with underlying global economic conditions. One way to reduce risk of overheating in the United States without explicitly raising interest rates is to allow the dollar to appreciate.

Whatever economic events drive financial markets over the coming years, we can be sure there will be some surprises. That most of the surprises regarding conditions underlying US equity markets have been favorable over the past several years says nothing about whether future surprises will be pleasant or unpleasant. Therefore, market prices will continue to be unpredictable. In view of that inescapable fact, we may find that, in 1997, central bankers and government officials may be less inclined to speculate about appropriate levels of equity markets, interest rates, or exchange rates. That would be a pleasant surprise.

Notes

1. Alan Greenspan, "The Challenge of Central Banking in a Democratic Society" (speech, Annual Dinner and Francis Boyer Lecture of the American Enterprise Institute, Washington, DC, December 5, 1996), https://www.federalreserve.gov/boarddocs/speeches/1996/19961205.htm.

2. The Nasdaq (National Association of Securities Dealers Automated Quotations System) is an electronic stock exchange, meaning that stocks are traded through an automated network of computers instead of on a trading floor. Based on market capitalization, the Nasdaq is the world's second-largest stock exchange.

—⏀—

Tension Rising

AUGUST 1999

In this piece, written in 1999, seven months before the tech bubble burst, Makin examined many of the contradictory signals coming from various economies. He saw interest rates falling, the stock market rising, and the dollar weakening. He concluded, "The equity market bubble has virus-like properties." The bubble, he said, will almost certainly burst, and the Fed will face some tough choices. The Fed, he wrote, is "now in the unenviable position of having embarked on a tightening journey with no clear destination." If the economies elsewhere in the world start to recover, the inflows of capital into the US that were propping up the stock market would slow. High interest rates, he predicted, would eventually end the stock market's rise. History, Makin warned, suggests that the aftermath of a bursting bubble leads to deflation and world depression.

The tension is rising in US and global financial markets. On June 30, the Federal Reserve took a timid first step toward tightening US monetary policy by raising the federal funds rate by 25 basis points—from 4.75 to 5.0 percent. It also rescinded the bias toward tightening that was articulated in May. The US stock market rallied by more than 5 percent in two weeks, while long-term interest rates fell by 20 basis points from where they had been before the Fed "tightened."

With US interest rates starting to fall again and the stock market rising, the incipient extra rise in US demand growth—and in the US current account deficit—is weakening the dollar. On July 19–20, the dollar fell by more than 3 percent against the yen and the euro, even before the May trade deficit was reported at $23.9 billion, a monthly record.

Meanwhile, in Japan, the economy has stopped deteriorating purely on the strength of the massive fiscal stimulus the government thrust on it during the first half of the year. Monetary policy is still too tight, as evidenced by the more than $30 billion in dollar purchases by the Bank of Japan required to avoid further appreciation of the yen. When an economy that can't sustain growth without massive fiscal stimulus experiences a strengthening currency, monetary policy is too tight. The dollar buying by the Bank of Japan should be allowed to increase growth of the money supply. The Bank of Japan is preventing that and is offsetting (sterilizing) its currency intervention's impact on the money supply.

The major engines of Europe—Germany and Italy—continue to experience weakening economic growth. The euro[1] has, until late July, drifted downward against the dollar, searching for a level that will reignite growth in Germany's and Italy's export-oriented economies. The euro may resume its fall unless German growth picks up. Meanwhile, the interest-rate-sensitive peripheral economies in Europe—Spain and Ireland in particular—thrive on monetary conditions that are too unrestrictive to balance demand with supply growth in those prospering areas.

The Perils of August

With all these tensions in the background, we find ourselves in the month of August, when major economic misalignments are often addressed by policymakers or markets. In August 1971, the Richard Nixon administration ended the Bretton Woods system by unilaterally breaking the link between the dollar and gold. In August 1982, the Mexican finance minister Jesús Silva Herzog announced to a discomfited American Treasury that Mexico could no longer meet the interest payments on its rapidly expanding debt. In August 1990, Saddam Hussein attacked Kuwait, initiating a tense six-month crisis that ended in the liberation of Kuwait and the start (in March 1991) of the current US economic expansion.

These crises, appearing at intervals approximately a decade apart, may contrast with the pattern of annual crises that has emerged since 1997. The Asian crisis began in June 1997 and intensified rapidly over the summer, although by September of that year the delegates to the International Monetary Fund (IMF)–World Bank annual meetings were congratulating themselves for having contained a crisis that was to spiral out of control by the end of the year with the collapse of a major bank and brokerage house in Japan and the virtual collapse of the Korean financial sector.

After a brief celebration during the spring of 1998 of the end of the Asian-Latin crisis, the crisis reemerged with a vengeance in August, when the Russian government, having received its $5 billion loan from the IMF, devalued its currency and defaulted on its debt. Those measures set off the shock waves that culminated in the near collapse of Long-Term Capital Management in September. Ironically, the Asian crisis and the Long-Term Capital Management crisis gave the US expansion a boost by lowering commodity prices, pushing safe-haven capital to the United States, and inducing the Federal Reserve to cut interest rates by 75 basis points.

Now, in the summer of 1999, we are witnessing the unraveling of the unexpected bonus provided to the US economy by the Russian and Long-Term Capital Management crises of the summer of 1998. The real question facing the US and global economies is whether the US stock market bubble—and yes, it is a bubble—will be deflated endogenously (that is, by natural market forces) or by the Fed ever-so-gently raising interest rates, while Chairman Greenspan suggests to markets, as my parents used to tell me, "This spanking is for your own good."

The Fed's Dilemma

The basic problem the Fed faces is the high likelihood that the bubble will burst and the certainty that someone will be blamed when it does. If the Fed raises rates quite a lot and the stock market then collapses, the Fed will be blamed and could be subjected to a curtailment of its quasi-independence by an angry Congress looking for scapegoats. Alternatively, if the Fed raises rates by only 25 or 50 basis points, the bubble will grow ever larger, and when it bursts, "irrational market forces" will be blamed. Then the US Congress will seek to pass a set of new laws that, while not doing anything to prevent future crises, will certainly hobble the economy's performance.

In considering whether it's to be the Fed or market forces that reduce the bubble before it gets even larger, it may be worthwhile to lay out the scope of the task that probably faces the Fed if it is going to bring US growth back into line with long-run potential. The realities underlying US growth in mid-1999 suggest that the federal funds rate will have to be raised to at least 6 percent over the coming year.

Slowing growth by a full percentage point—from, say, the current annual average of 4 percent to 3 percent (the Fed's long-run target)—would normally require about 150 basis points of Fed tightening over a year. If we calculate from the 4.75 percent federal funds rate that prevailed in June 1999, that would leave the federal funds rate at 6.25 percent by next June. Any extra acceleration of the consumer price index or wage increases would, of course, call into question whether the Fed could proceed along a smooth glide path and gradually raise rates to bring the growth down to a sustainable level.

Aspects of the Current US Economy

On an underlying basis, the US economy is in a classic investment-led expansion. The ongoing high-tech revolution in the United States, especially in communications and data processing, and rapidly falling computer prices have been part of a broad investment-led expansion that has seen the share of investment in the US. Gross domestic product (GDP) rose from 12 percent in 1990 to more than 17 percent in 1999. Neoclassical growth theory is clear on the consequences of the rising share of investment in GDP. A larger capital stock eventually reaches the point of diminishing returns, so that the marginal product of capital begins to fall and thereby compresses profits on the revenue side. Some business managers might call it a lack of pricing power; others will be disappointed ultimately with revenue projections undertaken at the time the decision was made to add to the capital stock.

The further by-product of a rising capital stock is a rising ratio of capital to labor that pushes up the marginal product of labor and thereby pushes up real wages. Real wages that are consistent with productivity increases are acceptable, but, as the capital/labor ratio continues to rise, the ability of more capital to add to the product of each unit of labor goes down and productivity growth begins to slow.

The other aspect of the US economy that is gaining great attention is America's rising current account deficit. Many see this as a pressure point that could interrupt the steady rise in US equity prices and, thereby, US consumption growth and the strong US expansion. Unfortunately, the current account is not an unambiguous guide to gauging the sustainability of the US expansion. The current account deficit of the United States measures the sum of public-sector dissaving and private-sector dissaving. Since public-sector dissaving—the US government budget deficit—has turned to a surplus while the current account deficit has continued to rise, it must be true that private-sector dissaving has jumped sharply.

Indeed, that is true. But part of the jump is entirely rational. Households that have experienced large gains in equities have been converting some of those gains into purchases of durable goods, especially housing, automobiles, and appliances. Although spending on automobiles and appliances is counted as consumption, it includes a savings component because durable goods last more than a year and represent a stock of future consumption services, just as savings of financial assets may do. However, durable goods are less liquid than financial assets, and their value falls with depreciation, whereas, on average, financial assets appreciate on earning either interest or capital gains.

The stylized version of a US financial collapse tied to the rising current account deficit is that foreigners "simply refuse to continue lending to the United States." This view is problematic. Rather, foreigners will continue lending $250–$300 billion per year to the United States only at higher and higher US interest rates, with the required rate going higher as opportunities outside the United States become more attractive. On the other side of the ledger for the US currency, a sudden cessation of capital flows to the United States would cause the dollar to collapse, making US producers (already highly competitive) even more competitive in a world where excess capacity exists in many areas, like autos and steel. Japan is already struggling (the $30 billion buying intervention) to avoid the dollar depreciation that results from its too-tight monetary policy coupled with some additional investment by global portfolio managers and selected Japanese equities.

Japan and Europe would be hurt if the United States becomes a major exporter of deflation. Germany, for example, would fare badly if the dollar collapsed and the euro appreciated back to 120. So far, the euro's depreciation against the dollar, from that level down to virtual parity, has failed to produce enough of a resurgence in the export sectors of Germany and Italy to reignite noticeable growth in their economies.

Is the US Equity Bubble Ready to Burst?

Despite these tensions, the US equity bubble is at levels that are more stretched than they were in October 1987. Ironically, this line was crossed just after the Fed's "tightening" on June 30, when relief at removal of the Fed's bias toward further tightening caused the equity market to rally more rapidly than the rate at which interest rates fell. Stocks in the United States are now at levels that are either unsustainable or, alternatively, suggestive of a radical new paradigm in the valuation of equities, as postulated by James Glassman and Kevin Hassett in their forthcoming book *Dow 36,000*.[2] I have suggested that part of the reason for the high valuation of US equities is the market's perception of an implicit guarantee from the Fed, based on its behavior last fall, that stock market drops of more than 20 percent will be cushioned by Fed rate reductions or huge liquidity injections. Glassman and Hassett argue rather that past models of equity valuation have become inappropriate as households come to believe that stocks are really less risky than bonds and, as a consequence, attach a lower and lower risk premium to the returns required to hold stocks instead of bonds.

The problem with all these arguments is that they are frightening when run in reverse. If the stock market collapses because of the lack of profitability or, alternatively, because the Fed simply pushes rates up to a level that forces stock prices to fall, all the factors that have been magnifying and justifying the high valuation of US equities are undercut. A drop in the stock market by more than 30 percent, without cushioning from the Fed, would de facto undercut the Glassman-Hassett argument that stocks are really less risky than bonds. When stocks are rising at 20 percent or more a year, bondholders earning their 5 or 6 percent look like fools. When stocks are falling at 20 percent a year, bondholders earning 5 or 6 percent look like geniuses. The characterization can shift rapidly when greed turns to fear.

The Fed is now in the unenviable position of having embarked on a tightening journey with no clear destination. It is entirely possible, and even likely, that inflation will not provide a dramatic signal of the need to tighten.

Further, a rate increase of more than 100 basis points, which is more than twice what markets are expecting, could actually be insufficient to cause a stock market collapse.

Once an equity market bubble starts to rise, it is quite robust. If approached delicately by a timid central bank, the equity market will shrug off small increases, just as it did the initial one on June 30, 1999. The equity market bubble has virus-like properties. The mere prospect of higher interest rates administered by the central bank is pored over by market participants, so that by the time the central bank does raise rates, the market has immunized itself to their impact. Of course, there is a limit to this process, but the market's ability to anticipate and prepare itself for Fed rate increases probably accounts for the resilience of most bubbles in the face of central bank tightening.

Undoubtedly, the market will be resilient to the well-telegraphed messages of the Greenspan Fed to raise interest rates. In June, Chairman Greenspan, in effect, overprepared the market for a rate increase and a possible asymmetric bias, and when the market saw just a rate increase in July, it shrugged and roared higher.

So how does the bubble eventually burst? History suggests that the pressure usually comes from economic strength outside the United States that creates competition for the capital that is driving up the stock market or from a Fed that can no longer tolerate the financial risks of a rapidly rising bubble. The alternative—inflation pressure that gives the Fed a traditional rationale to raise interest rates—has seldom been the means by which a bubble is eventually burst. Indeed, the absence of inflation pressure is a necessary condition for a bubble to emerge. I have already suggested that the Federal Reserve, absent inflation, is not in an aggressive or preemptive mood, and even if it were and it raised rates by another 125 basis points, that, too, based on historical comparisons with Japan in 1989–90 and the United States in 1928–29, might be insufficient to burst the equity market bubble. So we are left with the possibility of a rapid resurgence of growth in another major economy that pushes up US interest rates and creates competition for capital fueling the US stock market bubble.

Here, the most viable, and perhaps increasingly likely, candidate to produce a shock is Japan. Since the United States is a heavy importer of savings from Japan, a recovery in Japan would cause a reduction of US capital inflows at current interest rates. If Japan begins to recover, higher US interest rates will be required to sustain the high level of imported savings from Japan and elsewhere, and this rise in US interest rates will put increasing pressure on the US bubble. Indeed, a rapid recovery in Japan could see interest rates there rise by more than 200 basis points, which would require an equal or larger increase of interest rates in the United States. No equity market bubble of the scale we now see in the United States has withstood that kind of interest rate increase.

The Effects of Global Recovery on the US Economy

A global recovery, however moderate, would mean that the current level of capital flows to the United States will not be sustainable at an interest rate that supports the current level of the stock market. In short, as capital flows to the United States are redirected elsewhere, US interest rates, without any help from the Fed, will rise on their own to a point that eventually will cause a sharp fall in US equity prices. A sharp fall in US equity prices will produce a sharp drop in US demand growth and will require further rapid easing of monetary conditions in Europe and Japan. Otherwise, the collapse in the US stock market will administer a deflationary shock to the world economy that will dwarf the shock from Asia during 1997 and 1998. The past failure of central banks to recognize the need to offset deflationary shocks implicit in equity market collapses has led to world depressions. We can only hope that the outlook of major central bankers in Japan and Europe will be transformed by the time world market conditions require additional liquidity creation from their institutions.

A strange and, I fear, as-yet-unrecognized dilemma faces the central banks of Japan and Europe. If they don't ease, the world economy can't prosper without the demand boost from a US stock market bubble that, in turn, implies a rising US current account deficit. Then again, it is also true that if they don't ease, the US stock market will fall, because the interest rate required to enable financing of the US current account deficit will rise until the US equity market collapses.

Perhaps it is this kind of paradox that eventually brings bull markets to an end. Either markets put interest rates up too high for the stock market to bear or central banks do. My guess is that the markets will do it.

Notes

1. The euro was introduced for the core European countries in January 1999.
2. James Glassman and Kevin Hassett, *Dow 36,000: The New Strategy for Profiting from the Coming Rise in the Stock Market* (New York: Crown Business, 1999).

How the Bubble Bursts

JANUARY 2000

Makin detailed the precise causes of the emerging tech-stock bubble, which by late 1999 was pushing some equities to almost absurd levels that were clearly unsustainable. Drawing on his background, Makin explained why and how stocks rose to be so high by delving into the motivations and outlook of investors, fund managers, and policymakers—delivering a clear explanation of the phenomenon of bubbles. He further explained the predicted effects on the economy of the inevitable busting of the tech bubble, such as sharply higher interest rates.

Since October, money managers in the United States and worldwide have faced a choice: either buy the skyrocketing shares in the tech and communications services sector or risk going out of business. Every investor knows what is hot and wants to own it. As a result, many money managers have simply sold "value" (or other) stocks whose prices are related to the earnings prospects of a company or to interest rates and have purchased high-tech stocks whose prices are "momentum" driven. That means everyone expects the stocks to keep going up, and so everyone wants to own them until they don't go up anymore. And when they don't go up anymore, the bubble bursts.

The Tech-Stock Craze

The momentum for "momentum stocks" has grown pretty strong. Money managers who have not traditionally been investors in equities and those who have focused on sectors of the market other than high tech have begun to violate pacts with their investors to buy the high-tech stocks. Although they seem unprincipled, such actions have become a matter of survival for money managers. Investors are comparing virtually every form of investment to the high-tech sector and are rushing to buy into it. They sell other investments to raise more funds to finance the purchase of high-tech stocks.

This tech-craze phase of the stock market strengthened dramatically in the last eight weeks of 1999. While US interest rates have risen by more than 40 basis points across the US yield curve (normally a death knell for the stock market), the S&P high-tech sector has gone from being up a healthy 20 percent on the year in October to being up 50 percent on the year late in November. Meanwhile, the Nasdaq index, heavily weighted with high-tech stocks, has gone from being up 30 percent on the year in October to being up 80 percent on the year in late December.

Furthermore, the broader S&P 500 index has gone from being up just a few percent on the year early in October to being up about 15 percent on the year late in 1999. That move is attributable almost entirely to the high-tech sector of the S&P. Fewer than 10 percent of the stock sectors in the S&P 500 are above their 40-week moving average, though that narrow "breadth" of the stock market is at unprecedented levels. By contrast, during the second quarter of 1999, nearly 70 percent of stock sectors in the S&P were above their 40-week moving average.

Such remarkable moves of the broad indexes contain some truly breathtaking increases in the component stocks of the indexes. Among the hottest stocks, Qualcomm, which has risen to over 2 percent of the capital weighting in the S&P high-tech index, is up 1,500 percent from its level early in January. The stock had risen a mere 700 percent from its January level by early November and then redoubled the 700 percent increase during the last eight weeks of the year.

Slower-moving tech stocks like Amazon.com, Intel, and Microsoft are up between 40 and 60 percent since January, while the hotter Yahoo has risen by about 160 percent, with two-thirds of that increase coming since early November. Even the tech stocks are breaking down into the really hot ones, such as Qualcomm (up 1,500 percent), Real Network (up 700 percent), or CMGI (up 700 percent), and the "older" hot high-tech stocks, such as Amazon.com, Microsoft, and Intel, that have risen merely in the 50–100 percent range for 1999.

Is the high-tech sector in a bubble? You bet it is. At its peak in 1989, Japan's Nikkei 225 had reached a level 700 percent above the level 14 years earlier, when the Nikkei began its gradual ascent in 1977. In 1929, the Dow Jones index was about 275 percent above its level 14 years earlier. By the same yardstick, the S&P high-tech index is up over 850 percent. The S&P

high-tech sector is clearly in a bubble that is distorting both the allocation of capital and the behavior of the overall economy. Many of the high-tech companies are promising, but their prospects have not doubled or tripled during the past eight weeks, though the stock prices have.

The tech-sector bubble is not confined to the United States. While Japan's overall stock index, the Nikkei, has been about flat since October and up about 50 percent on the year, tech stocks have performed more spectacularly. Japan's telecommunications giant, NTT, rose by 100 percent from the beginning of the year to October. Since then, it has jumped even more sharply, to a level 350 percent above its level at the start of the year. Even hotter is Japan's Softbank Corporation, which was up a mere 600 percent by October and since then has reached a level 1,200 percent above its level at the beginning of the year. These incredible tech-stock surges have also appeared in Hong Kong and Singapore markets—and pushed up the overall indexes with incredible price moves that, in turn, increase the weighting of the rapidly rising tech stocks in the indexes.

The process whereby the leadership in stock markets becomes narrower and narrower as a smaller and smaller subset of stocks rises faster and faster is a classic late-equity-cycle phenomenon. As the favorite stocks rise spectacularly in value by factors of 10 and 15, their weighting in the overall index becomes larger and thereby provides support for the index. That support conceals an ever-weakening performance by a broader and broader sector of "unfavored" stocks in the index. The number of New York Stock Exchange stocks at new 52-week lows has soared to 1,200 over the past eight weeks, which is about the level reached in autumn 1999.

Today, investors look at their "typical" portfolios and find the values either flat or falling—even as they read newspaper headlines about the spectacular performance of tech stocks. As a result, they migrate to funds that are labeled as tech-sector mutual funds. Since the capital weighting of such mutual funds has historically been very small, the funds quickly find themselves overwhelmed with investors, and, because of constraints of management and other scale factors, some are forced to limit the flow of funds into their firms. Meanwhile, desperate managers of funds that have traditionally had nothing to do with high-tech stocks suddenly discover that tech stocks somehow match their original investor mandate and start to buy the stocks. More and more investors begin to chase fewer and fewer stocks, and the result is the spectacular increase in prices of a few favorite stocks.

The tech-stock surge has nothing to do with broader arguments about the valuation of typical stocks. My colleagues James Glassman and Kevin Hassett have argued in *Dow 36,000* that stock prices relative to earnings may indeed rise, on average, to levels three times their current levels, based on an elimination of the risk premium between stocks and bonds. A lower risk premium on stocks should push up nearly all stock prices. But the average price-earnings multiple on the S&P 500 has actually dropped slightly from its high of around 34 this summer to about 29 now. That is partly because typical S&P shares have been sold to finance purchases of high-tech shares.

In 1999, a strong stock market, propelled by unusually sound fundamentals like strong earnings growth and an absence of inflation pressures, was transformed into a stock market driven by a true bubble in the technology and communications sectors. With all investors eager to add to their holdings of tech stocks by selling, as necessary, less-favored sectors, serious distortions are beginning to arise. Traditional small cap stocks with price-earnings multiples below 25 are facing a higher cost of capital than the overall S&P index with a price-earnings multiple of 29. More broadly, analysts who attempt to place a value on stocks that is conditional on earnings prospects and returns on alternative assets such as bonds have given up those criteria as a means of allocating scarce capital. Rather, the need to survive has simply driven them to purchase tech stocks irrespective of the absence of earnings or the ominous rise in interest rates in the United States and Europe.

The US Economy and the Bubble

The macroeconomic consequences of the tech-stock bubble in the United States are beginning to emerge, and they are making the Federal Reserve governors distinctly uneasy. By the broadest measure, the US economy, which was growing at about a 2.5 percent annual rate during the first half of the year, accelerated to a 5 percent growth rate during the second half of the year, with the rise in growth driven by stronger consumption spending. US aggregate demand growth exceeded US output growth during the first three quarters of 1999 and looks set to do the same during the fourth quarter.

Optimists about the US economy say there is little cause for worry, given the acceleration of US growth, and suggest that neither wages nor prices are rising rapidly. Although the rises are moderate by historical standards, inflation is, in fact, rising. The consumer price index, which began in 1999 rising at a year-over-year rate of 1.6 percent, hit a 2.6 percent year-over-year rate in October. Wage growth, while not torrid, is running between 3.5 and 4.5 percent, depending on which measure one chooses.

The tech-sector bubble has been superimposed on a powerful rise in the overall US stock market. Between the second quarter of 1998 and the second quarter of 1999, the higher prices of stocks and a derivative increase in home prices pushed up the net worth of US households by $2.5 trillion (from about $31.5 trillion to $34 trillion). The rise in net worth means that, thanks to rapidly increasing share prices, the assets of US households have risen even more rapidly than the households' rapidly rising liabilities. There is a borrowing boom going on in the US household and corporate sector, but the increase in borrowing (liabilities) has, so far, been overshadowed by the extraordinary rise in assets, thanks particularly to higher equity prices.

In this latest phase of the US stock market boom, a high-tech bubble has pushed up wealth even further over the past eight weeks, although the increases are probably more narrowly concentrated on those who happen to either work for or own shares of companies in the high-tech sector. But the rise in tech stocks has been spectacular enough to preserve 15–20 percent increases in the overall indexes and thereby continue to support a high level of spending growth in excess of income growth.

Viewed broadly, American balance sheets will look fine as long as stocks stay at current levels. The big concern is that stock prices could drop rapidly, and the bubble in the high-tech sector is not a comforting sign. Assets will be eliminated while liabilities remain in place, and US spending will have to be cut even more rapidly than a drop in wealth alone would dictate.

It is asset inflation—higher private wealth from higher share and house prices—that is driving the US economy in this vibrant, investment-led expansion, which is closer to a 19th-century boom than anything we have seen in this century. The resulting strain on output capacity is showing itself in a rising current account deficit (American borrowing from the rest of the world) that will require still higher interest rates to induce further growth and foreign lending to American individuals and companies. A global configuration of accelerating American demand growth, driven by higher asset prices, and Japanese repatriation of foreign investments has created an unsustainable situation.

If the world's largest borrower, America, has to borrow more as its current account deficit rises, driven higher by faster demand growth that in turn reflects a stronger and stronger stock market, and the world's biggest lender, Japan, wants to lend less as its losses on foreign-asset holdings mount because of a rising yen, US real interest rates have to rise further—probably by a full percentage point, to 5 percent. Add that to a 3 percent inflation rate, and you have US market interest rates approaching 8 percent next year. That will place a heavy strain on the stock market and especially the tech-sector bubble.

The tech-sector bubble being created atop a US equity market that is already 50 percent above normal value (given current earnings prospects and interest rates) is dangerously unstable. Increasingly rich market players, who bid up house prices at more than 20 percent a year while buying bonds that are pricing long-term inflation at 2 percent, are living with a contradiction that cannot persist. Market interest rates of 8 percent will be needed to eliminate the contradiction, unless a stock market plunge cuts spending and the rising US current account deficit. A currently "unimaginable" 8 percent level for interest rates—markets are looking for current rates of not much more than 6 percent to be the limit—will strain the Goldilocks American economy and markets to a breaking point.

When the Crunch Comes

Having said this, I should add that the party will no doubt last at least until the next Federal Reserve Open Market Committee (FOMC) meeting on February 1, 2000. The FOMC left rates unchanged at its meeting on December 21, 1999, not wishing to introduce any additional strains as markets struggle to cope with actual or imagined Y2K problems. However, beyond early February, the US tech bubble, and with it the US stock market, could run into some serious problems. Among them are the already mentioned probable rise in US inflation rates to more than 3 percent and a continued strain on world assets markets from the tendency in Japan to repatriate funds. Japanese credit markets are still priced for deflation because the Japanese economic recovery, which was expected to materialize during the second half of 1999, has failed to appear.

If history is any guide, the US Federal Reserve will ultimately be forced to prick the bubble in the US tech sector. The huge increases in wealth created by the tech-sector bubble atop a 50 percent overvalued broad US equity market will push up US demand at an unsustainable pace. Inflation may not be as serious in registering the unsustainable growth of US demand as a rising US current account deficit may be. We shall probably see a moderate rise in inflation, along with a rapid rise in the US external deficit; the two together will press the Fed to raise interest rates to slow US demand growth. Usually, equity markets are the first to fall when the central bank moves to restrain excessive demand growth or its symptoms. That was the case in 1929 in the United States and in 1989 in Japan—and, as noted above, the US tech-sector bubble has exceeded by a wide margin the valuations of the US Dow Jones in 1929 and the Japanese Nikkei in 1989.

As heady as the run-up in the US tech sector has been, elimination of the bubble will come as a relief to most US financial managers, who currently have no choice but to buy tech stocks on the supposition that the next buyer will pay even more for the stocks. That is neither a good nor sustainable way to allocate capital. An important question facing US investors—and investors and economies worldwide—is how the broad US equity market will behave after the tech-sector bubble bursts. If US stocks were to return to normal valuations conditional on interest rates and expected earnings, they would fall by 40–50 percent from current levels. That is not an unreasonable outcome, since the tech-sector bubble is essentially an anti-valuation approach to the stock market that is pricing stocks with no reference to fundamentals. Once that bubble bursts, investors will probably return with considerable fervor to employing fundamentals in the pricing of the equity market.[1]

The macroeconomic problems associated with a sharp drop in stock prices will be formidable, though not impossible to overcome. US balance sheets will look considerably worse, and spending growth will have to be cut, to rebalance assets and liabilities.

Looking back, historians may conclude that the emerging-market crises of 1997–98 were the root cause of the US equity bubble in 1999. By cutting the demand for raw materials and capital in the rest of the world while inducing the Fed to cut interest rates, the emerging-market debt crisis provided a tremendous tailwind for the US economy and stock markets. Consistently, but somewhat ironically, the return of emerging markets to economic health during 1999 has begun to place powerful stresses on the sustainability of the US stock market boom. An additional challenge, the Y2K problem, has probably delayed a Fed tightening by several months. Normally, an interval of that length would not be significant, but this time it may have been. The emergence of a true tech-sector stock market bubble in the United States required only eight weeks during the last part of 1999. It could grow considerably larger during the first month of 2000. By then, the Fed will be playing catchup on the need to tighten, and subsequent rate increases will be more than simply a "take back" of the anti-crisis rate cuts that were undertaken during the fourth quarter of 1998.

Notes

1. By the end of 2000, the Nasdaq was off more than 50 percent from its peak in March 2000. It wouldn't surpass that peak until 2015.

Bubble Trouble

NOVEMBER 2000

The equity bubble began to burst in March 2000, and by the end of the year, like dominoes, other sectors were collapsing as a result. Stocks were in a free fall, and it was becoming clear that the US economy would soon hit economic turbulence. Makin, of course, had for years warned that the "golden age" would end at some point. Writing in May 1995 ("Is This the Golden Age?"), he explained:

> *The stock market bubble—inadvertently fed by a central bank that believes it is performing well by keeping inflation moderate although prices actually ought to be* falling *in a supply-led recovery—begins to expand so rapidly that the increase in wealth from that bubble causes demand to run away. Demand growth quickly comes to dominate supply growth, and the central bank is forced to collapse the bubble to avoid a runaway inflation.*

In this piece, he described how bubbles burst—and correctly forecasts that the tech-stock collapse "could well cause a US recession next year." As it turned out, economists would later say the US was in a recession from March through November 2001. He went on to describe how the stock surge of the late 1990s destroyed Americans' saving ethos and predicted that as stocks returned to sensible levels, consumption would fall and start an unusual recession. The upside, he said, was that capital would be better allocated, but he voiced his fear that "too many decisions are being made on the expectation that stock prices will continue to rise—an expectation in turn based on unrealistic predictions."

A stock market bubble exists when the value of stocks has more impact on the economy than the economy has on the value of stocks. The US stock market bubble is bursting—hot sector by hot sector, starting with the internet bubble, which has already burst, and continuing with the IT communications sector bubble, which is in the process of bursting.

The collapse of the hot sectors has also pulled down the stocks of brokerage houses and banks that have been cheerleading for and financing those sectors. Finally, the contagion will spread to more basic stocks such as Home Depot, whose shares dropped sharply after announcing an earnings disappointment in mid-October.

The collapse in 2000 of the hottest sectors of the stock market will probably spread to other sectors and could well cause a US recession next year and possibly a global recession. Even though the broadest stock indexes are down "only" 10 percent so far this year, a flat or modestly lower broad stock market is far from what US households and businesses expected at the start of the year. Those expectations drove spending and borrowing to levels that were imprudent, because they required higher stock prices to be viable. The result of such imprudence will be sharply lower investment and consumption spending, probably starting by early next year.

The negative effects of the sharp drop of demand will be compounded by a contraction of credit, whose extension has been predicated on ever-rising stock prices. That the credit shrinkage is already underway has been signaled by the spread in October 2000 of 700 basis points between junk bonds and treasuries, higher than the 680 basis points reached in October 1998 during the Long-Term Capital Management crisis.

The onset of the US recession will be unusual in form because of the unusual nature of the investment-led expansion that has driven stock prices and, in turn, economic behavior to extremes. The recession will be sharp. It will not be caused by Federal Reserve tightening, though the Fed will be blamed, but instead by a collapse of demand (investment and consumption) in turn driven by the simple failure of equity prices to rise with economic behavior that could only be validated by higher stock prices.

The Usual Recession Scenario

Most recessions are caused by overheating. As the economy gets stronger and keeps growing, households and businesses keep spending more until demand growth outruns output growth. Then prices start to rise, and the Fed keeps pushing up interest rates and restricting liquidity until the economy slows down. Sometimes it takes a recession to convince the happy spenders to slow down, as in 1990; sometimes it just takes an economic slowdown, as in 1994–95.

The current expansion looked like a classical demand boom for a brief period, from late 1999 to early 2000. During that period, the Fed raised short-term interest rates by 175 basis points, about one-half of what it usually takes to slow the economy. Final sales—that is, demand—slowed from a 6.7 percent annual growth rate in the first quarter of this year to a 3.9 percent rate in the second quarter. The Fed stopped raising rates after a half-point boost in May, and now markets actually expect—or at least hope for—a rate cut by early spring 2001.

Stocks and Spending

As Election Day approaches, there are signs of a sharp slowdown of investment and consumption growth that has little to do with the level of interest rates and a great deal to do with the level of the stock market. The extraordinary rise in the US stock market has been fueled by strong growth of investment and productivity coupled with strong consumption growth that has, in turn, had to rely on a zero level of saving out of income by American households.

But now, the stock market—and especially the once-favored internet and IT sectors—is signaling an end to the investment boom. The Nasdaq index, which contains many of the most favored internet and IT stocks, is down 20 percent since January and down 40 percent from its April highs. Attendant falls in the Dow Jones and S&P 500 indexes have left the broadest averages of equity prices about 10 percent below their levels at the end of 1999.

Signs of weakness in the IT sector, including stocks like Microsoft, Intel, and Cisco Systems, are especially significant for the outlook of the US and global economies. This is far more significant than is typical for a particular sector of the economy. The IT sector has accounted for most of the extraordinary growth of investment and productivity over the past several years, not to mention its disproportionate contribution to rising household wealth.

The huge wealth increases generated by rising stock prices and the attendant, though much less spectacular, increases in real estate and bond prices have increasingly led American households to rely on asset appreciation (rather than saving out of income) to achieve their savings goals. During 1999, wealth gains totaled $5.15 trillion, and saving fell to 2.2 percent of disposable income, far below the long-run average of around 7 percent. This year the wealth gains are so far zero or negative, and saving out of income has fallen yet again. Americans in 2000 are spending more than their after-tax incomes.

Households are borrowing more to finance spending in excess of income because the huge rise in equity prices and wealth during the 1990s created an average annual wealth increase from 1990 through 1999 of $2.64 trillion. The year 1999 was extraordinary because nearly two years of the annual expected household wealth increase occurred in just one year. In 2000, households have so far felt comfortable spending all their disposable income and then some because they achieved two years of wealth accumulation with the extraordinary rise in the stock market during 1999. Further, many appear reluctant to sell stocks and pay capital gains taxes, preferring instead to borrow against them to finance continued strong spending.

The most important questions about the outlook for the US and global economies are these: Will the US stock market end this year flat or down? What will that outcome imply for investment and spending behavior next year? The current consensus for a modest slowdown in spending overlooks the powerful negative effects on investment and consumption that could result from an absence of stock market gains, let alone a broad drop in stock prices.

Up until a decade ago, Americans wondered at the start of each year whether the stock market would go up or down. They saved about 7 percent of after-tax income to ensure that wealth would at least be maintained even if stock prices fell. By 2000, after nearly a decade of rising stock prices, Americans started the year wondering by how much the stock market would rise and saved nothing out of income, but relied instead on expected wealth gains to do their saving for them. American businesses experienced a similar transformation of expectations about stock prices over the decade and undertook more aggressive spending and borrowing plans in 2000 as a result.

This transformation of expectations implies magnified wealth effects from stock market behavior during this year and next. The transformation also means that the American economy is vulnerable to the extraordinary volatility generated by investment-led booms of the sort prevalent in the 19th century and the early part of the 20th century.

Investment Booms

An investment boom starts when a new discovery or new technology opens up immense opportunities for wealth creation. Investment growth surges and output capacity are enhanced by more capital and greater productivity of capital. Growth accelerates, but inflation does not, thanks to higher productivity growth. The rising stock of more productive capital increases labor productivity faster than wages rise, so that the real cost of labor falls and profits rise. The "new economy," with faster growth and stable or falling prices, excites investors to bid up stock prices of new-economy companies. Another round of investment follows, thanks to the low cost of capital implied by a voracious appetite for new-economy stocks. The first phase of a new economy appeared after 1995, when growth of productivity accelerated from 1 percent annually to nearly 3 percent.

The second phase, after a 1998 global scare that actually benefited the United States with lower raw materials costs and lower financing costs enhanced by a Fed rate cut, began in 1999. It crested when dot-com companies could raise billions of dollars merely by suggesting an idea about using the internet. Who wanted to build an old economy refinery in 1999 when there were hundreds of new-economy dot-coms in which to invest? In other words, the white-hot phase of the new economy investment boom is reached when normal investments are starved for capital by a headlong rush into new-economy companies with seemingly limitless possibilities. There is too much investment in the new-economy sector and too little in the old economy. Bottlenecks, like inadequate refining and drilling capacity and inadequate supplies of fuel or electric power, begin to slow the economy just as excess capacity emerges in much of the new-economy sector.

Investment does not slow down when excess capacity appears. It stops. The capacity embodied in new capital equipment cannot be laid off. It has been bought and paid for (probably through borrowing). If too much IT equipment, meaning an amount that will not allow its buyers to recoup its cost, is on hand, IT orders are eliminated, not reduced. That is why investment-led booms end suddenly, with a collapse of investment spending.

If IT investment, which has accounted for virtually all investment and productivity growth since 1996, drops to zero, total US growth will be cut by 1.5–2 percentage points. Productivity growth would also drop sharply, perhaps back to 1 percent. Real labor costs would rise, and a combination of rising labor costs and reduced pricing power (weakened by excess capacity) would depress profits. Stock prices would fall rapidly—especially in the face of dashed hopes of earnings growth rates of 30 percent per year or higher.

Wealth, Saving, and Consumption

These stylized facts comport well with the behavior of dot-com stocks in April and May 2000 and with the behavior of many IT stocks in September and October. The main implication of these events for households has been no wealth creation during 2000. If the absence of wealth gains in contrast with extraordinary expected wealth gains causes a sharp drop (as yet unseen) in US consumption, the second and decisive feature of an end to the US investment-led boom will fall into place, and we shall experience a sharp recession.

How plausible is the heretical yet immensely dangerous notion of a sharp drop in US consumption? If the stock market merely stays at current levels, it is quite plausible. If it falls another 15 or 20 percent, it is a virtual certainty. If stocks go back up to their April highs or beyond, the boom will end later and more painfully, after another surge in consumption.

During the 1990s, capital gains came to augment saving out of income as the way in which American households accumulate wealth. On average, the sum of saving out of income plus expected capital gains (calculated as a smooth version of average annual capital gains during this expansion) has constituted about 15 percent of after-tax household income.

With after-tax disposable income at about $7 trillion in 2000, the 15 percent rule would call for $1.05 trillion in saving. The fact that measured saving out of income is zero so far this year is consistent with the hypothesis that households in 2000 have not yet lowered their long-term expectation of substantial gains in wealth from higher stock prices.

The Role of the Fed

No analysis of the entry into a recession after an unconventional investment-led expansion would be complete without examining the possible options facing the Federal Reserve. A crucial question involves the degree to which households' and businesses' expectations of continued substantial increases in stock prices and wealth are contingent on the expectation that the Federal Reserve can and will move aggressively to stem a collapse of share prices. The Fed's objectives, to maintain price stability and orderly financial markets while avoiding systemic risk, coupled with its actions in 1998 in response to what it deemed systemic risk in the Long-Term Capital Management crisis, leave open the likely nature of its response to a rapid drop in share prices.

The Fed's problem is complicated by the stagflationary shock from higher energy prices and by the fact that the United States is borrowing over 4 percentage points of gross domestic product from the rest of the world to finance an investment boom. If that investment boom ends for legitimate reasons tied to the underperformance of investments in the new economy, part of the approach to stabilizing the dollar would be to engineer a sharp drop in US spending growth that, in turn, reduces American borrowing requirements with respect to the rest of the world.

If the limited past experience of the role of central banks at the end of investment-led recoveries is any guide, the best the Fed can hope to do is avoid making a bad situation worse. That would probably involve gradually lowering short-term interest rates and providing enough liquidity to avoid unwarranted solvency problems, but not to underwrite excessive borrowing.

However it proceeds, the Fed must find a way to move households and businesses steadily away from the situation in which the stock market's behavior has a bigger impact on the economy than the economy does on the stock market. That situation is untenable because it leaves the Fed in the uncomfortable position of having to target the stock market to control the economy. Many market players already believe the stock market is so important that the Fed must and will put a floor under stock prices to avoid a recession. The only way the Fed can move back to a situation in which it aims for bedrock objectives like price stability is to allow the stock market to reflect underlying economic realities.

Once it has given a clear signal that it is not in the business of supporting any particular level of stock prices, the Fed can begin to move to stabilize the economy and encourage a resurgence of growth based on the sound economic fundamentals that still prevail in the US economy. At that time, tax cuts could be helpful as a stimulative measure.

The problem facing the Fed is not that US economic fundamentals are unsound or that inflation is about to burst forth. Rather, the problem is that too many decisions are being made on the expectation that stock prices will continue to rise—an expectation in turn based on unrealistic predictions about the pace of earnings growth in the new economy.[1]

Notes

1. See "Is This the Golden Age?," May 1995.

Japan's Lost Decade: Lessons for America

FEBRUARY 2001

With the US showing signs of entering a recession, Makin drew on his deep knowledge of Japan's experience in the 1990s to offer advice. The key to a US recovery, he wrote, "is to avoid Japan's serious policy errors of the 1990s." Even though Japanese leaders could have followed the guidance of John Maynard Keynes and Milton Friedman from decades earlier on avoiding post-bubble monetary policy errors, they ignored that advice—with disastrous results.

On the monetary side, the lessons from Japan are to maintain stable monetary base growth, avoid targeting nominal interest rates, and prevent deflation. Makin also warned, "In monetary policy, the most fundamental challenge will be to modulate the slowdown in the real economy without creating another bubble in the US equity market." On the fiscal side, Makin said, the government should avoid wasteful spending and should maintain "lower and more uniform marginal tax rates" to ensure that government policy doesn't distort the private sector and help maintain currency stability.

As the United States enters a recession amid growing signs of excess capacity after a surge of investment spending, inevitable comparisons arise with Japan's 1989–90 collapse and the disastrous decade that followed for its economy. While the American recession will be painful (like all recessions), it need not be followed by a decade or more of serious economic underperformance like that still suffered by Japan. One of the keys to a normal US recovery is to avoid Japan's serious policy errors of the 1990s.

The most reassuring conclusion to emerge from examining government policies, especially monetary and fiscal policies, that followed this century's major equity market bubbles (including Japan's in 1989 and America's in 1929) is their extraordinary ineptness. Such mistakes should be easy to avoid, yet a need for caution arises from the fact that Japan made such mistakes even with the benefit of lessons provided by John Maynard Keynes' monumental *The General Theory of Employment, Interest, and Money*, published in 1936, and Milton Friedman and Anna

Schwartz's *A Monetary History of the United States*, published in 1963. These important works provide a comprehensive guide to avoiding post-bubble mistakes in monetary policy. While America's grave monetary policy errors in the early 1930s were made without benefit of the lessons articulated by Keynes and Friedman, Japan chose to ignore these lessons, compounding its economic pain with major errors of fiscal policy in the 1990s.

Given that Japan's experience is both more recent and more disconcerting, because known tenets of monetary policy were ignored, the focus here will be on lessons for US policymakers from Japan. It is important to avoid the possibility, however remote, that American policymakers might fail to learn from the past just as Japan's policymakers have done.

Lessons of Monetary Policy

Three basic lessons of monetary policy follow from Japan's recent experience and from the analyses of monetary policy by Keynes and Friedman: (1) maintain stable monetary base growth; (2) avoid targeting nominal, or market, interest rates, especially while inflation rates are falling or negative; and (3) do not let deflation, a falling price level, take hold.

The need to maintain stable growth of the money base is clearly illustrated by problems resulting from the high degree of volatility exhibited by Japan's money base growth in the 1980s and 1990s. The Bank of Japan allowed money base growth to rise rapidly from about a 6 percent annual rate in 1987 to more than 12 percent at the end of 1989. The bank's staff and leadership have, since then, been unrelievedly mortified by the realization that a rapid surge in money growth fed Japan's late 1980s equity market bubble. It came when confidence in Japan and its economic future was as high as it would be 10 years later in the United States, especially in late 1998 and 1999. Indeed, it is probably true that the rapid acceleration in money base growth supplied by the Federal Reserve—first, after the Long-Term Capital Management market crisis of October 1998 and, second, during the lead-up to the end of 1999 and its Y2K[1] concerns—contributed to the extraordinary surge in US equity prices that began in the fall of 1999.

A change of leadership and remorse over allowing the equity market bubble to develop led the Bank of Japan to slam on the monetary brakes in 1990, dropping the growth rate of the monetary base from 12 percent to below 2 percent during most of 1991, 1992, and 1993. This acute monetary contraction caused the equity market in Japan to collapse. The Nikkei index dropped first from close to 40,000 to around 24,000 during 1991 and then dropped further to about 16,000 in 1992. Japan's equity bubble burst rather than deflated. Consequently, a sharp rise in the cost of capital caused private investment growth to collapse and subtract between 1 and 2 percentage points from overall growth during the three years following the early part of 1991.

The Bank of Japan was misled about the intensity of monetary tightening by a rapid fall in Japanese interest rates, which created an impression of easy monetary policy—an illustration of the danger of gauging the stance of monetary policy solely from the behavior of nominal interest rates. Actually, the drop in interest rates was a reflection of falling inflation expectations and falling real interest rates that accompanied the collapse in Japanese investment spending.

The Bank of Japan has also tended to look with satisfaction on a strengthening yen and a rising current account surplus as signs of a sound economy. Actually, the rising current account surplus mirrored a collapse in domestic investment spending coupled with a sustained high level of domestic savings. Japan ran out of investment opportunities at home while its households continued a high level of saving. For a time, consumption spending held up reasonably well while the high level of domestic saving made it easy for the Japanese government to begin a series of public works spending packages financed by the sale of government bonds to Japanese savers.

The Bank of Japan's failure to maintain adequate monetary growth after the bursting of the equity bubble naturally led to its third major mistake: allowing deflationary psychology to develop. After allowing a modest run-up in money base growth rates from 2 percent during the 1992–93 period to 6 percent in the middle of 1994, the Bank of Japan again began to restrict growth of the money base—dropping growth abruptly to below 4 percent by early 1995.

The result was the closest thing to a deflationary crisis witnessed by any major industrial country in the postwar period. By the spring of 1995, Japan's equity market was plunging—dropping from above 20,000 in 1994 to below 15,000 by May 1995. Private consumption began to contract rapidly, while the yen appreciated sharply, briefly reaching a high of just 79 yen per dollar in the spring of 1995.

The combination of a falling stock market, collapsing consumption, and a strengthening currency is a dangerous one, indicative of a rapidly emerging deflationary psychology. Rising expectations of deflation shrink profit prospects, and equity prices fall. As consumers expect prices to continue falling, they hold off on spending and accumulate cash. The desire to add to liquid balances that appreciate at the rate of deflation also reduces capital outflows and causes the currency to appreciate. The currency appreciation is itself a deflationary event and thereby reinforces the trend toward further deflation.

Finally, confronted with what amounted to a deflationary crisis, the Bank of Japan relented and accelerated money base growth from about 3 percent to more than 10 percent in late 1995 and early 1996.

The reacceleration of money growth coupled with continuing fiscal stimulus from higher public works spending combined to produce a sharp recovery in Japanese growth in late 1995 and 1996. The move toward deflation was stopped, and the yen weakened back to more than 100 yen per dollar. Ominously, land prices in Japan continued to fall; by 1996 they had sunk to about half their level at the peak of the bubble.

While the Bank of Japan's insensitivity to gyrations in the growth rate of the monetary base may seem hard to explain, the reason lies clearly in its tendency to focus on the level of interest rates as a guide to monetary policy. The danger of doing this in an environment of disinflation, deflation, and weak investment spending was clearly articulated in Friedman and Schwartz's *A Monetary History of the United States*, which focused on the US experience during the 1930s. Market interest rates reflect underlying real returns on investment and market inflationary expectations. After an equity market collapse accompanied by sharply lower investment spending, real interest rates drop, signaling economic weakness, not easier monetary policy.

Lessons for Fiscal Policy

After 1993, the Japanese government pursued a series of fiscal stimulus packages that, by 1999, reached a cumulative total of over $1 trillion. The budget deficit approached 10 percent of gross domestic product (GDP)—the equivalent of a trillion-dollar deficit in the United States. Government debt has risen to 130 percent of GDP, the highest in the G7.

The additional spending was largely directed toward public works projects, shoring up a weak financial system, and subsidies to the weakest of Japan's businesses, which, in retrospect, ought to have been allowed to fail. In short, Japan followed a decade of overinvestment in the private sector in the 1980s with a decade of overinvestment in the public sector in the 1990s. While the direct stimulus of government works projects and subsidies to weak businesses kept the economy from falling back into negative growth for a time, the weakness resumed once the direct stimulative effects of the spending packages wore off. This is hardly surprising considering that the large stimulus packages went to finance wasteful public works projects and simultaneously abetted the serious misallocation of resources by supporting weak industries rather than strong ones.

As soon as the Japanese economy began to recover, in the wake of powerful monetary and fiscal stimulus after the deflationary crisis of 1995, the Japanese government moved rapidly to raise the tax rate applied to consumption in Japan. This flirtation with fiscal orthodoxy (an attempt to reduce budget deficits by taxing household consumption in a deflationary environment) proved disastrous and threw the Japanese economy back into a sharp recession in 1997. Subsequently, private investment and consumption weakened, and another large program of fiscal stimulus was initiated in 1998 and again temporarily boosted the economy. But the recession resumed in 1999—resulting in yet another stimulus package. That stimulus package boosted the economy, once again temporarily, until Japan's growth rate turned negative during the second half of 2000.

The most basic lesson about fiscal stimulus to be learned from the Japanese experience is to avoid wasteful government spending. Rather, it is better to reduce tax rates to encourage private demand and private work effort and investment. Japan's wasteful demand stimulus created nothing but temporary relief from a chronically depressed economy resulting from underlying deflation and monetary policy that was too tight. The spending in support of public works projects, such as tunnels under Tokyo Bay and railroad lines to underpopulated parts of Japan, would never have been undertaken by the private sector.

In effect, the Japanese government used Japan's huge flow of trapped savings, pushed into government bonds by high levels of economic uncertainty and fear of investing abroad, to finance immensely wasteful expenditures. Had Japan instead reduced tax rates in 1992 to encourage investment and additional work effort, the economy would likely have begun to recover, provided that the Bank of Japan did not keep monetary policy too tight. In fact, Japan's only forays into tax policy raised consumption taxes in 1997 while increasing payroll taxes to finance health insurance programs. Both measures reinforced the deflationary pressures from tight monetary policy.

Japan's tendency to use stimulative fiscal policy with the Bank of Japan's invariably tight monetary policy pushed up real interest rates and thereby caused the currency to strengthen, which reinforced the deflationary tendency already present. Curiously, the Japanese government was never able to recognize the dangers inherent in this deflationary policy mix. Furthermore, advice from the American Treasury Department reinforced this misguided policy.

Will the United States Repeat Japan's Mistakes?

It seems highly unlikely that American policymakers will repeat the post-bubble mistakes of Japanese policymakers. But difficult problems still face the designers of both monetary and fiscal policy in the United States.

In monetary policy, the most fundamental challenge will be to modulate the slowdown in the real economy without creating another bubble in the US equity market—particularly in the dot-com and IT sectors. The stimulative monetary policies pursued by the Federal Reserve in late 1998 and late 1999 probably contributed to the late 1999 bubble in parts of America's equity market. One of the big problems with such a bubble that goes unrecognized for a time is that it creates too much investment because rapidly rising stock prices make it tempting for managers to expand capacity too rapidly. Simultaneously, resources are misallocated by the bubble's sectoral nature. The surge in dot-com and IT stocks meant that adequate funding was unavailable to expand oil-drilling capacity or electricity-generating capacity. Who wants to invest in oil-well drilling when the price of oil is low and the cost of capital is high?

Now that America's sectoral equity market bubble has burst, there is too much capacity in some areas and too little in others. Resources need to move out of the IT and dot-com sectors and back into the basic industry sector. Government policies should not interfere. In particular, if the tax code is opened up this year to reduce marginal tax rates, pleas for special support for "needy" industries should be avoided. The pleas from dot-coms and IT companies may be especially loud in view of the excess capacity problems and the rapid deterioration in conditions in those industries. The Japanese government yielded to the siren call to help weak industries at the expense of sound industries, thereby accentuating resource misallocation rather than gradually eliminating it.

The Federal Reserve probably understands well the need to guard against deflationary tendencies like those that have emerged in Japan. The basic lesson arising from Japan's experience is to avoid a situation in which a falling stock market and weakening consumption are accompanied by a stronger currency, as happened in Japan in 1995. The fact that the dollar has remained stable while the US economy has slowed rapidly over the past several months is not a bad sign in view of the negative implications of a US slowdown for global growth.

The biggest lessons for the US flowing from Japan are in fiscal policy. The Bush administration proposal to reduce tax rates will help stimulate both demand and supply, with the latter being helped by the encouragement of more work effort and investment in basic industries. Lower and more uniform marginal tax rates will allow the US government to collect taxes with less distortion of the private sector. Fiscal stimulus through lower tax rates also helps stabilize the dollar by strengthening both supply and demand in the private sector.

America in 2001 is remarkably well supplied with policy options to contain recession. With the federal funds rate, the policy interest rate of the Federal Reserve, just half a percentage point below its recent 6.5 percent high, ample room remains to cut rates another 3 percentage points if necessary. Tax rates are clearly too high with government revenues at over 21 percent of GDP (a postwar record) and a surplus of over 2 percent of GDP, or about $250 billion annually. Lower tax rates make eminently good sense even without a recession. With one, they become a necessity. The notion of paying down America's debt (the lowest in the G7) instead of lowering tax rates as we enter recession is absurd, akin to Japan's disastrous flirtation with fiscal orthodoxy when it raised tax rates in 1997 and precipitated a sharp recession.

Finally, the Federal Reserve must take care not to cling too hard to a fear of inflation. Should the end of America's investment boom precipitate a sharp recession, inflation rates will fall faster than interest rates. Real interest rates will rise and monetary policy will be tightening even as market interest rates fall. Should this happen, the Fed will have to be aggressive in pushing down market interest rates, using faster money growth to signal its desire to achieve stable, not falling, prices. The lesson that stable prices are best but falling prices are highly dangerous is the most important lesson American policymakers can learn from Japan's sad experience since 1990.

Notes

1. The term "Y2K" was shorthand for the year 2000. It became a reference to the two-digit computer code for the year, which had been used since the 1960s and was expected to cause widespread computer failures as 1999 changed to 2000. The fear was that computers would revert to January 1, 1900, instead of January 1, 2000.

A Primer on Depressions

APRIL 2001

Writing in the middle of what would turn out to be the 2001 recession, Makin reported that "US equity market losses over the past year have totaled over $4.5 trillion. That wealth loss amounts to about 60 percent of a year's household disposable income and over 12 percent of total US household wealth from all sources," and he warned that the worst was not over. He drew on history and the more recent experience of Japan to assess the odds of a depression. It's not impossible, he said, and it can happen at the end of an investment-led boom followed by a stock market collapse. Avoiding such a severe downturn, Makin wrote, requires a reorientation of fiscal and monetary policy geared at aggressively stimulating growth. In hindsight, that's what policymakers did, in the form of what would become the George W. Bush tax cuts of 2001 and sharp cuts in the federal funds rate throughout the year.

A depression follows a period of euphoria about the outlook for the economy and the future earnings of "new" companies. The euphoria becomes unsustainable, and the stock prices of the new companies collapse. Large wealth losses replace large expected wealth gains. Consumption growth slows, then turns negative, and stock prices of more companies fall because weaker demand erases pricing power and, with it, prospective profits. Demand falls further, and deflation sets in.

In a depression, the central bank discovers (to its horror) that stock prices, not interest rates, become the major transmission mechanism running from financial markets to the real economy. That is because after a bubble, earnings fall faster than any central bank can, or will, cut interest rates, and when earnings—or more ominously, expected earnings—fall faster than interest rates, stock prices fall.

Earnings expectations for Nasdaq companies have fallen by more than 75 percent in many cases. The Federal Reserve is expected to have cut interest rates by 2 percentage points by May, from 6.5 to 4.5 percent, or by about 30 percent. That would be a large move by historical standards, but not enough to stabilize equity prices. So the Fed is left looking powerless, cutting interest rates aggressively but failing to stabilize equity prices.

Economists are shy about mentioning the word "depression." If they do mention it, they "hasten to add" that it is "contained," as in Japan, or that it "can't happen here," as in the United States. I have used these words myself. But history, specifically the aftermath of the 1929 stock market crash in the United States and the aftermath of the 1990 Japanese stock market crash, offers little consolation to those claiming that depression is not inevitable after an investment-led boom that ends with a stock market collapse. In the United States after 1929 and in Japan after 1990, the only two instances in this century in which stock market collapses followed investment booms, depression resulted.

Yes, Japan is in a depression complete with rapidly falling prices, zero interest rates that are not low enough to stimulate spending, public works expenditures on counterproductive projects with negative marginal products, and paralyzed policymakers at the Finance Ministry and the central bank. The nightmare that John Maynard Keynes wrestled with in *The General Theory of Employment, Interest, and Money*—an economic equilibrium consistent with self-reinforcing falling prices, employment, and output—has settled over Japan like an invisible cloud of poison gas. Little wonder that Kiichi Miyazawa, Japan's elderly but still acute finance minister, uttered recently before the Japanese Diet that Japan's government finances were close to a "catastrophic situation."

The Link Between Financial Markets and the Real Economy

The bursting of an equity market bubble that leads to a prolonged collapse of the real economy is the manifestation of a most basic and enduring theme of macroeconomics: the link between financial markets and the real economy. A powerful negative shock to the financial sector, like the collapse of a stock market bubble, sets in motion a deceptively straightforward set of events that seems, somehow, to leave policymakers caught like deer in the headlights.

Leading up to the bubble, a virtual prosperity mania sets in, with households contemplating undreamed-of wealth, firms bidding for and stockpiling precious skilled labor, and governments marveling at—and promptly spending—tax revenues that far exceed their most optimistic expectations. The end comes, as it did during the past year in the United States, after extraordinary events like expected, unfailing growth of 25–30 percent per annum have come to be seen as ordinary. That perception makes investors view as unremarkable the purchase of equities at prices 200 times current earnings, or at more than 10 times the normal price-earnings multiple. Such pricing cannot be sustained.

The most recent and spectacular example of the insanity that accompanies equity market bubbles is the experience of Yahoo, a company whose primary source of revenues is online advertising. Not only have Yahoo's profits failed to grow, but they have collapsed—virtually to zero in 2001 with a hoped-for rebound to $60 million in 2002—down sharply from earnings of nearly $300 million in 2000. Since Yahoo's share price surged because of an expected perpetual acceleration of earnings growth, the reality of a sharp deceleration in earnings growth has brought the stock from a high of about $240 early in 2000 to $17 on March 9, the first anniversary of the 5,000-level peak of the Nasdaq. The Nasdaq itself, with its collection of dot-com and internet stocks, fell by 60 percent, from 5,000 to 2,000, from its March 2000 peak to March 2001. The Yahoo swoon alone wiped out nearly $80 billion worth of wealth, while the more general Nasdaq collapse has erased over $2.5 trillion in wealth.

Taken altogether, US equity market losses over the past year have totaled over $4.5 trillion. That wealth loss amounts to about 60 percent of a year's household disposable income and over 12 percent of total US household wealth from all sources.

Bubbles Can Mislead Policymakers

An insidious feature of a post-bubble period is the unusual and—at first—deceptively benign behavior of the real economy. Such benign behavior creates serious problems for policymakers.

The onset of the US growth slowdown over the past six months manifests a classic post-bubble pattern. Since excess capacity resulting from accelerated, bubble-driven capital formation quickly becomes a problem after the bubble bursts, capital-spending growth slows. Indeed, US capital-spending growth went from a 21 percent annual rate in the first quarter of 2000 to a –0.6 percent annual rate in the fourth quarter.

The initial reaction of markets is to embrace the idea of a capital inventory correction that can be remedied quickly with lower interest rates. Many commentators, especially those eager to sustain flows into stock market investments, suggest that the slowdown in capital spending is a healthy sign of the economy's ability to regulate itself. The central bank consoles itself with similar notions of the therapeutic effect of a slowdown in capital spending. Although consumption slows, it does not collapse in an environment identified as a beneficial correction. Indeed, US consumption spending, which grew at an extraordinary 7.6 percent annual rate in the first quarter of 2000, slowed only to a still-respectable 2.8 percent annual rate in the fourth quarter.

But the extraordinary investment surge that characterizes an investment-led boom carries the seeds of its own destruction. Normally, investment growth accounts for about one-sixth of the total growth of the economy. From 1959 through the end of 2000, investment growth accounted for 0.6 percentage points of an average 3.5 percent growth rate. However, during the 12 quarters ending in the first quarter of 2000, the peak of the investment boom, investment spending accounted for 1.5 percentage points of the 4.6 percent overall growth rate, or nearly a third of all growth. At the end of an investment boom, a sharp slowdown in investment spending produces an unusually sharp drop in gross domestic product (GDP) growth. The 5 percent annual growth rate at the beginning of 2000 became a 1 percent annual growth rate by the fourth quarter of 2000, with an unusually large portion of that slowdown attributable to a slowdown in investment growth.

Consumption Will Fall Next

The outlook for US consumption growth is bleak. In the November *Economic Outlook*, I asked:

> How plausible is the heretical yet immensely dangerous notion of a sharp drop in US consumption? If the stock market merely

stays at current levels, it is quite plausible. If it falls another 15 or 20 percent, it is a virtual certainty.

Since November, the Wilshire 5000 index (the broadest measure of equity value) has dropped by 18 percent.

The link from wealth to savings and consumption suggests strongly that large equity losses will cut consumption spending as households add to savings out of income in an attempt partially to compensate for the severe damage to their balance sheets. During the 1990s, when capital gains came to augment and then dominate saving out of income as the way in which American households accumulated wealth, on average the sum of saving out of income plus expected capital gains (calculated as a smoothed version of average annual capital gains during this expansion) constituted about 15 percent of after-tax household income.

The assertion that the United States could experience a year of negative growth is certainly a long way from saying the United States will enter a depression. It is not moving—and need not move—inexorably in that direction. Rather, the United States is probably moving toward an unusually intense recession wherein the growth slowdown will be longer and deeper than many have been willing to admit. It is the dangers inherent in making the transition from unusually good times to unusually bad times that need to be recognized. Spending will remain depressed for some time as the realization sinks in that the acquisition of wealth requires some saving out of income and not simply the acquisition of "hot" stocks whose value seems to rise inexorably.

Aggressive Stimulation Needed

Policymakers need to move away from a state of complacency about the need for stimulative measures. In 1962, a Democratic president, John F. Kennedy, proposed tax rate cuts equal to more than 2 percent of GDP to stimulate economic growth. He did this at a time when the ratio of publicly held debt to GDP was 44 percent and the deficit was higher than 1 percent of GDP. The US economy was entering an expansion, but Kennedy wanted tax reform and sustained economic stimulus from a better-designed tax system. Today, as the US economy enters what looks to be a serious recession, a Republican president is proposing tax rate cuts and a modest fiscal stimulus equal to barely 1 percentage point of GDP while the ratio of publicly held debt to GDP is 33 percent and falling and the surplus is approaching 3 percent of GDP.

Today's protests about tax cuts being too large because the debt paydown[1] is threatened are the result of a dangerous, mistaken idea that somehow debt paydown caused the prosperity of the 1990s. In truth, the prosperity of the 1990s caused the debt paydown. Tax rate reductions are an even better investment in 2001 than they were nearly 40 years ago in 1962. Note that although the Kennedy tax cuts were not enacted until February 26, 1964, three months after the president's assassination, they helped sustain three years of noninflationary growth averaging 6.6 percent from 1964 through 1966. The Kennedy-inspired tax and tax rate cuts of 1964 were part of a fiscal revolution and ably chronicled by the late Herbert Stein.[2]

In 2001 the negative pressures on the US economy, not to mention the global economy, are serious enough to justify far more aggressive tax rate reductions that, in fact, target moderate budget deficits and an attendant moderate rise in the ratio of debt to GDP. Some movement in that direction will occur when the sharp slowdown in the US economy over the coming months turns fiscal policy debate from a quarrel about whether tax cuts are too large into a contest between Republicans and Democrats to determine who can cut taxes by the larger amount.

Monetary policy is also disconcertingly complacent in view of the dangers facing the US economy. Although reductions in interest rates cannot eliminate the recession, they can cushion it. Holding the federal funds rate at a still-restrictive 5 percent (even after a reduction of 0.5 percent on March 20) throughout the onset of a recession when a stimulative 3–3.5 percent is needed will unnecessarily prolong economic weakness. In addition, Fed Chairman Alan Greenspan's advocacy of a destabilizing fiscal measure that raises tax rates in a recession—the debt trigger mechanism—only reinforces the misplaced leaning toward restrictive fiscal policy at a time when stimulative measures are needed. Both monetary and fiscal policy will have to be sharply reoriented toward stimulation of the economy in coming months. A failure to do so would only reinforce the uncanny tendency toward depression after equity market bubbles have burst.

Notes

1. After several years of budget surpluses, the government had been paying down the national debt. Some worried that tax cuts would detract from this effort.

2. Herbert Stein, *The Fiscal Revolution in America*, 2nd ed. (Washington, DC: AEI Press, 1986).

—⁂—

The Fed Didn't Cause the Stock Market Bubble

OCTOBER 2002

With the benefit of more than two years of insight about the stock market bubble of the late 1990s, Makin defended the Fed and rebutted claims from critics who sought to blame the Fed for the huge run-up in stock prices and their subsequent collapse. Instead, Makin pointed to a different cause: the repeated bailouts and ensuing moral hazard[1] created by the US Treasury and International Monetary Fund in Asia and Russia and with Long-Term Capital Management. The Fed's role "was, at most, peripheral," while the actions of other institutions "created a strong perception that aggressive investments in risky markets were more attractive than usual."

Federal Reserve Chairman Alan Greenspan has been widely criticized for claiming in his August 30 address at Jackson Hole, Wyoming, that the Fed is not at fault for failing to deflate the US stock market bubble. Specifically, Greenspan, who was addressing the Federal Reserve Bank of Kansas City Symposium on Rethinking Stabilization Policy, asserted that an interest rate increase sufficient to deflate the bubble would have done significant damage to the economy at large: "The notion that a well-timed incremental tightening could have been calibrated to prevent the late 1990s bubble is almost surely an illusion."[2]

Chairman Greenspan raised an important issue, suggesting that we need to understand better the role of equity risk premiums in asset bubbles, and he urged "productive discussion of these and other issues related to stabilization policy"[3] at the symposium. In fact, little discussion followed of either the causes of the late 1990s bubble or the appropriate role of central banks in dealing with bubbles. Nor was additional insight on these difficult issues offered by critics who dismissed Chairman Greenspan's remarks as an ill-advised apologia for the Fed's role in addressing the stock market bubble.

Intervention and the Risky Asset Bubble

A close look at the role of governments in markets during the last half of the 1990s suggests that the Fed's role in creating preconditions for a stock market bubble was, at most, peripheral and that the Fed did undertake to cool an overheating economy in 1999. The fact that equity risk premiums, the expected higher total return on stocks above returns on "riskless" government bonds, were falling sharply while the US equity market bubble was inflating suggests that the real contributor to the global bubble was the proactive role of policymakers in rescuing markets from the fallout of the Asian bubble in 1997–98, including the Long-Term Capital Management (LTCM) crisis in October 1998.[4] While the Fed played a subordinate role in all these events, the proactive role of the US Treasury and the International Monetary Fund (IMF) was more decisive in creating a moral hazard problem that led global financial markets first to be shocked and driven from risk exposure by the Russian default and devaluation in August 1998 and then to be overly inured to risk after the rescue of LTCM in October 1998.

An understanding of the forces leading up to the US equity market bubble during the late 1990s requires a careful examination of global economic conditions before its emergence. A good place to begin this story is with the collapse of the Mexican financial markets late in 1994, which was followed by an aggressive IMF-led and US Treasury–sponsored rescue for Mexico early in 1995. The Mexican rescue, widely hailed at the time as a great success, established the model whereby the US Treasury and the IMF worked in tandem to ensure financial stability in emerging markets.

During the following two years, a speculative bubble developed in Asia where the emerging markets of Indonesia, Korea, Taiwan, and Thailand had come to be seen as economies with unlimited upside potential. Capital flowed rapidly to the region, and a speculative bubble developed in real estate and a variety of other investment types. Strains began to show in 1997 as widespread signs of excess capacity emerged.

Simultaneously in the United States, records of Fed meetings show that some Fed governors, including Lawrence Lindsey, had begun to raise concerns about the rapid increases in US equity prices. In September 1996, the Fed held lengthy discussions internally concerning possible speculative excesses in US equity markets. Chairman Greenspan's December 1996 reference to the possibility of "irrational exuberance" was an external reflection of those discussions, even though in his speech Greenspan linked irrational exuberance to the Japanese equity market bubble in the late 1980s. Even though most measures of fair value for stocks failed to show overpricing late in 1996 and early in 1997, the Fed was concerned enough to begin raising US interest rates in March 1997, when it boosted the federal funds rate by 25 basis points to 5.5 percent.

Asian Crisis Invites Moral Hazard

The emergence of the Asian crisis late in the spring of 1997 marked the start of a period of financial instability that constrained Fed actions over the following two years and probably, thereby, contributed to the Fed's role in the eventual emergence of the 1999 US equity market bubble. But the primary role was played by the US Treasury and the IMF and their ever-increasing role in bailouts that ultimately failed to prevent either the Russian collapse or widespread devaluations in Asia and Latin America.

To understand the timing of the Asian collapse, it is important to remember events in the largest Asian economy—Japan. The Japanese economy had, after 1995, experienced a recovery, including a resurgence of investment spending that appeared to place Japan on the path for a sustainable recovery. However, in April 1997, Japan implemented a sharp increase in its consumption tax and in payroll-withholding taxes for retirement and health benefits. The negative impact on demand growth in Japan sharply weakened the Japanese economy and caused Japanese financial institutions to reduce their loan portfolios in Asia. Thailand was the weakest of the once-booming Asian economies, and when Japanese banks refused to roll over credit lines to Thailand late in the second quarter of 1997, the Asian crisis began to intensify.

The summer of 1997 saw intense denial that an Asian crisis was emerging. The September 1997 IMF meetings were largely devoted to empty testimony to the resilience of the region. Subsequently, during the fall of 1997, the Indonesian and Korean bubbles collapsed. Efforts to repair the damage with substantial Treasury-sponsored IMF rescue packages were not very successful. The Korean rescue package cobbled together late in 1997 failed at the end of the year.

Treasury Intervention and Moral Hazard

In January 1998, Treasury Secretary Robert Rubin summoned leading global bankers to the boardroom of the New York Federal Reserve Bank and enlisted an additional $25 billion in aid for Korea to stem the then-burgeoning Asian crisis, thus solidifying the role of the US Treasury and the IMF as a guarantor of global investors. There followed a powerful recovery in global financial markets during the first half of 1998 capped by a large bond issue for Russia, which was underwritten by Goldman Sachs in June 1998. Reassured that a proactive US Treasury and IMF would not allow a nuclear power to default, investors celebrated by purchasing high-yielding Russian bonds. Unfortunately, the government in Russia failed to get the message and in August 1998 devalued the currency and defaulted on its obligations to global lenders.

Another event in June 1998 contributed to deflationary pressure in Asia. During the spring of 1998, the value of the Japanese yen, the currency of a weakening economy in a weakening region, fell sharply. The consequent improvement in Japan's competitive trade position in Asia alarmed the Chinese, ever vigilant of their dominant role as an exporter within Asia. The Chinese insisted that the yen's depreciation be ended. The Chinese pressed their demands vigorously on the eve of a trip to China and Japan by then-President Bill Clinton and suggested that the Chinese visit would not go smoothly unless the United States took decisive measures to terminate the depreciation of the yen.

In mid-June 1998, the US Treasury directed the Federal Reserve to join the Japanese in selling dollars, thereby ending the drop in the yen and ultimately resulting in a period of yen appreciation that contributed substantially to the deflationary environment both in Japan and Asia overall. Once again, the proactive role of the US Treasury was hailed as a reassuring event, but the deflationary implications for Japan and Asia of a stronger yen were largely unnoticed and then forgotten in the wake of the dismaying devaluation and default by the Russian government in mid-August.

Russian Default Kills Appetite for Risk

So unnerving was the Russian default, not only to the hapless holders of Russian bonds, many of which were purchased just two months earlier, but more broadly to financial risk managers worldwide, that decisions were quickly made to reduce sharply the exposure of private financial institutions to global markets. After the proactive successful role played by the US Treasury–IMF team in Latin America and Asia, the Russian default suggested bailout impotence. As a result, the spreads between emerging-market bonds and US Treasuries and other indicators of risk exploded during September and early October as a flight to quality ensued. The world's largest volatility risk-spread trader—LTCM, which had huge bets that widening spreads between riskier assets and US government securities would narrow—was wiped out by the flight to safety that caused those spreads to balloon.

Once again, in September 1998, the offices of the New York Federal Reserve Bank were offered to provide to private financial markets the implicit approval of the Fed and the US Treasury of efforts to craft a rescue package that financial markets could not manage on their own. The decision to accommodate the rescue of LTCM was a difficult one. Clearly, financial markets were disrupted by the events leading up to the virtual collapse of LTCM. Numerous banks and investment banks were substantially exposed to financial risk, both through their direct involvement with LTCM and through the broad role that they played in what had become highly volatile financial markets.

The rescue of LTCM, or more accurately the reduction of the widespread exposure to LTCM's activities, was accompanied by rapid rate cuts by the Fed. The federal funds rate was reduced by 75 basis points between the end of September and mid-November 1998 in what became part of a successful effort to restore more normal spreads and lower levels of volatility in financial markets.

LTCM Rescue Rebuilds Appetite for Risk

By the end of 1998, relative calm had been restored to global financial markets. More significantly, the confidence of markets that governments stood ready to intervene in cases of extreme financial stress was underscored. The feelings of abandonment that had arisen in global markets after the Russian default and devaluation were erased by the rescue of LTCM and the Fed's rapid rate cuts.

The year 1999 was the real bubble year in US and global financial markets. The focus was on what might have been viewed as riskier stocks in the US IT sector. As I wrote in the January 2000 *Economic Outlook*, "How the Bubble Bursts":

> This tech-craze phase of the stock market strengthened dramatically in the last weeks of 1999. . . . The Nasdaq index, heavily weighted with high-tech stocks, has gone from being up 30 percent on the year in October to being up 80 percent on the year in late December.

Emerging markets boomed as well, with risky assets rising most rapidly. As Chairman Greenspan noted, the equity risk premium in the US stock market fell, consistently with the idea that higher returns on risky assets were attractive if governments, the IMF, and, after October 1998, the Fed were prepared to underwrite additional risks.

Because conditions in 1999 were good for financial markets and especially for riskier assets, a bubble developed, most dramatically affecting the shares of riskier companies in the IT sector. In the aftermath of the Asian bubble with its attendant excess capacity, cheaper raw materials were available for US producers, including those in the high-tech sector. The Fed easing of 75 basis points, which had been induced by the LTCM crisis, provided a further tailwind, as did an additional flow of safe-haven capital to the United States, which was newly anointed as the world economic champion. The cost of capital for tech ventures was pushed nearly to zero as dot-com shares were snapped up regardless of earnings or prospects for earnings. Excess capacity expanded rapidly.

By mid-1999, the party was heating up enough so that the Fed began to apply restrictive policy. From June 1999 through March 2000, it increased rates in 25 basis-point increments five times to 6 percent. In May 2000, it followed up with another 50 basis-point increase two months after the peak of the bubble and during a period of sideways movement of most stock market indexes.

Bubble Bursts

While 1999 was the exhilarating bubble year for the US and other global financial markets, 2000 saw the start of a period when the bubble became self-correcting as the underlying conditions supporting it melted away. By the fourth quarter of 2000, US growth had dropped to 1.1 percent from an extraordinary 7.1 percent growth rate in the fourth quarter of 1999. The fourth quarter of 2000 also witnessed the first of what was to become a string of seven negative quarters of investment growth lasting through the second quarter of this year and perhaps beyond. Investment growth slowed because excess capacity had been generated by the costless capital available courtesy of the stock market bubble. Excess capacity meant falling prices for IT products whose stock price increases had been the greatest. Expected profits in the stock market began to fall sharply, and by December 2000, the Nasdaq index had been cut in half to just below 2,500 from its high of 5,000 in March.

The steep drop in the stock market was accompanied by an abrupt slowdown in United States economic growth driven largely by an inventory sell-off and continued falling investment spending. The US entered a mild but unusual recession, with consumption sustained but investment weak, early in 2001 and saw negative growth during the first three quarters of that year. As growth slowed and unemployment rose, the Fed cut rates rapidly beginning in January 2001 from 6.5 percent down to 3 percent by August. The sharp rise in uncertainty associated with the September 11 terrorist attacks on New York and Washington, DC, led to another rapid sequence of cuts totaling 125 basis points between September 17 and December 11.

The Fed has left the federal funds rate at 175 basis points during all of 2002. A consumption surge at the end of 2001 fueled by tax cuts and lower interest rates boosted growth to about 5 percent in the first quarter of 2002. However, by the second quarter, growth had slowed back to 1.1 percent, largely supported by modest inventory building.

Bubble Lessons

Looking back over the past half decade, it becomes clear that the global equity market bubble of 1999 was one of a series of bubbles that emerged in the last half of the 1990s. The proactive response of government, especially the US Treasury and the IMF, along with the cooperation of the Federal Reserve, appeared by 1999 to have created a strong perception that aggressive investments in risky markets were more attractive than usual by virtue of the apparent willingness of the US Treasury and the IMF to underwrite those risks, coupled with the Fed's willingness to maintain an accommodative stance for monetary policy when such rescue efforts were underway. This classic moral hazard problem may have been responsible for the compression of risk premiums in US equity markets that Chairman Greenspan mentioned in his Jackson Hole address. Certainly, risk premiums in other risky investments, such as those for bonds of emerging markets, were also compressed during 1999.

The important question still facing the global economy is not so much who caused the bubble but, rather, whether stimulative monetary and fiscal policy can produce sustained economic growth and with it sustained growth in profits that will enable financial markets to recover as part of a credible resumption of global demand growth.

We remain in a global economic environment best described as a "post-bubble era," in which investment spending drops sharply and then excess capacity and the need to preserve profit margins force down employment and consumption. That the Federal Reserve has confined itself (so far in 2002) to hoping for a recovery, while the European Central Bank perversely continues to believe that inflation is lurking just below the surface and the Bank of Japan has openly declared its impotence to do anything further to help the Japanese economy, is discomforting at best. If history is any guide, look for the aftermath of the bubble to display dismayingly consistent economic weakness that leads the Fed to resume interest rate cutting,[5] probably by another 75 basis points over the balance of 2002. Subsequent dollar depreciation may well force the European Central Bank to ease while the government of Japan is pressed to increase liquidity further.

Notes

1. See "Interference with Free Markets Causes Global Crisis," October 1998.

2. Alan Greenspan, "Economic Volatility" (speech, Federal Reserve Bank of Kansas City, Jackson Hole, WY, August 30, 2002), https://www.federalreserve.gov/boarddocs/speeches/2002/20020830/default.htm.

3. Greenspan, "Economic Volatility."

4. Long-Term Capital Management was a Connecticut-based hedge fund that was bailed out by a plan organized by the Federal Reserve Bank of New York in 1998.

5. The Fed did cut rates throughout 2002, and they bottomed out in 2003.

12

THE WEALTH OF MODERN NATIONS: WEALTH ACCUMULATION AND DESTRUCTION

America's Destabilizing Wealth Explosion

MAY 2000

By mid-2000, America's financial picture seemed divided: Economic growth remained strong, but the stock market, which had surged in the fourth quarter of 1999 and kept accelerating until March 2000, was showing signs of strain and had started collapsing. Makin assessed the unusual circumstances in this period and found that the sudden explosion of wealth, "while exhilarating, has upset the balance of the economy."

During the fourth quarter of 1999, the real net worth of American households rose by a massive $3 trillion (from $33.5 trillion to $36.5 trillion), an increase of nearly 9 percent—a 36 percent annual rate— due almost entirely to rising stock prices. Subsequently, during the first quarter of 2000, the Wilshire 5000 Total Market Index (the broadest measure of the wealth effect from US household equity holdings) rose by another 4 percent. Even the underperformance in the volatile tech sector did not put a dent in overall American financial wealth during the first quarter of 2000.

But a mid-April plunge in the stock market erased nearly $2 trillion of net worth in a week and was followed by huge oscillations of stock prices. Like most "too much, too soon" events, the wealth explosion, while exhilarating, has upset the balance of the economy. It is not sustainable, and, as the jump in the March consumer price index reminded us, more than just oil prices are rising. Perfection could turn to stagflation—slower growth and higher inflation—in coming months, thereby inverting the growth-without-inflation combination so characteristic of this remarkable expansion of output and wealth.

An Unprecedented Rise in American Wealth

The $3 trillion increase in American wealth during the fourth quarter marks a new phase in the unfolding of America's extraordinary "golden age" that appeared in 1995. It is unprecedented, being equal to the wealth increase during the entire decade of the 1960s when the previous record-long (nearly nine-year) American economic expansion occurred. The increase in household wealth attributable to the housing boom during the entire decade of the 1970s was just $2 trillion. That decade contained 40 quarters, while now we have seen a $3 trillion wealth increase (in real terms, not current dollars) in just one quarter.

Other historical comparisons are also useful. From 1960 through 1990, real US household net worth rose at an average annual rate of 3.5 percent, which was great by historical and international standards. From 1990 to 1998, the annual rate of increase of US wealth rose sharply to 6 percent a year. None of these respectable figures even approaches the extraordinary 36 percent annual growth rate for household wealth during the fourth quarter of 1999.

The extraordinarily rapid pace of wealth accumulation witnessed at the end of 1999 will not continue. Indeed, some of it has been reversed. Based on the performance of the broad Wilshire index since March, typical household stock portfolios have fallen by around 10 percent from their highs. Still, compared to the end of 1998, with the Russian crisis and the Long-Term Capital Management collapse still in mind, American households understandably entered 2000 feeling far more financially secure than they had during the previous year. It is not an exaggeration to say that America's golden age reached a new and higher plateau at the end of 1999, and, as yet, the extraordinary rise in wealth associated with that new phase has, for the most part, remained intact.

Imbalances Could Turn Perfection into Stagflation

The dangerous underpinnings by financial markets of the 6-percent-plus growth rate of the US economy constitutes a familiar story replete with potential problems. Those problems are being studiously ignored by US markets that have been priced for perfection and a soft landing. The Federal Reserve's excruciatingly slow "no surprises" approach to raising US interest rates is beginning to look like a policy mistake that will see US demand growth continue to outstrip the willingness of the rest of the world to lend the United States $1.3 billion a day at recent interest rates and exchange rates.

It is somewhat ironic to note that the Japanese government, struggling to revive its own economy, has provided some $85 billion of financing for the US current account deficit since July 1999 by selling yen and buying dollars. This generosity has been undertaken to avoid a sharp yen appreciation that would endanger Japan's weak recovery. A significant recovery in Japan or other interruption of these large flows would, once again, raise the problem of a falling dollar, rising US inflation, and slowing US output growth. Such a combination of a falling dollar, falling stocks, and falling US output would signal a rapid transition from the current state of perfection to stagflation, a combination of slower growth and higher inflation that we left behind at the end of the 1970s.

The high praise for the Fed's brilliant handling of the economy—so far—could evaporate quickly under any one of the conditions that might end the current unsustainable combination of rapid demand growth, stable prices, a stable dollar, and falling interest rates. Such a transition would be particularly awkward for the Fed and for Democrats before the upcoming election in November. It is important to bear in mind that the ensuing financial sector disorder that might accompany such adjustments would not change that the United States still can have a healthy economy that grows between 3.5 and 4 percent a year without disruption. It is the extra 2 percentage points of growth that have emerged from the huge wealth surge at the end of 1999 and the fact that its continuation is priced into financial markets that will cause problems in the financial sector that could harm the real economy.

The Wealth of Modern Nations

JANUARY 2007

In this piece from 2007, Makin pondered an idea that was as important today as it was then: the role of the US and China as economic superpowers. Building on Adam Smith, Makin surveyed the two countries and delved into their strengths and weaknesses—especially in their crucial financial sectors—with respect to their abilities to move from wealth creation to wealth preservation. He also examined the tensions that arose between the US and China because of their differing abilities to preserve wealth. While these differences tempt policymakers on both sides to react, he counseled that the best path forward is to continue free trade—for the US, to remain open to Chinese goods and, for China, to allow US investment, especially in financial services. These themes are still current some 14 years later.

Top economic policymakers from China and the United States met in Beijing in mid-December 2006 for the first round of what has been called the US-China Strategic Economic Dialogue. A lot more is at stake than the level of China's currency when the world's premier economic sprinter—China—meets with the world's premier economic long-distance runner—America. The fundamental issue at hand is the creation and preservation of wealth of two nations, each of which has much to teach the other. The right outcome from the dialogue would provide a substantial boost to the global economy in coming years, while the wrong outcome would threaten the continuation of global prosperity.

Wealth Creation and Storage

In his monumental treatise *An Inquiry into the Nature and Causes of the Wealth of Nations*, Adam Smith does not directly address wealth creation (the "natural progress of opulence," as he calls it) until book three, about 350 pages into his lengthy analysis. For Smith, "the natural course of things" is first agriculture, then manufacturing, and finally foreign commerce.

Smith's treatments of wealth creation and wealth storage—the role of the financial sector—may be inadequate to address fully the growing economic and financial relationship between America and China. Better scholars than me may be able to demonstrate that what I have to say here was, for the more discerning reader, all fully articulated by Smith. If that is so, I only suggest that, given the rising risk of acrimony in the economic dialogue between the United States and China, the points being raised here about the synergy between the real and financial sectors of modern economies bear repeating.

Smith's triad of steps on the progress of opulence seems remarkably apt as a characterization of today's star economy—China. That nation is consistently growing at a rate of nearly 10 percent a year as tens of millions of workers are being absorbed into a manufacturing sector that has come to dominate global production of goods.

Simultaneously, foreign commerce has drawn capital and market skills into China that have, in turn, further enhanced the growth that the country has achieved with the employment of vast, heretofore underemployed agricultural labor.

China is today's most rapidly growing large economy, exceeding both in pace and scale the rapid growth of Japan's economy during the 1960s and 1970s. And, like Japan, since Chinese growth creates more goods than Chinese households can absorb and more savings than Chinese financial institutions can invest domestically, both its goods and savings flow into the global economy.

The surfeit of Chinese goods at low prices creates benefits for consumers and trade tensions, as producers in other countries are forced to eliminate, redirect, or relocate production facilities. The surfeit of Chinese savings creates risks of overinvestment and misdirected investment inside China while fueling demand growth in countries, such as the United States, to which the excess savings flow and encourage dissaving.

The tensions associated with American dissaving are largely associated with what have come to be known as "unsustainable deficits," or more mundanely, a persistence of national expenditure in excess of national income. The problem, if there is one for America, is not so much that such "imbalances" are unsustainable but that they may be eminently sustainable. They can persist as long as China's financial system is too underdeveloped to manage capital allocation domestically while private capital outflows are largely prohibited by government fiat.

The wealth of modern nations and its enhancement requires a well-developed financial sector, something not much explored by Adam Smith. China's emergence as the world's preeminent producer of goods alongside the United States—which, while still a major goods producer, is the world's preeminent supplier of financial services—has given rise to tensions and opportunities.

One can hope for a positive-sum game between America and China. Much is to be gained by understanding "the natural progress of opulence" that emerges from closer ties between the world's preeminent "real" economy, China, and the world's preeminent financial economy, the United States.

The Crucial Role of the Financial Sector

Fundamentally, successful economies do two things: organize and carry out efficient production of goods and services and, once past subsistence, allocate capital among alternative uses while storing wealth. Economic development and attainment of "durable advanced economy" status require the symbiotic, ongoing growth of both the real and financial sectors of the economy. Contrary to populist demagoguery as practiced by Lou Dobbs[1] and others, people "work for a living" in both the real and financial sectors of the economy. Each is necessary for sustained economic growth and wealth enhancement.

Indeed, the most difficult part of the transition to status as a durable advanced economy is the development of a resilient financial sector. The British economy thrived during the century before World War I in no small part because, after the Industrial Revolution had transformed the operation of the real economy in England, a more advanced financial order emerged. The gold standard and its management by the Bank of England formed the basis for a stable British financial system that operated imperfectly at times, but on balance functioned remarkably well to reallocate capital and store wealth for well over 150 years.

Postwar Japan worked, saved, and invested to achieve remarkable success of the "real" economy during the 1970s and 1980s but failed to develop an efficient financial sector. By the late 1980s, the massive flow of Japanese savings, without the benefit of a modern financial system to allocate capital and store wealth, drove the real return on capital to zero. The resulting collapse of the stock market in 1990 and the land market in the several years thereafter erased Japanese wealth equivalent to about three years of national income. That would be the equivalent of an astounding $40 trillion for today's American economy. The Japanese did not allow much capital to flow out of the country and inefficiently allocated the huge stock of funds locked inside. The result was a financial disaster followed by more than a decade of substantial real economic weakness.

Today, China is sustaining 10 percent economic growth and massive investment, both conventional earmarks of a powerful real economy. But China's financial sector remains dangerously underdeveloped. Capital allocation is still far too arbitrary, largely directed by poorly staffed state banks with limited experience in identifying viable investments. Political expediency drives too much of China's capital allocation. Beyond that, the surfeit of private capital is largely trapped inside China because of restrictions on capital outflows imposed by China's nervous Communist oligarchs.

The important relief valve for China's excess savings is the huge flow of capital from China's government to US and European capital markets. This, however, results from persistent undervaluation of the currency and restrictions on private capital outflows. China's underdeveloped financial sector has forced the Chinese government to import wealth-storage and management facilities from the United States and Europe. The dominant role of the United States in this activity accounts for the "sustainable" US current account deficit and, in part, for the extraordinarily low 4.5 percent long-term US interest rates in the face of the Fed's boost of short-term rates from 1 percent to 5.25 percent between June 2004 and June 2006.

Despite China's decision to store its $1 trillion–plus foreign exchange reserves, equal to an extraordinary six months of income, at least two fundamental problems remain. First, China's domestic investment, exceeding 40 percent of gross domestic product, remains far too large and too poorly allocated among alternative uses to sustain the country's growth. The result, as Japan discovered after its own decade (the 1980s) of excessive and poorly allocated investment directed by government bureaucrats, will be financial turmoil that weakens the real economy.

Second, China's undervalued currency is resulting in overinvestment in its traded-goods sector that generates, in turn, politically charged rising trade surpluses. The issue is not so much whether a floating yuan will reduce China's trade surplus or America's trade deficit but whether it will help balance investment flows between China's traded and non-traded sectors while diffusing rising trade tensions that could result in protectionist legislation. Such legislation represents yet another avenue of potential damage to the real economy resulting from imbalances in China.

America's Lessons for China

For close observers, China's economy serves as a mirror that reflects the factors behind the remarkable success of the American economy over the past 25 years. As already noted, China lacks a modern, private financial sector. America possesses the world's most advanced financial sector, which offers a sometimes bewildering yet attractive array of wealth-storage facilities.

The symbiosis between America's financial sector and its real economy has been enhanced by a sharp reduction in the level and volatility of inflation, a change engineered after 1980 by the Federal Reserve System under Paul Volcker and sustained by Alan Greenspan. Simultaneously, deregulation has enhanced the US financial system's ability to become more innovative.

The lower and more stable level of inflation rate going back to the early 1980s has greatly improved the functioning of America's economy while providing more opportunities for financial integration. The term "Great Moderation" refers to this phenomenon. It has many features, but most broadly, it describes sharp reductions, after 1983, relative to the previous postwar years since 1947, in the *volatility* of economic growth and inflation. Simultaneously, the *level of growth* was maintained, and recessions were sharply curtailed and moderated. In the 24 years since 1983, the US economy has spent only 16 months in recession, after having spent more than 50 months in recession during the 24 years before 1983.

China may have wished to peg its currency to the dollar, in effect, to make the Fed, as author of the "Great Moderation" in America, its central bank. In principle, this is a sound idea, but in practice it requires dismantling controls on private capital outflows and development of a modern financial system in China. These steps will require time for China to complete, but it is important to initiate movement toward a stronger financial system now if China is to escape Japan's post-1980s collapse resulting from too much poorly allocated investment at home. Some further Chinese movement along the path to currency flexibility would also help buy time and smooth the flow of resources from the production of traded goods into production of goods for China's domestic consumption.

Lessons for America and China

Adam Smith made clear 230 years ago the important yet now seemingly obvious insight that the primary goal of a market economy, driven by enlightened self-interest, is wealth creation that accrues to workers in the economy. Today, we recognize perhaps a little more clearly that wealth creation emanates from the financial sector as well. Wealth, once created, must be reinvested if it is to continue to support consumption and further capital formation. The success of America's advanced economy and the growth of its financial system are perhaps best illustrated by the extraordinary growth and preservation of wealth in the more stable environment that has prevailed since the mid-1980s.

During the volatile and inflationary 1970s, American real net worth grew at an average of 2.57 percent per year. During the 1990s, the annual growth rate of wealth more than doubled to 5.25 percent per year before being interrupted by the stock market crash in 2000. Such corrections are inevitable in a modern financial system. The important thing is recovery. Growth in American wealth has recovered to a 4 percent rate over the year ending in the third quarter of 2006, the latest period for which we have comprehensive data.

The path to symbiotic development of the American and Chinese economies is clear. America needs to continue to maintain open markets for goods to benefit from China's vibrant real economy. China needs to open its capital markets and allow American investment in its banks to benefit from America's vibrant and innovative financial sector.

The path, while clear, will not be an easy one to follow because of vested interests in both countries favoring restrictions on trade and financial flows. But persistence and flexibility by governments, businesses, and financial institutions in America and China, aimed at integrating the real and financial sectors of the two economies, would do a great deal to enhance the wealth of modern nations. Adam Smith would be proud, of both America and China.

Notes

1. Lou Dobbs is a television commentator, author, radio host, and anchor who has worked for CNN and Fox News Network.

—⁓—

Wealth Enhancement and Storage

MAY 2008

As the US headed into what became known as the Great Recession, Makin stepped back to explain the fundamentals of storing and enhancing wealth. In the late 20th and early 21st centuries, Americans had many more assets available for wealth storage than humans have historically had. In the 1990s, households turned to stocks. In the aftermath of the bursting of the tech bubble in the mid-2000s, investors sank money into American real estate and real estate–derived investments, while the problem of American dissaving persisted. Those high-flying investments upended the traditional understanding that "the way to enhance wealth was to live well within one's income." Yet with the housing bubble bursting, Americans would be forced to save more—inviting a deep and, as Makin predicted here, lengthy recession.

The desire to enhance and store wealth has been present ever since income rose above subsistence levels. In ancient times, before the creation of symbolic financial claims on wealth, wealth storage was, quite literally, the storage of intrinsically valuable articles in temples, pyramids, or other such formidable structures. Even today in Tibet, which was long a theocracy, a major repository of wealth can be seen in religious statues of solid gold resting in temples.

The enhancement and storage of wealth by individuals—as opposed to kings or religious organizations—grew rapidly after the Middle Ages. Italian and Dutch traders amassed great fortunes in the 15th and 16th centuries. After the Industrial Revolution, large fortunes were accumulated in England.

The accumulation of great wealth always brought with it problems of enhancement and storage. Enhancement often meant moving into businesses unrelated to those that first created the wealth for an individual or family. When the desire for wealth enhancement (as opposed to wealth storage) grew too intense, fortunes were sometimes lost. Striking the right balance has defined successful wealth management.

The dangerous stage for many wealth managers arises when the prospects for wealth enhancement (as opposed to storage) seem to become overwhelmingly attractive. Bubbles arise, be they tied to the price of tulips, tech stocks, or Miami condos. A bubble occurs when investors believe that purchasing a particular means of storing wealth will yield such strong returns that a substantial rise in living standards will be possible much sooner—and for many more people—than previously imagined. Journalist Samuel Crowther's 1929 interview with General Motors financial executive John J. Raskob, published in *Ladies' Home Journal* under the title "Everybody Ought to Be Rich," comes to mind. It cited an expected annual return on stocks of 24 percent. Contemporary examples abound in print and on television about how to grow rich in real estate. Some people do. Many do not.

The prevalence of post-bubble regrets notwithstanding, there is substantial evidence that the United States enjoyed a remarkably strong period of wealth creation during the 1990s. That experience convinced many households that wealth enhancement did not require saving out of disposable income, as evidenced by a substantial drop in the personal savings rate from a long-term average of around 8 percent of disposable income between 1960 and 1990 to just 2 percent by 2000. Thereafter, by 2004, a credit boom, which enabled households to convert rapid gains on home values into cash, was associated with a drop in the measured savings rate virtually to zero.

A major question surrounding the outlook for the US economy, in terms of the length and depth of the current recession, concerns the pace at which Americans will restrict spending relative to (falling) income, first to arrest the drop in accumulated wealth and subsequently to restore wealth.

Old-Fashioned Wealth Management

In 19th-century England, wealth management, at least viewed retrospectively a century and a half later, was relatively simple. As England industrialized, the middle class, which built the factories and railways and conducted England's growing global trade, accumulated wealth and stored it in British consols. Consols were long-term bonds issued by the British government, and their yield varied roughly between 5 percent at the start of the 19th century and 2.5 percent at the end. The long-term drop in yields on consols was largely associated with a century of relative peace after the British victory at Waterloo in 1815. The absence of war meant the absence of wartime finance and inflation.

There were minor wars and accompanying oscillations of yields on consols throughout the century. A primary day-to-day preoccupation of British investors was the price of consols. Soames Forsyte, the main character in John Galsworthy's *The Forsyte Saga*, personified the attitude of the British wealthy middle class—as opposed to the upper class, whose wealth was based on land ownership. Soames' dinnertime conversation with his uncles about wealth management, as opposed to running businesses, centered mainly on the price of consols, since they were the primary vehicle of wealth storage for England's middle class during the 19th century.

Prices fell and yields rose upon the prospect of war, as in the cases of the Boer War in 1899 and World War I in 1914. The onset of peace and the prospect of easier government finances usually produced a rally in consol prices. Throughout such cycles, the underlying presumption remained that the way to enhance wealth was to live well within one's income so that asset holdings could grow. The rich grew richer if their spending grew more slowly than their income from wealth. The same was true for the not-so-rich.

Britain's new wealthy in the latter half of the 19th century had generally worked hard in business, accumulated wealth, and meant to maintain it or enhance it in perpetuity for themselves and their heirs. One wanted to accumulate enough assets so that the yield on those assets would pay for a handsome lifestyle without cutting into capital, the stock of wealth that yielded the income on which to live. A person described as having "£100,000 a year" was a person with assets the income from which amounted to £100,000 a year. At 3 percent, that meant holdings of consols and other assets worth over £3.3 million—a substantial fortune—in the hundreds of millions of dollars in today's world.

There were, of course, other assets available to British investors, some with considerably higher rates of return and more risk. Inflation was low and stable in the 19th century and drifted downward toward the end of the century, thereby enabling the nominal yield on consols to fall as purchasing power remained steady.

Underlying Realities

Long-term real yields between 3 and 3.5 percent on low-risk assets like claims on stable governments constitute a sort of a norm in the world of wealth storage and enhancement. Jeremy Siegel reports that between 1802 and 1997, the real return on long-term government bonds averaged about 3.5 percent. Between 1871 and 1997, that real return had dropped to 2.8 percent, partly reflecting the downward drift in returns during the 19th century. Underlying a long-term real return of about 3 percent on low-risk assets is the return on investment in real and human capital. Those willing to forgo current consumption to accumulate assets on average earn real returns of 3–4 percent for low-risk investments and higher rates for high-risk investments. Stocks are more volatile than government bonds and therefore riskier. Over that same long period from 1802 to 1997, the average real return on stocks was 7 percent, or roughly twice the average real return on bonds. The standard deviation of returns on stocks is roughly twice that on bonds, so that risk-adjusted real returns on stocks and bonds over long periods of time are roughly equal.

The postwar American experience with wealth accumulation and storage has been more complex than the British experience in the 19th century. The array of assets—means for wealth storage and enhancement—available to American households, especially since the 1960s, is far greater. Beyond that, inflation has been more volatile than was typical in 19th-century Britain because the gold standard no longer operates as an anchor on prices. The postwar period in America has seen more substantial demands on the government in the form of broadly expanded social programs begun first in the 1930s and expanded dramatically in the 1960s under Lyndon Johnson's Great Society.

The 1967 "guns and butter" budget resulting from Johnson's simultaneous pursuit of the Great Society and the Vietnam War created more than a decade of higher inflation that persisted until 1980, when the new Federal Reserve chairman, Paul Volcker, took drastic steps to bring inflation back down. The subsequent two-and-a-half decades of falling inflation, at least until 2000, broadly coincided with higher and less volatile economic growth and enhanced returns on assets. As we struggle with the collapse of the housing bubble and recession in 2008, however, American households may be coming to terms with a more difficult environment for wealth accumulation and storage.

American Wealth Expansion

Between 1960 and 2007, the real net worth of American households compounded at an average annual rate of 3.68 percent per year. That figure includes the appreciation of stocks, bonds, and real estate over the period. From 1990 to 2000, the average growth rate of real net worth for American households was 5.3 percent per year. For the growth rate of real net worth of households in the world's largest economy to have persisted for a decade at a level nearly 44 percent above its average rate during the 47 years from 1960 to 2007 was nothing short of extraordinary. During that period, a steady rise of house prices coupled with an extraordinary rise, particularly later in the decade, of stock prices combined to increase the growth rate of wealth of American households at an unprecedented rate.

That unusually rapid pace of wealth accumulation was accompanied by a substantial drop in savings rates by American households and by rapid innovation in American financial markets. From 1990 to 2000—the period of most rapid American wealth accumulation—the measured savings rate out of disposable income fell to 2 percent from its long-run average of 8 percent. With real returns on investments rising at twice the normal rate—certainly twice the rate enjoyed by British households in the 19th century—American behavior adjusted to what was perceived as a new reality. Disposable income could be virtually all consumed while wealth accumulation took care of itself through investments in the stock market and, later on, in housing. A generation of American heads of households has grown up under the impression that wealth accumulation can be left to the natural appreciation of stocks or houses.

The notion of autonomous wealth creation through the stock market suffered a severe blow in 2000, when the tech bubble burst and the broader stock market fell sharply from the highs achieved after nearly two decades of steady growth crowned by a surge of tech stocks. Between late 2000 and late 2002, the broad stock market, measured by the S&P 500 index, fell by nearly 50 percent. Still, the savings rate remained low and subsequently fell to zero after 2004 as the housing boom took hold.

The search for an alternative vehicle for wealth accumulation, coupled with the remarkably easy credit conditions that emerged in the wake of the stock market crash, may have pushed American households into investments in housing as an alternative vehicle of wealth accumulation. There was plenty of help from the American tax code, which favors housing with full deductibility of interest on mortgages and favorable tax treatment of capital gains on residential real estate. Beyond that, the innovative mortgage sector had, by 2003, begun to expand radically the amount of leverage available for households wishing to purchase real estate. By 2005, the need for down payments, income documentation, and even timely mortgage payments had been largely eliminated, so that home buyers became accustomed to the notion of purchasing real estate with no money down and no need to make interest payments on a timely basis. With all this help from the credit sector—and because a strong predilection existed that there ought to be an investment that yields at least 20 percent a year—house prices, particularly in markets such as Las Vegas, Los Angeles, Miami, New York, and other major metropolitan areas, soared at annual rates of 20–40 percent per year.

American Wealth Contraction

Despite the surge of house prices in major metropolitan areas and the extraordinarily easy credit conditions that enhanced it, American households have been unable to recapture the extraordinary pace of wealth accumulation enjoyed during the 1990s. Between 2000 and 2007, the real net worth of American households rose at 2.29 percent per year—less than half the 5.3 percent annual growth rate of wealth during the 1990s, despite a concentration of double-digit house price gains in major metropolitan areas.

The current situation facing American households intent on accumulating wealth to sustain spending of 100 percent of disposable income is difficult. The front page of the March 26, 2008, *Wall Street Journal* reminded investors that stocks had not offered much help over the past decade, pointing out that the S&P 500 had risen only about 1.3 percent a year after dividends and inflation were factored into returns. For the last eight of those years, the number is even more discouraging: –1.4 percent a year. Currently, the S&P 500 is oscillating at levels between 11 and 18 percent below its October 9, 2007, record close. Just as stocks are flirting in bear-market territory, house prices are dropping according to the Case-Shiller Price Index at a rate of 11 percent a year, with the prospect of a drop from peak to trough now over 25 percent. With the prices of two major assets—stocks and housing—both falling at double-digit rates, American households are turning from strategies of wealth enhancement to wealth preservation and risk avoidance.

A Long Recession

The difficult experience of American households with wealth accumulation and storage, especially over the past year, has profound implications for spending behavior. The presumption that emerged during the decade ending in 2000, when real net worth was rising at a rate well above 5 percent a year and saving seemed unnecessary, will have to be reexamined.

Even a modest effort by US households to increase savings could cut US growth substantially. Just 2 percent of US disposable income is $200 billion. If US households attempt to boost the savings rate from the current zero level to 2 percent, the drag on gross domestic product would be about 1.5 percentage points. That drag, coupled with the equal drag from deleveraging in the US financial sector (allowing for some overlap between the two impediments to growth), could cut US growth by 3 percentage points over the coming year. Even after that retrenchment, American households would still have a traditionally measured savings rate of only about 2 percent of disposable income.

The Fed's measures in March 2008 to avoid a credit meltdown that would have resulted from the collapse of Bear Stearns[1] and perhaps other investment banks has helped calm credit markets. But the US economic crisis resulting from a collapse of the housing bubble and falling stock prices that combined to hammer US household balance sheets is just beginning. Even the Federal Reserve has acknowledged that US growth will probably be negative during the first half of 2008. The Fed still foresees a rebound in the second half of the year. While tax rebate checks may boost growth slightly in the third quarter, the persistent drag from wealth losses as house prices and stocks fall and households begin saving again—coupled with bank deleveraging—will undercut the Fed's forecast for a sustainable growth rebound. Instead, a prolonged US recession looks like the more probable outcome.

Notes

1. Bear Stearns, established in 1923, was an American investment bank that collapsed in March 2008 during the 2008 financial crisis. As the nation's fifth-largest investment bank, its collapse shocked the financial world and marked the beginning of the financial crisis.

The Global Financial Crisis and American Wealth Accumulation: The Fed Needs a Bubble Watch

AUGUST 2013

Building on earlier observations about savings, consumption, and the economy, Makin explained in 2013 why the recovery was so tepid five years after the housing bubble burst. The recession wiped out 22 percent of American wealth, which resulted in weaker spending and investment that were still reverberating through the economy. US consumption, he noted, had been lower than usual in a recovery. Evaluating the economy's recent experience with stock and housing bubbles, Makin recommended that the Fed "pay more attention to the tricky problem of identifying speculative bubbles before they burst" by creating a "viable Fed bubble watch program."

The global financial crisis destroyed over one-fifth of accumulated American wealth (real net worth of households and nonprofit organizations) in just one year: 2008. That huge loss was on top of a far more modest but still significant 1.62 percent wealth loss in 2007. Both the US stock market bubble burst in 2000 and the housing bubble implosion of 2008 contributed to the current situation, reinforcing the need for a Federal Reserve "bubble watch" program. If we could recognize patterns that lead to these bubbles, we could see them coming and adjust policy to protect wealth accumulation and the economy as a whole.

A wealth loss of the magnitude of the one in 2008 is unprecedented in post–World War II America. The previous record year was 1974, with a 9.14 percent loss, reflecting the extreme disruptions tied to the "oil shock," when oil prices quadrupled in just a year. The three years from 2000 to 2002 saw a total wealth loss of 9.9 percent, less than half the one-year 2008 loss.

This substantial policy stimulus notwithstanding, the post-2008 recovery of American wealth, not to mention the American economy, has been gradual with some setbacks, notably including a 1.26 percent wealth drop in 2011. From the 2008 low through the first quarter of 2013, real net worth grew by 20.5 percent, or at an average annual rate of 4.23 percent. This outcome occurred with the help, especially post-2011, of rising equity markets and a modest recovery in home prices.

The high post-2008 growth rate is a bit misleading since it occurred from a very low 2008 base that followed the 22 percent 2008 wealth collapse. By the end of the first quarter of 2013, US wealth still stood 8 percent below its 2006 peak. A longer-term perspective on the devastating impact of the global financial crisis on US wealth arises from the sharply reduced 1.2 percent annual pace of American wealth growth from 2000 Q1 to 2013 Q1. Over the past 13 years, American wealth has risen at a pace just above a third of the 1960–2007 pace and just above a fifth of the 5.39 percent pace during the 1991–99 "golden age." The bursting of the stock bubble in 2000–02 and of the housing bubble in 2008 has taken its toll on American wealth.

Wealth Losses Weakened the Recovery

In my May 2008 *Economic Outlook*, published just after the Bear Stearns collapse but a few months before the more spectacular Lehman collapse,[1] I identified "the pace at which Americans restrict spending relative to (falling) income, first to arrest the drop in accumulated wealth and subsequently to restore wealth" as a major factor affecting the outlook for the US economy. My prediction later in the piece of "a long recession" was disquieting yet prescient. I continued:

> The US economic crisis resulting from a collapse of the housing bubble and falling stock prices that combined to hammer US household balance sheets is just beginning. Even the Federal Reserve has acknowledged that US growth will probably be negative during the first half of 2008. The Fed still looks for a rebound in the second half of the year. While tax rebate checks may boost growth slightly in the third quarter, the persistent drag from wealth losses as house prices and stocks fall and households begin saving again—coupled with bank deleveraging—will undercut the Fed's forecast for a sustainable growth

rebound. Instead, a prolonged US recession looks like the more probable outcome.

It is useful to note from reading that last paragraph written in May 2008 that the Fed was still in a business-as-usual mode after the Bear Stearns crisis. While acknowledging some slowdown, the central bank was still looking for a second-half recovery, as it is doing again, perhaps unwisely, this year. The Lehman crisis and subsequent economic collapse were nowhere to be seen in May 2008.

The recession that followed the Lehman collapse was intense. Although it technically ended in June 2009, the subsequent recovery, as is now well-known, was tepid and disappointing. Understanding the specifics of the actual post-2008 paths of consumption, investment, saving, and policy measures is important to examining both the effect of large wealth losses and the possible direction of future growth five years into the extended post-financial-crisis period of the recovery.

Before the onset of the 2008 financial crisis, the US personal saving rate had been on a long-term downward path since the late 1970s. During and after the crisis, in the recession that accompanied its onset and aftermath, the US personal saving rate rose sharply from about 3 percent to more than 6 percent and has held at that level at least until the current year. Shocked by wealth losses, American households restricted spending even after the recession technically ended in June 2009. The by-product was weak growth of aggregate demand, offset in part by aggressive monetary and fiscal measures.

The personal saving rate spiked late in 2012, given the accelerated distribution of dividends in anticipation of higher tax rates on such income that took effect in early 2013. Since then, the personal saving rate has dropped somewhat, back to a level of around 4.5 percent, perhaps because of increasing confidence that rising home prices and equity prices will support future wealth accumulation. Relative to past cycles, the US personal saving rate since 2009 has been low. However, this largely reflects that the personal saving rate was substantially higher in the 1960–80 period, even relative to the elevated levels after the 2008 global financial crisis.

A look at the path of personal consumption expenditures explains how US households could elevate saving rates even in a period of slow growth.

From June 2009 to the present, the path of US consumption has been substantially below that of a typical recovery. As consumption continues to lag, the gap between the path of consumption in this tepid recovery and the benchmark of weaker recoveries—a standard deviation below typical recoveries—has grown wider, proving that consumption during the current recovery has been especially weak.

The large wealth losses during 2008 prompted American households to restrict consumption to help restore wealth losses through a higher saving rate. The by-product of this, of course, has been a slow pace of gross domestic product (GDP) growth and a subpar recovery. The rationale for high levels of fiscal and monetary stimulus has been that it is necessary to try to replace the lost demand growth, given the restricted spending patterns of American households.

The path of investment before, during, and after the financial crisis is similar to the path of wealth accumulation because investment, in addition to the capital stock, is a form of wealth accumulation. Before and during the crisis, investment fell sharply. Thereafter, from a very low base, the recovery of investment, or capital formation, has proceeded along the lines of a normal economic recovery. This reflects the desire of companies conserving on hiring of labor to replace labor with capital. It also reflects the ongoing need to replace depreciated capital as companies aim to increase output to keep up with moderate growth of domestic demand and help expand exports.

As with wealth accumulation, although the postrecession path of investment has been average, real capital stock is still probably below its level before the global financial crisis, largely because of the sharp drop in investment in the year before and during the crisis. Going forward, sustained growth will require further capital accumulation and some policy measures, such as lower tax rates on capital, that encourage that activity.

Of course, the overall result of reduced levels of consumption and investment growth has been a subpar recovery. The growth rate of GDP experienced an unprecedented drop during the crisis in 2008 and has been sharply below the average recovery growth rate. Even now, five years into the recovery, the pace of GDP growth remains below typical levels, and accumulated losses of output are substantial.

Going forward, it will be impossible to sustain higher growth without stronger consumption growth. That, in turn, is made less likely by the fiscal drag introduced early this year and the tapering of monetary stimulus under consideration at the Fed. Indeed, we have reached a point, 50 months into a recovery, where typical postwar recoveries begin to falter.

We Need a Fed "Bubble Watch"

Notwithstanding the devastation of American wealth and the modest pace of the recovery since 2008, Americans are uniquely blessed with wealth accumulation opportunities. As an excellent place to store wealth, the United States remains a major exporter of wealth storage instruments. Such facilities need to provide liquid, mobile, stable, and long-lived assets, all qualities possessed by a number of American offerings. Between 2006 and 2011, the Chinese availed themselves of wealth storage facilities in the US Treasury market, helping support American consumption in the post-crisis period.

However, the two major avenues of American wealth accumulation, financial assets and owner-occupied housing, have been both a help and harm to American households over the past half century. The unique convenience of wealth accumulation through homeownership became so compelling after the equity bubble burst in 2000 that the housing bubble developed with considerable government encouragement from tax preferences during the decade after 2000. The bursting of the stock bubble early in 2000 left American households searching for another avenue of wealth accumulation, and with considerable encouragement from banks and brokers, American households turned to real estate to accumulate wealth.

As history has shown, the financial asset and housing approaches to wealth accumulation have their drawbacks, particularly manifest in bubbles that, upon bursting, have set wealth accumulation back a long way. Policymakers' sensitivity to financial and housing markets and their desire to support those avenues of wealth accumulation have probably contributed to the bubbles in both sectors during the past half century. It may be better to allow the pace of wealth accumulation in those sectors to slow somewhat to avoid the disruptions that inevitably accompany the bursting of such bubbles.

In any case, the Fed needs to pay more attention to the tricky problem of identifying speculative bubbles before they burst. Any prospective Fed chairman needs to step up to the challenge of creating a viable Fed bubble watch program. Over to you, Larry and Janet.

Notes

1. Lehman Brothers was an investment firm that had developed broad exposure to the housing market. When the subprime mortgage crisis began in 2008, Lehman was forced into bankruptcy—the largest bankruptcy in US history.

13

THE HOUSING BUBBLE

Greenspan's Second Bubble

APRIL 2005

In this piece from 2005, Makin was early to identify the emergence of the housing bubble that would eventually lead to the global financial crisis that began in 2007. He says that the bubble results mostly from missteps from the Fed and a unique combination of circumstances that caused people to believe that housing prices would continue to rise. He said the Fed's responses to specific crises since 1998 had created a "macroeconomic moral-hazard syndrome" that led to "a conviction among market participants that the Fed would not allow a serious drop in broad asset prices." He urged the Fed to move quickly and speak clearly to address this obvious bubble because of the "possible systemic risk associated with the growth and eventual bursting of a bubble in housing prices." He wrote: "It is a simple matter of pay me now or pay me later, but it is less expensive to pay the price now."

I knew Alan Greenspan had his first bubble in late 1999 when cabdrivers were too busy talking to their brokers on cell phones to talk with customers. The "cabdriver test" flashed its second bubble warning light to me just recently when I arrived in Key West for the annual winter vacation with my family. Without any prompting, our cabdriver told us of a Key West real estate market on fire. Condos that were selling a year ago for $600,000 could not be touched for $1 million today, while the units under construction were sold four times over before anyone even thought of occupying them. The old hotels were being torn down to be replaced by condos that were selling like hotcakes before construction had begun.

Meanwhile, room rates and rental rates in Key West had hardly budged. The implied return on investment in real estate is tied to an expectation of ever-rising prices, not to income from property.

Although Greenspan and his Federal Open Market Committee colleagues may not have the opportunity to come to Key West and talk to the cabdrivers about real estate, they could have heard similar stories over the past several years in the red-hot real estate market around Jackson Hole, Wyoming, where they gather annually for central bankers' summer camp.

Lest I be accused of being unscientific, there is more objective evidence of a housing bubble in the United States than that linked to the opinions of cabdrivers. Between 2000 and 2004, house prices, nationwide, rose by more than 40 percent—the fastest rate of increase on record since World War II. Moreover, the pace is accelerating. During 2004, the value of real estate on household balance sheets rose by 12.5 percent. That is far short of the 30–40 percent increase in prices evident in some markets over the past 12–18 months, but it denotes a substantial and widespread acceleration in the price of owner-occupied real estate. Meanwhile, the ratio of average yearly rents to house prices has been dropping steadily, from about 5 percent nationwide in the 1990s to 3.5 percent in 2004, reminiscent of the way earnings plunged relative to soaring equity prices before the tech bubble burst in March 2000. Rental yields in the hotter markets are even lower.

What Caused the Housing Bubble?

Bubbles in any market feature expectations for price increases that catch fire, so that more and more people begin to chase the market based on only the expectation of ever-rising prices. This bubble has some clear and proximate causes, none of which by itself would have been sufficient to cause a bubble, but which together create a compelling set of preconditions for a housing bubble.

The key underlying elements contributing to the new-millennium housing bubble are the Fed's responses to a series of unique events over the past seven years: the Long-Term Capital Management crisis in the fall of 1998, the collapse of the Nasdaq stock market in March 2000, the September 11 attacks, and the corporate scandals beginning with the 2001 Enron debacle. In the background, the emergence of China as a new mass supplier of inexpensive traded goods has also forced the Federal Reserve to respond to a 2003 deflation scare.

All these events combined to create a conviction among market participants that the Fed would not allow a serious drop in broad asset prices. The "systemic risk" warning flag would be unfurled should markets be threatened, resulting in an extended period of very low interest rates. The aim was to avoid an asset market meltdown while addressing a deflationary problem of global excess capacity in the traded-goods sector.

The housing bubble, together with a pervasive underpricing of risk, is a by-product of a set of compelling and arguably necessary monetary policy responses to a powerful series of market-unfriendly events, each of which potentially constituted a systemic threat to the global financial system. It may be true that the Fed has played the systemic-risk card so frequently since the fall 1998 Long-Term Capital Management rescue that a macroeconomic moral-hazard syndrome has emerged. Specifically, it would be understandable if an asset market participant observing the operation of the Federal Reserve over the past seven or eight years concluded that risk should be sought aggressively as a means to enhance returns because any financial accidents lead to a declaration of systemic risk and accommodation by the Federal Reserve that amounts to free insurance for aggressive risk-taking.

The Fed followed its accommodative response to the Long-Term Capital Management crisis in the fall of 1998 with a brief period of tightening in 1999. After the collapse of the Nasdaq in March 2000, the Fed began rapid easing that accelerated in the aftermath of the September 11 tragedy. That was followed by the 2003 deflation scare, which was due partly to the massive excess capacity in the traded-goods sector driven largely by China's emergence as a major producer in the area. This resulted in the Fed's decision to consider buying long-term bonds to avoid deflation and then later to predetermine that its tightening pace should be slow.

The Fed's need to target its ultra-accommodative monetary stance—the real federal funds rate was negative during the two and a half years before its cautious initiation of tightening in June 2004—to combat a disinflationary trend in the traded-goods markets ballooned the US real estate market. Tax law changes that allowed households repeated exemptions of up to $500,000 on housing capital gains coupled with an innovative mortgage market that simplified withdrawal of accumulated gains, even from unsold housing, added to the fire under the housing market. As a result, housing replaced tech stocks as the "hot" way to accumulate wealth for most American households.

The current US housing bubble is the result of two aspects of Fed policy. First, as I have already noted, the Fed needed to keep rates very low (negative in real terms) for an extended period that included an underlying disinflationary impulse from the global excess capacity problem. Second, possible systemic risk in the face of exogenous shocks from Long-Term Capital Management to the Nasdaq collapse, September 11, and corporate scandals rightly or wrongly has made the housing bubble intensify further on the notion that the Fed would also act to avoid a housing meltdown that threatened to erase trillions of dollars of household wealth.

The Fed, however, is not supposed to target asset markets for the very reason that it would result in too much risk-taking. Yet who doubts that a sharp drop in the market for housing or the stock market would cause Fed tightening to stop or even be reversed? The Greenspan Fed has been willing to spike the punch bowl when the party threatened to end for asset markets. Is it willing to remove it when the party gets too rowdy?

The Fed began to tighten in June 2004 with a commitment to raise rates at a "measured pace" until policy no longer remained accommodative. So far, the measured pace of Fed tightening has left financial conditions remarkably easy as the dollar has dropped and long-term rates have risen a little while, of course, a housing boom has boosted household net worth by $6 trillion since 2000. That said, the Fed faces a difficult task as it tightens in this cycle. Excess capacity in the traded-goods sector continues to exist, somewhat exacerbated by China's refusal to allow its currency to appreciate, while the liquidity flowing into China is being recycled back into US financial markets through heavy purchases of US government securities.

In retrospect, there are plenty of reasons to account for the emergence of a housing bubble, and no single one, save perhaps for the Long-Term Capital Management rescue, can be described as an inappropriate or inflationary action by the Federal Reserve. Like so many difficult issues, the housing bubble has emerged from an unusual combination of events. The

Fed's response to each is defensible. However, taken collectively, those responses have encouraged what is arguably a worldwide housing bubble.

The wealth created in the housing sector may be distorting investment decisions and boosting aggregate demand so that even goods prices are starting to rise at a faster pace. The most recent report on the core personal consumption expenditures deflator, the Fed's favorite index of inflation, showed a modest rise to a 1.6 percent year-over-year increase. But the annualized inflation rate over the past three months has been 2.1 percent, and it is fairly easy to see the year-over-year rate rising above 2 percent, the top end of the Fed's permissible range, by the end of this year.

What Should Be Done?

The reason to end the housing bubble proactively is straightforward. If it is a real bubble, it will grow bigger and burst of its own accord with even more disruption to financial markets than would be caused by a preemptive strike from the Federal Reserve. It is a simple matter of pay me now or pay me later, but it is less expensive to pay the price now.

The Fed should proceed in two steps to remove accommodation while minimizing risks to asset markets. First, it must remove the precommitment lag, which has been included in the statement following its periodic rate-setting meetings. The phrase "accommodation can be removed at a measured pace" has been interpreted by markets as a signal that Fed rate increases will proceed at 25 basis points per meeting until an unknown, neutral level of the federal funds rate is achieved. This precommitment by the Fed suggests a fear of lower asset values. If the Fed is prepared to temper its tightening pace for the sake of asset markets, then, so some believe, it will slow or reverse its tightening process if asset markets fall. Because of the Fed's implicit guarantee, the return on risky assets has been driven far below normal. The same has happened to the return on low-risk assets, as indicated by the sub-2-percent real yields on 10-year Treasury notes that have yielded long-run average real returns well above 3 percent.

The Fed should eliminate the "measured pace" language from its statement and simply indicate that monetary policy is currently accommodative and that accommodation will be removed at a pace dictated by the future path of growth and inflation. Second, if growth remains at or above a 3.5 percent trend rate and inflation creeps closer to or above 2 percent, the Fed should raise the federal funds rate by 50 basis points, perhaps at its midyear meeting in June. That would put the federal funds rate at 3.5 percent (assuming another 25-basis-point increase in May) and leave the real rate at roughly 1.5 percent, which would still be accommodative. More important, the Fed would unambiguously have shown markets that the precommitment era is over.

The decision to end its precommitment strategy to a measured 25-basis-point per meeting pace of tightening brings the Fed up against a basic issue. The Greenspan Fed has always been prepared to consider asset markets in distress with attendant possible systemic risk as a relevant consideration in accelerating the pace of easing. A housing bubble puts the shoe on the other foot. If there is an asset market bubble, is the Fed prepared to alter its pace of tightening to address the possible systemic risk associated with the growth and eventual bursting of a bubble in housing prices?

Only by addressing this question and suggesting that the systemic-risk consideration works both ways in the asset markets can the Fed remove a long-building moral-hazard problem from asset markets in which the price of risk is simply too low. Greenspan's decision is whether to bite the bullet now or leave the hard work to his successor.[1]

Notes

1. Alan Greenspan retired on January 31, 2006, having been appointed by Ronald Reagan in August 1987.

Housing and American Recessions

DECEMBER 2006

With signs of a weakening housing sector at the end of 2006 and the possibility of a resulting recession, Makin turned to the relationship between the housing sector and recessions. History, he said, shows a strong link between the two—and he thoroughly explored that link to show the dilemma the Fed faced in attempting to confront the damage.

A weak housing sector has accompanied every American recession since 1965, but not every episode of housing weakness has accompanied a recession. An annual drop in the growth rate of residential investment (a good measure of home-building activity) of more than 10 percent has coincided with a recession five of the seven times it has occurred since 1965. (In 1967 and 1995, declines in residential investment occurred without a recession.) A significant drop in residential investment therefore appears to be a necessary, but not a sufficient, condition for a US recession.

Housing slowdowns tend to lead recessions rather than result from them. During the second quarter of 2006, fixed residential investment fell at an 11.1 percent annual rate, followed by a 17.4 percent rate of decline in the third quarter. The intensity of the fall in US residential investment during the middle two quarters of 2006 is approaching potential recession territory. The year-over-year drop reached nearly 8 percent during the third quarter. Moreover, moving into the fourth quarter, the housing slowdown is intensifying. Housing starts, another important measure, fell by nearly 15 percent during October, bringing the three-month (August through October) annualized rate of decline to nearly 50 percent.

Still, the chances of a recession in 2007 caused by housing weakness are probably only about one in two. Understanding how recessions result from a weaker housing sector helps determine the odds of an upcoming recession.

Weakness in the US housing sector poses the sternest test of the self-stabilizing capacity of the US economy. That is because residential construction, although it is not a large part of the economy, can be volatile.

Housing construction is like investment insofar as product must be built ahead of demand, which means that a slowdown in the demand for housing can create sharp disruptions in the housing construction industry. Because residential real estate is the major asset of most households, changes in its value can affect spending on all items. To begin with, spending on housing is tied to spending on home improvement and furnishings, so an abrupt slowdown in home building and home purchases spills over with extra intensity into those sectors of the economy.

A Primer on Housing

Spending on housing construction constitutes a small portion of gross domestic product (GDP). At $573 billion, fixed real residential investment was 5 percent of GDP in the third quarter of 2006. However, spending on furniture and household equipment, which is closely related to sales of both new and existing homes, constitutes another 5 percent of GDP. Taken altogether, the housing sector represents about 10 percent of the economy.

The contribution of residential investment to GDP growth has been unusually large during the five years since the end of 2001. During that time, residential investment accounted, on average, for about 0.3 percentage points of an average total GDP growth rate of 3.1 percent. During the much longer period since 1947, residential investment accounted for only about 0.1 percentage points of growth out of a total average of 3.5 percent growth in GDP.

The potential for changes in residential investment to precipitate a recession results from the sharp volatility in residential construction that can occur at the end of a housing boom. I shall examine this volatility more closely below when I investigate the proximate sources of the recent slowdown in GDP growth.

The purchase of new and existing homes is accompanied by large purchases of furniture and household equipment. In fact, the official government statistics on housing outlays tend to understate the impact of residential construction on the economy by excluding kitchen and bathroom appliances and furniture and carpets fitted by house builders in new homes. Instead, these items are treated as part of personal consumption expenditure on durables. Therefore, it is important to remember that a large part of the $553 billion spent annually on furniture and household amenities is really closely tied to expenditure on housing.

Another large potential effect of the housing sector on the overall economy comes from its significant role in household wealth. Between 2000 and 2006, the value of US real estate rose by about $10 trillion to $22 trillion. Over the past year alone, the value of real estate on household balance sheets rose by $2 trillion. The total value of real estate at $22 trillion constitutes nearly 40 percent of household net worth. Consequently, changes in the value of housing can substantially affect household wealth and, in turn, affect consumption.

Broadly speaking, if the current housing downturn were to take house prices back to their values of mid-2005, representing a drop of about $2 trillion or 10 percent of the current value of the housing stock, households would feel worse off and probably consume less. The best estimates of the impact of housing wealth on consumption suggest that a 10 percent decline in the value of housing wealth would reduce consumption by about 0.6 percent. That, in turn, would translate to a drag of about 0.4 percentage points on overall GDP growth. The estimates of the impact of housing wealth on consumption are naturally subject to some error, but it is reasonable to assume that the impact on GDP growth from a loss of $2 trillion in housing wealth would range from, say, 0.3 percentage points to 0.5 percentage points.

The direct impact of declining residential construction and associated spending on furniture and household equipment typically subtracts about 1 percentage point from GDP growth for a number of quarters during a housing slowdown. If weaker residential investment imparts a drag on consumption through weaker spending on furniture and household equipment, weaker consumption growth can place a substantial additional drag on GDP growth, as it did during the 1990–91 recession. The loss of wealth that accompanies a housing slowdown and falling housing prices puts an additional drag on consumption—perhaps amounting to half of a percentage point of GDP. Still, given that underlying US growth averages just over 3 percent, a housing slowdown confined largely to the impact on residential construction and spending on household equipment would ordinarily lower growth by about 1.5 percentage points but would not cause a recession.

The Fed's Role

A housing sector slowdown usually results from a combination of the effects of a rapid run-up in housing prices and the higher interest rates that result from the Federal Reserve's attempt to slow the potentially over-heating economy that may be part of a housing boom. Between June 2004 and June 2006, the Fed raised short-term interest rates by 425 basis points, thereby boosting borrowing costs for prospective home buyers, although the continued low level of longer-term interest rates has helped cushion the impact of the Fed's tightening on the housing sector.

Perhaps a more compelling reason for the recent slowdown in housing has been waning affordability. The cost of a typical home relative to disposable income per capita has gone from about 100 percent in 2000 to nearly about 140 percent today. This puts much of the housing stock out of reach for many households, despite the accommodative financing that has been available from the mortgage industry. As potential buyers wait for lower prices, inventories of new and existing homes begin to rise, and prices start to fall. The median sales price of single-family new homes fell 10 percent in the year ending September 2006. Meanwhile, median sales prices of existing single-family homes went from an annual increase of more than 15 percent in 2005 to -4 percent in mid-2006. Clearly, a combination of higher borrowing costs and a lack of affordability has caused a sharp drop in housing prices, a sharp slowdown in home building, and consequently a large buildup in inventories of unsold new and existing homes.

The Fed's "wait and see" stance on the outlook for US growth and inflation could still be accompanied by self-stabilizing market moves that prevent a recession. US markets are searching for the combination of financial conditions—specifically, interest rates, exchange rates, and equity prices—that will stabilize the housing sector, and with it overall growth at around 2.5 percent. These rates and prices are currently predicated on an expected federal funds rate of about 5 percent by the middle of 2007.

The Two Previous Housing Slides

The last two housing slowdowns provide a useful backdrop against which to gauge the intensity of the current one. The 1994 housing slowdown was not accompanied by a recession, while the 1990–91 slowdown was. During the 1994–95 mid-cycle slowdown (between the third quarter of 1994 and third quarter of 1995), the cumulative drag on GDP growth from weaker residential construction was 1.3 percentage points. That amounts to just over 0.3 percentage points per quarter spread over four quarters. At the end of that period, during the second quarter of 1995, GDP growth bottomed out at 0.7 percent. Consumption growth bottomed out in the first quarter of 1995 with a growth contribution of just 0.4 percentage points related, in part, to some negative spillover from weaker housing activity. That said, the moderate 1994–95 decline in residential construction produced neither a negative reading on consumption growth nor a recession.

The downturn in residential construction leading up to the 1990–91 recession was more severe, although it is important to bear in mind that the first Gulf War began on August 2, 1990, and probably contributed to the onset of recession. Leading into that recession, residential investment had been weak during all of 1989, subtracting 1.2 percentage points from growth over four quarters, close to the four-quarter drag in 1994–95. Nevertheless, growth averaged 2.65 percent with consumption holding up reasonably well.

The first quarter of 1990 saw solid growth at 4.7 percent. Thereafter, however, the housing slowdown intensified. During the second and third quarters of that year, the cumulative total drag on growth from residential investment was 1.7 percentage points, a handicap on the economy more than twice as severe as the housing drags in 1989 and 1994–95, each of which was spread over four quarters. That, together with an inventory drag of 0.8 percentage points during the third quarter (and disruptions tied to the first Gulf War), produced zero third-quarter growth—even as consumption contributed 1.1 percentage points to growth, about half its normal pace.

Recession followed in the fourth quarter of 1990 and the first quarter of 1991 with negative annualized growth rates of 3 percent and 2 percent, respectively. Residential investment subtracted another total cumulative

1.7 percentage points from growth during the recession, while consumption fell sharply, subtracting a cumulative total over two quarters of 3.1 percentage points from overall growth. (During the 2001 mini-recession, consumption supported overall growth. In fact, consumption has not declined in any quarter since the fourth quarter of 1991.)

In 2006, the release of weak third-quarter residential investment data indicated a housing slowdown comparable in intensity to the slowdown that preceded the 1990–91 recession. During the second and third quarters of 2006, the cumulative drag on GDP growth from falling residential investment was 1.8 percentage points (an average of 0.9 percentage points per quarter), marking the most intense two-quarter drag since 1981.

Prospects for a Recession

So far, in the fourth quarter, there are only tentative signs of a sharp drop in consumption. Spending on furniture and household equipment slowed in September and October. While markets are not expecting a recession in 2007, there are as yet no signs of an end to the drag on the economy from falling residential construction. As already noted, housing starts (and permits) fell sharply in October. With starts at the lowest level since December 1997, we can expect at least another quarter in which home building retards GDP growth by more than a percentage point. That outcome would take a three-quarter cumulative drag on growth close to 3 percentage points, a level that in the past has been accompanied by a spillover into weaker consumption growth and an elevated chance of recession.

Containment of the economic drag emanating from sharply falling residential construction will depend largely on how rapidly financial market conditions adjust to cushion the negative impact on demand growth and on how the Fed responds, or is expected to respond, to a weakening housing sector. During the two episodes in 1967 and 1995 when a residential construction slowdown was not associated with a recession, the behavior of the labor markets was unique. In both episodes, the unemployment rate did not rise. In the current cycle, the unemployment rate, currently at 4.4 percent, is at a cycle low and has, as yet, given no sign of rising.

Therefore, it is possible to suppose that markets, and with them the Fed, will be skeptical that this housing slowdown can result in a recession.

The last point to remember about housing and American recessions is that no two cycles are ever the same. For example, part of the reason for the persistent drop in the unemployment rate during this cycle is that labor force participation rates have dropped, so the growth of the labor force has slowed to a point at which fewer jobs need to be found to maintain a stable rate of unemployment. The economy is, in effect, slowing along with growth of the labor force, so the attendant rise in the unemployment rate is muted.

The path of consumption growth over the next two quarters will determine whether the housing slowdown creates a recession or just a growth pause at around 1.5 percent, about the growth rate already recorded during the third quarter. The Fed's judgment will play a crucial role in the final outcome. As already stated, one wishes that inflation growth were in the Fed's comfort zone so the Fed could move quickly to cut rates given any signs that the weakness in housing was depressing consumption growth. That said, the prospect of a real housing-led recession is probably frightening enough to cause the Fed to ease aggressively should the housing slowdown threaten to create a recession, notwithstanding the level of inflation. The Fed's rationale would be simple. If the economy is heading for recession, even with core inflation at nearly 3 percent, sharply slower growth should quickly eliminate the inflation problem.

Inflation at current levels presents the Fed with a dilemma. If it moves aggressively enough by cutting rates to revive growth promptly, then the US economy would exit the current slowdown with core inflation well above the "comfort zone." In view of that possible outcome, it is difficult to escape the conclusion that the economy needs to grow at a below-trend rate for several quarters to bring inflation down gradually. The Fed needs a weaker housing sector, but it cannot be too weak or recession will result.

No one ever said that avoiding recession after a housing bubble would be easy. It is not.

Risk and Return in Subprime Mortgages

MARCH 2007

As the housing sector continued to falter in 2007, the subprime mortgage market began to fall apart, beginning in February of that year. Writing the following month, Makin provided a clear and thorough examination of what would become the subprime crisis—detailing risk, explaining the theory behind high-yielding assets, and showing how such "shoddy and absurd" lending practices might endanger a wider section of the economy. He also foresaw the danger of "moral hazard"—increased risk-taking because of the anticipation of a government backstop. He urged the Fed to indicate clearly "the activities for which they would hold financial intermediaries individually responsible and for which they would not provide systemically oriented relief" as a way of inducing financial institutions to "undertake a normal evaluation of risk and return in connection with their mortgage lending activities."

The slowdown in the housing sector that began early in 2006 subtracted more than a percentage point from gross domestic product growth during the second half of 2006. Now, in 2007, analysts have declared that the worst of the housing slowdown is over. However, early in February, more serious problems emerged in the subprime mortgage market, the rapid growth of which supported the later stages of the housing boom in 2005 and 2006. Subprime mortgages are risky loans to weak borrowers who usually have to borrow the down payment on a home purchase, leaving them with mortgage obligations equal to 100 percent of the purchase price.

Two companies, HSBC Holdings PLC and New Century Financial, disclosed early in February increased provisions for losses on subprime loans. The stock price of New Century Financial, which had been drifting lower, having fallen by about 15 percent between November 2005 and January 2007, dropped by 36 percent in one day on February 8, 2007, when its subprime lending problems surfaced. By February 9, New Century shares were down 46 percent on the year.

The weakest subprime loans are tracked in a credit market index known as the ABX subprime index that tracks loans rated BBB–.[1] That index dropped 7 percent in one week early in February. The ABX BBB spread, the gap between interest rates on subprime loans and Treasury securities, went from about 250 basis points (early in December 2006) to over 800 basis points by early February 2007 and has continued to rise. Clearly, the perceived risk on subprime loans has increased sharply.

While problem loans in the mortgage sector are largely concentrated in the subprime area, concern has spread to the housing market as well. Prices of shares in the S&P home builders' sector had rallied by about 20 percent from November 2006 to the end of January 2007, but then sold off by about 10 percent during the week in which problems began to emerge with subprime mortgages. Said Jeffrey Mezger, chief executive of KB Home, a large US homebuilder: "If subprime tightens up and underwriting tightens up, it's going to impact [housing] demand."

More Return, More Risk

The behavior of the subprime mortgage market, at least in the months leading up to the disclosure of more defaults early in February 2007, was typical of the behavior of many classes of risky assets, including loans to emerging markets and junk bonds in the corporate sector. Subprime loans can be viewed as household-sector junk bonds issued with the help of specialists operating to expedite the lending process and then repackage the subprime loans into tradable securities. The tradable securities yield a higher rate of return than claims on less risky assets and constitute a more attractive investment outlet for managers who are keen on higher rates of return and are less concerned about risk. The widely noted subprime problems that have emerged early in 2007 are, of course, a reflection of doubts that the higher returns on such mortgages will be paid. The market manifestation of more shakiness in the subprime sector is a sharp increase in the interest rate paid on the securitized claims on that sector, which, in turn, reflects elevated risks.

While the sell-off of risky assets in the junk-bond class for households— subprime mortgages—may be contained, it is symptomatic of a broader issue tied to risk-taking by investors incessantly searching for higher returns. Understanding its implications requires an understanding of the principles behind additional risk-taking in that context.

Understanding Risk

Taking on risk means increasing investments with a broader range of possible outcomes, positive and negative, in the hope of capturing the more positive outcomes without suffering too many of the negative ones. According to Peter Bernstein, "The word 'risk' derives from the early Italian *risicare*, which means to 'dare.'"[2] Investors "daring" to risk negative outcomes expect, on average, to earn high rates of return. Higher expected returns are meant to compensate investors for assuming more risk. They are not, of course, a guarantee that bad outcomes will not occur.

In financial markets, risk is tied to volatility. An investment that yields an average return of 10 percent in a market where yields range from –2 percent to +22 percent may be deemed "risky" compared to an investment yielding, say, 5 percent in a market where yields range from 3 percent to 7 percent. The investor choosing the expected 10 percent return option "dares" to risk negative returns to access a higher expected return.

Remember, however, that risk and return figures are expressed as expected values to be realized over a finite period, usually a year. Expected values are derived from past experience. Outcomes may differ from expectations and thereby modify forward-looking expectations. Risk rises with both an increase in the range of possible outcomes based on current information and possible further modification of such outcomes that may be tied to new information yet to be received.

The key to undertaking successful investment in risky assets is the price paid for the riskier assets. If, for example, an investor buys a BBB-mortgage security yielding 250 basis points more than the yield on Treasury notes, he or she is betting that conditions surrounding the underlying subprime mortgages will not deteriorate and, in fact, may improve. If conditions remain the same, the investor earns an extra 2.5 percentage points over what would have been earned on low-risk Treasury notes, while if conditions improve, the investor earns an even higher rate of return. However, implicit in the higher rate of return is the possibility that conditions will worsen.

As conditions have deteriorated in the subprime mortgage market, their value has fallen by enough to more than wipe out the extra return earned over Treasury notes. In other words, after the fact, investors' evaluation of risks in the subprime mortgage market, at least in February 2007, has proven to be too optimistic. Losses have to be acknowledged, earnings have to be written down for the owners (such as HSBC Holdings and New Century Financial), and prices of related stocks have had to fall. Moreover, doubts about the viability of financing the housing sector have spread to home-building stocks in general, and those stocks have fallen in value as well.

Hindsight, of course, is easy. To evaluate the intensity of the appetite for risk in search of higher rates of return, it is worthwhile to have a better understanding of what was known about subprime loans while investors were bidding eagerly for the bonds tied to those loans.

A Primer on Subprime

"Subprime mortgage" is a term used in financial markets to describe, euphemistically, mortgage loans that are largely uncollateralized and undocumented. "Uncollateralized" means there is no asset being purchased with the loan's proceeds that could be seized and presumably sold by the mortgage lender should the borrower fail to make payments on the loan. The collateral asset, the home being purchased, is already pledged to the primary mortgage lender, not to the secondary or subprime lender who is probably lending to pay the down payment on a home purchase. "Undocumented" means the mortgage loan is granted without verification of the prospective borrower's income and assets that might be used to pay interest on the loan or eventually repay the loan.

Many of the uncollateralized or undocumented loans in the subprime sector were, in a world of "innovative" mortgages, initiated as "negative amortization loans." Such loans allow the borrower simply to skip inconvenient payments of interest or principal, with such omissions being added automatically to the amount borrowed, in many cases without collateral or documentation. The result is a larger loan to an already unqualified borrower who has no equity cushion in the purchased home, having already borrowed the down payment. If the loan is an adjustable-rate mortgage, when the rate rises (as has started to occur in recent months and could well continue), the borrower will probably be unable to pay the higher rate.

If such lending practices seem shoddy and absurd, so be it. They are shoddy and absurd. But they produce high-yielding mortgage products in a world where high yields are harder and harder to find. Investors just keep buying more and more high-yielding product as if it carried just a little more risk than lending to the US Treasury in a world of low and stable inflation.

Of course, every binge has its limits, and the rush to acquire high-yielding, subprime mortgages has recently turned into a rush to exit, or to "write off" such loans. No matter how you describe it, lending to mortgage borrowers who simply cannot pay any interest (never mind principal) or who cannot make mortgage payments unless interest rates keep falling or property values keep rising is unwise. Once rates stop falling or house prices start to fall, the game is over.

Now that interest rates have risen a little and property values have definitely stopped rising—and in some cases have dropped sharply—subprime borrowers cannot even get a loan from subprime lenders. Compounding the difficulty facing these borrowers is that most subprime loans have pre-payment penalties. If the subprime loan is structured as an adjustable-rate mortgage, after a period of time—say, one or two years—the interest on the mortgage is boosted above the initial "teaser" rate. But in most cases, even if the borrower wants to pay off the loan, a prepayment penalty makes it more costly to do so. By virtue of the prepayment penalty, the borrower has an incentive simply to walk away from the loan, leaving it to be declared nonperforming.

The subprime mortgage market, by itself, is not large enough to constitute a systemic risk to the banking or financial system unless a "contagion effect" boosts rates on all mortgages. Such subprime loans constitute about 10 percent of the $9.5 trillion mortgage market, or about $950 billion, with the lowest-quality subprime loans only a small portion of that nearly trillion-dollar figure encompassing all subprime loans. Still, in view of the possible risks to the broader mortgage market and to the housing sector overall that are implicit in problems in the subprime sector, it is worth asking how and why mortgage lenders would wish to actively accumulate subprime loans, some of which are uncollateralized and undocumented and therefore highly likely to default.

Why So Much Subprime Lending?

Why has subprime lending grown so much? The answer, at least partly, lies with the incessant search for yield among highly liquid financial managers. Subprime loans grew rapidly late in the housing boom because there was a strong demand, especially in California, among households that could not really afford to latch on to property in the booming housing market. An inability to raise any cash toward a down payment on a house or inadequate income to qualify for a mortgage under normal standards were deemed "no problem" by subprime lenders. Many of the originators of subprime loans were simply intermediaries who then resold the loans that were repackaged into credit tranches (parts of a larger, diversified bond portfolio) and securitized for sale to investors seeking higher returns. The ultimate holders of the claims on high-risk borrowers may or may not have known they were buying what were, in some cases, uncollateralized or undocumented loans. In its February 8, 2007, article on problems in the subprime market, the *Wall Street Journal* quotes HSBC executive Tom Detelich saying, "We made some decisions that could have been better."[3]

The role of government regulators in the mortgage market has been to attempt to discourage some of the practices that led to granting subprime loans, but as has become clear, given the size of the problems that have emerged, regulators could not prevent rapid expansion of such loans. With the emergence of additional problems in February 2007, market forces followed by regulators tightening loan standards have made it much more difficult and expensive to get a loan in the subprime market.

There is a broader message in the fiasco that has emerged in the subprime market. That is the growing "moral hazard" problem in the financial markets and in the approach to those markets by banks and other financial intermediaries that may be tied to official policy toward asset market bubbles. A number of speakers from the Federal Reserve System, including Chairman Ben Bernanke and new board member Frederic Mishkin, have articulated the Fed's policy on housing or other asset market bubbles. Basically, the policy is that since bubbles are impossible to identify before the fact, the central bank should not attempt to deflate alleged asset market bubbles. However, if the bubble bursts and asset markets are hurt to a degree that threatens the financial system or economic growth, the Fed should step in and provide support to prevent systemic risk, as was done after the Long-Term Capital Management collapse in the fall of 1998 and, with a lag, after the tech-stock collapse in 2000.

There is sound logic to this view of the central bank's role with respect to asset markets, since bubbles are difficult to identify before they burst and can be problematic for financial markets after they burst. However, the compression of risk premiums (i.e., the earlier tightening of the spread between BBB-mortgage paper and Treasuries to 250 basis points) suggests a willingness on the part of many financial intermediaries, including some leading banks and mortgage brokers, to overpay for risky assets. This is, perhaps, tied to a general sense that the Fed will act as a cushion if credit markets swoon. Of course, if one's competitors are willing to overpay for risky assets—and during the run-up in the prices of those assets they out-perform the market—then the pressure to participate in the rush into risky assets may attract more buyers. That said, the moderate scale of the problems in the subprime market (some 10 percent of the total mortgage market), coupled with the extremely imprudent behavior of leading financial institutions that has created such problems, may present an opportunity to the Federal Reserve to begin to mitigate the moral hazard problem tied to its obligation to avoid systemic risk.

A Proposal

The Federal Reserve should, as part of its oversight activity for the American banking system, prepare a report on the growth of the subprime mortgage market. The report should include the activities of mortgage specialists, such as New Century Financial and HSBC Holdings. If there are jurisdictional issues with respect to responsibility for different segments of the mortgage market, those should be resolved by producing a joint report with other institutions.

The report should document, in detail, the activities in the mortgage sector that have led to the difficulties in the subprime sector. The Fed and its potential coauthors should clearly indicate the activities for which they would hold financial intermediaries individually responsible and for which they would not provide systemically oriented relief. The aim would be to force financial intermediaries to undertake a normal evaluation of risk and return in connection with their mortgage lending activities.

This would be a messy and difficult endeavor. A myriad of reasons—jurisdictional, practical, and others—will be found not to undertake it. However, the alternative is to allow some participants in the US financial system simply to continue to seek return irrespective of foreseeable risks, confident that any resulting financial disaster would be prevented by the Federal Reserve as soon as someone cried "systemic risk."

Notes

1. A BBB-mortgage security is a "medium grade assigned to a debt obligation by a rating agency to indicate an adequate ability to pay interest and repay principal." David L. Scott, *Wall Street Words: An A to Z Guide to Investment Terms for Today's Investor* (Boston, MA: Houghton Mifflin, 2003).

2. Peter Bernstein (1919–2009) was an economist, author, and financial historian. Peter Bernstein, *Against the Gods: The Remarkable Story of Risk* (Hoboken, NJ: John Wiley & Sons, 1996).

3. Carrick Mollenkamp, "In Home-Lending Push, Banks Misjudged Risk," *Wall Street Journal*, February 8, 2007, https://www.csus.edu/indiv/e/esquivela/documents/wsj%20in%20home%20lending%20push.pdf.

14

THE FINANCIAL CRISIS

Three Lessons from the Financial Crisis

SEPTEMBER 2009

With the worst of the financial crisis having passed, Makin took a step back in the second half of 2009 to explore its lessons. He explored three main ideas: that financial crises bleed into the real economy, that central banks are slow to respond but wield great power to combat crises, and that China's role in the global economy was on the rise. He said the lessons learned from the 2008–09 financial crisis should "provide guidance for a quicker policy response in future crises."

More than two years have passed since the US housing bubble burst. That event ushered in a financial crisis that was not only intense but also stunning. So stunning in fact, that in August 2008, just a month before the collapse of Lehman Brothers, the global economy was close to a crisis worthy of comparison with the Great Depression, yet neither the markets nor the Federal Reserve had much of an inkling of what was to come. The S&P 500 index had come down to about 1,300 from its October 2007 high of 1,576. Positive growth had just been reported for the US economy during the second quarter of 2008 at an annual rate of 2.8 percent (later revised down to 1.5 percent). Almost 1 percentage point of that growth came from US consumption, and government spending also contributed.

The wave of relief after the Bear Stearns scare in March 2008 provided a nice boost to the economy and markets. That boost was further enhanced by the substantial contribution to growth from net exports

(2.9 percentage points) thanks to what was then continuing strength in the global economy, especially in China, which had reported blistering 10.1 percent year-over-year growth in the second quarter of 2008. These and other positive components more than offset a drag from inventories and residential investment. In short, the real economy had not shown much evidence of damage emanating from the chaos that was churning in the financial sector.

The Fed's Open Market Committee met on August 5, 2008, and decided to keep the federal funds rate at 2 percent. Its statement following the meeting was cautiously constructive about the economy while expressing concern about inflation. The statement concluded by suggesting, "Although downside risks to growth remain, the upside risks to inflation are also of significant concern to the Committee."[1]

Three Lessons

Given the relative complacency of markets, the Fed, and other central banks during the period running up to the Lehman Brothers collapse and even in the midst of the July 2008 crisis involving Fannie Mae and Freddie Mac,[2] it is worth asking what lessons have been learned over the past year, in particular, because of the wrenching dislocations following the Lehman Brothers collapse. I hope this will provide guidance for a quicker policy response in future crises.

Three lessons stand out. First, financial crises produce powerful effects on the real economy. In a crisis, truly breathtaking dynamic and somewhat unpredictable causal connections, or nonlinearities, involving basic economic relationships come to light that policymakers need to appreciate more fully.

The second lesson is that central banks tend to be slow to react, partly because their models—which broadly exclude a financial sector—are based on linear relationships, not the nonlinearities that emerge after a financial crisis. However, an ancillary lesson is that while central banks may be slow to respond, they possess great power to contain a financial crisis, as witnessed by the experience during the six months following the chaotic market response to the Lehman Brothers collapse.

Finally, a third lesson that needs to be taken seriously in the current environment is that China has become an even bigger player in the global economy and financial markets than most people have realized. China's actions—not least the massive fiscal stimulus package announced in November that equals about 14 percent of gross domestic product (GDP)—can play a big role in helping stabilize the global economy and financial markets. Of course, China could destabilize as well, but the increasing integration of Chinese policymakers with G7 policymakers over the past year is an encouraging sign that China can, on balance, be a stabilizing force in the global economy.

Economic Harm from a Financial Crisis

The immense power of a financial sector disruption—such as the collapse of the housing bubble—to depress the real economy in a way that neither central banks nor financial markets anticipate was illustrated by the events following the September collapse of Lehman Brothers. That collapse, which symptomized the onset of the acute phase of the financial crisis, froze the global financial system and gave new meaning to the phrase "adverse feedback loop," whereby a paralyzed financial system causes real economic activity to contract sharply, which in turn further damages the financial system.

That said, it is important to recognize, in retrospect, that the Lehman collapse resulted from stresses that had been accumulating in the financial sector for well over a year. The Federal Reserve's inability to save Lehman indicated that the financial crisis had reached a stage that could not be contained; saving Lehman would not have saved the system. If the Lehman Brothers failure had not triggered the panic phase of the cycle, some other institutional failure would have done so.

The financial markets responded almost instantly to the onset of the acute phase of the financial crisis. By early October, the S&P 500 index had dropped by a third from its August level to a range between 875 and 900. The US economy was already weakening rapidly during the third quarter. Growth was recorded at a –2.7 percent annual rate, mostly the result of a 2.5 percentage-point drag from sharply lower consumption. Residential investment subtracted 0.6 percentage points from growth during the third quarter of 2008, with many analysts suggesting, incorrectly, that would be the maximum drag from the housing crisis.

The fourth quarter of 2008 and the first quarter of 2009 were among the most severe quarters of contraction seen in the United States during the postwar period. Both consumers and businesses froze spending: Consumption subtracted 2.2 percentage points from growth, and business fixed investment subtracted another 2.5 percentage points, with the overall growth rate at –5.4 percent. The slowdown accelerated into the first quarter of 2009 with a –6.4 percent growth rate, primarily reflecting an intensifying drop in investment spending that subtracted 5.3 percentage points from the total, while a deepening collapse in the housing sector subtracted another 1.3 percentage points. A panicky rush to reduce inventories in the face of collapsing aggregate demand subtracted another 2.4 percentage points from growth. The growth rate would have been far weaker had it not been for a 2.6 percentage-point positive contribution from net exports and a stabilization of consumption in the first quarter.

The nonlinear, negative response to the onset of the acute phase of the financial crisis was global. By the first quarter of 2009, the Japanese economy contracted at an extraordinary annual rate of –11.7 percent after falling at a 13.5 percent rate during the fourth quarter of 2008. Germany contracted at a similar pace of –13.4 percent during the first quarter of 2009 and –9.4 percent during the previous quarter. Capital flows to most emerging markets dried up, and growth fell sharply in those markets as well. The sharpness of the contraction was unprecedented and left policymakers scrambling to avoid a full-scale panic.

Alongside the collapse in investment spending, US employment contracted at a pace of 700,000 jobs per month during the first quarter of 2009. The job losses in themselves and also the wider effects of the confidence-sapping rise in the unemployment rate from 6.7 percent to 9.5 percent between November 2008 and June 2009 further weakened consumption spending. During the second quarter, despite extraordinary contributions to US household disposable income from government tax cuts and rebates, US consumption contracted, accounting for about 0.9 percentage points to the 1 percent overall drop in US GDP growth. In all, the government sector contributed a positive 1.1 percentage points to growth during the second quarter because of the stimulus package enacted in February 2009.

Central Banks: Slow but Powerful

The wave of policy measures enacted to stem the post-Lehman collapse was astonishing. Fiscal measures did not contribute much until the second quarter of 2009 because countercyclical fiscal policy measures need time to produce their effects. During the two quarters of the most intense contraction of the US economy, the last quarter of 2008 and the first quarter of 2009, the government contribution to annualized GDP growth was actually a modest 0.2 percentage points, substantially less than the average growth contribution from the government sector during the postwar period (0.6 percentage points). A financial crisis causes such a quick and powerful negative shock to the economy, raising the risk of further damage to the financial sector, that an extemporaneous response by the central bank—backed by fiscal authorities of the government—is the only viable option.

Notwithstanding the extraordinary request from Federal Reserve Chairman Ben Bernanke and Treasury Secretary Henry Paulson to Congress for $750 billion of Troubled Asset Relief Program (TARP) funds,[3] the Federal Reserve and other central banks did most of the initial heavy lifting. On October 8, 2008, a joint central bank statement was issued that included widespread reductions in policy interest rates, including a reduction in the federal funds rate to 1.5 percent, which was still cautious—at least viewed retrospectively—in view of the crisis that was unfolding. The Fed may have been tempted to keep some of its powder dry. At its regular meeting on October 29, the Fed cut the federal funds rate by another 50 basis points to 1 percent.

Meanwhile, the Fed's balance sheet expanded by nearly $1.5 trillion—that is, by nearly 200 percent—from its average level of $800 billion, while in October, as already noted, Congress passed the $750 billion TARP rescue package for banks. Of course, other governments and central banks initiated substantial monetary easing and additional fiscal stimulus measures, including China's measure (enacted in November) worth an advertised 14 percent of GDP.

While, viewed retrospectively, the response of central banks, particularly the Fed, to the rapidly unfolding financial crisis was slow, it did prove effective. After a breathless wait for the extraordinary policy measures enacted in late 2008 and early 2009 to take hold, the adverse feedback loop running from the financial sector was broken during the second quarter of 2009. The reversal was all the more remarkable because the fall in home prices and equities through the first quarter of 2009 had already erased nearly $20 trillion of American wealth—about one-third of the total. A combination of the stress tests for which most US banks received a passing grade in May and a second US fiscal stimulus package, totaling $775 billion over several years, helped calm investor psychology further. The appearance of less-than-disastrous first-quarter earnings reports—especially for US financial corporations, whose results were somewhat flattered by additional forbearance resulting from changes in accounting rules—further aided the respite from financial panic.

There are additional reasons for the stabilization of investor attitudes that appeared by March 2009, tied largely to actions taken by the Fed. Wisely, the Fed moved aggressively to assure that there were no runs on banks and that no depositors at federally insured institutions lost any money, unlike during the Great Depression. The sharp rise in the value of risky assets, including stocks and lower-grade corporate bonds, that began in March resulted from a relaxation of investor panic that had been tied to the potential onset of a global depression.

The Importance of China

The year 2009 may be the first in which China's economy has played a substantial role in determining the path of the global economy. Until the Lehman Brothers collapse in 2008, the Chinese authorities had been rapidly withdrawing liquidity from what appeared to be an overheating Chinese economy that was driving up commodity prices and energy prices in particular. The sharp nonlinear reversal in the path of the global economy that followed the Lehman Brothers collapse forced a rapid reconsideration by policymakers in China. Their response was among the quickest. In November, they announced their massive public works program that would, over about two years, be the equivalent of 14 percent of GDP—an extraordinary amount by any measure. Japan's largest stimulus packages during its "lost decade" seldom reached 4 percent of GDP, even when counted over periods of greater than a year.

The Chinese stimulus program produced immediate results. China's quarterly growth rate jumped from a 1.9 percent annualized rate at the end of 2008 to an 8.3 percent rate in the first quarter of 2009, and that was followed by a further acceleration to a 14.3 percent annual rate during the second quarter.

The sharp rise in Chinese shares was followed by a similar increase in Asian shares generally, and it could be said that China's aggressive stimulus measures and its positive impact on the export sector in Asia helped lead financial markets and the global economy higher during the second quarter of 2009. Surely 2009 is the first year during which it is possible to say that aggressive Chinese policy measures and the attendant positive responses of China's and Asia's equity markets helped lead global financial markets higher while boosting the global traded-goods sector. China's rapid expansion was aided by an aggressive increase in money and credit, especially during the second quarter of 2009, which further excited speculation in equity and property markets. While there may be concern about bubbles in the Chinese property and equity markets emerging late in the summer of 2009, no one can still doubt the power of Chinese policy measures to boost the economy and financial markets of China, Asia, and the G7 economies.

Looking Ahead

While the acute phase of the financial crisis has been truncated by aggressive measures of central banks and governments, and while economic activity in the traded-goods sector has stabilized, the outlook is somewhat uncertain. Coming full circle to the present, the consensus characterization of the real economy, especially in the United States, seems eerily similar to what it was a year ago. Most forecasts call for positive growth during the second half of the year, anticipating a substantial boost from the temporary surge in auto production tied to the federal government's $3 billion subsidy to encourage trading in older cars with poor fuel efficiency for new models. The Fed, having been chastened by the abrupt adverse turn of events during the fall of 2008, has signaled it will hold rates low for a substantial period while maintaining an enlarged balance sheet. The large boost to US disposable income resulting from enhanced tax cuts and transfer programs during the second quarter has ended. During June, the latest month for which data are available, real disposable incomes for US households fell by 1.8 percent, while real consumer spending fell by 0.1 percent.

The other big question mark going forward concerns China's increasingly important role in the global economy. We may well get a test of the "decoupling hypothesis," whereby Asia, and particularly China, is said to be able to keep growing even without growth in the United States, should US growth slow toward the end of the year.

The global economy is at an important juncture. The story of the year to date has been, first, the substantial power flowing from collapsing markets to a collapsing real economy in the fall of 2008 and a reversal of that process in the spring of 2009. With financial markets likely to be playing a smaller role in determining the path of the real economy, it is prudent to consider how the feedback loop may run from the real economy back to financial markets. If growth resumes on a sustainable basis (as many forecasters currently believe), financial markets will rise further, thereby providing additional reinforcement to positive growth in the real economy. Conversely, if aggregate demand fails to pick up and the real economy falters, financial markets will have a difficult time sustaining current levels and may even come to pose further downside risks to global economic activity.

Notes

1. Federal Open Market Committee, "Transcript of the Federal Open Market Committee Meeting of August 5, 2008," August 5, 2008, 103, https://www.federalreserve.gov/monetarypolicy/files/FOMC20080805meeting.pdf.

2. Fannie Mae and Freddie Mac are government-sponsored enterprises that help encourage mortgage lending. They played a major role in underwriting the housing loans that contributed to the crisis.

3. The Troubled Asset Relief Program was a proposal put forth by the Fed and the Treasury to help recapitalize banks after Lehman Brothers' collapse. Congress initially rejected it but eventually agreed it was necessary.

Financial Crises and the Dangers of Economic Policy Uncertainty

NOVEMBER 2012

Four years after the financial crisis, the US economy was still struggling to recover. Growth was tepid. Makin evaluated the circumstances and concluded that policy uncertainty, in both the fiscal and monetary sides, deserved a big part of the blame. Without clarity from Congress, the executive branch, and the Federal Reserve, businesses hoard cash, which keeps the country's economic future in limbo. Makin recounted the many different policies considered, abandoned, enacted, and still being sorted out, including Dodd-Frank,[1] the Affordable Care Act,[2] Cash for Clunkers,[3] and tax policy, and he called the Fed's quantitative easing part of "four years of extemporized monetary policy." He wrote: "Economic uncertainty is choking the economy simply because there is no clear path toward the next steps for monetary or fiscal policy."

Empirical research has shown that the economic benefits of steps to reduce economic policy uncertainty would be substantial. Economists have constructed a measure of economic policy uncertainty derived from a combination of factors, including the frequency of media references to economic policy uncertainty, the number of tax code preferences set to expire, and the degree of forecasters' disagreement over future inflation and government purchases. They then conducted a statistical analysis to measure the negative impact on employment and output arising from separate policy uncertainty shocks. They found the magnitude of policy uncertainty shocks arising between 2006 and 2011, the largest of which are linked to the post–Lehman Brothers financial crisis in the United States and Europe, to be sufficient to have cut private investment by 16 percent over three quarters, industrial production by 4 percent after 16 months, and employment by 2.3 million within two years.

The spike in policy uncertainty tied to the onset and aftermath of the 2008 financial crisis was unavoidable. That fact accounts largely for the intensity of what has come to be known as the Great Recession in the

United States. That said, since 2010, too many policy responses, including the debt ceiling debacle of mid-2011, the morass of indecipherable legislation in the Dodd-Frank Act, the Affordable Care Act, the latest quantitative easing experiment (QE3), and the fiscal cliff,[4] have all contributed to prolonging the recession, especially for American workers unable to find jobs. In addition, Europe's indecisiveness has precluded articulation of a clear path toward recapitalization of its ailing banks. Economic policymakers should begin to reduce uncertainty surrounding their responses to the financial crises in America and Europe.

What Uncertainty Does

It is important for policymakers to understand why policy uncertainty harms the economy. Uncertainty causes households and firms to delay decisions until the uncertainty is resolved or at least substantially diminished. Symptoms of responses to elevated uncertainty include reduced levels of spending on goods and services by households and reduced levels of investment and hiring by firms. Firms and households may respond to higher uncertainty by accumulating larger precautionary cash balances, as a way to both deal with a wider range of unexpected contingencies and have ready resources to employ once uncertainty is removed. Cash provides optionality, which becomes more valuable as the world becomes more uncertain.

The desire to increase optionality in states of elevated uncertainty complicates policymakers' work after an event like a financial crisis that increases uncertainty about the value of future real assets. Holders of these assets sell them for cash, whose future value is least sensitive to the state of the world, save for value changes related to uncertainty about the prospective rate of inflation. In a sense, a rush into cash that reflects less spending preordains a fall in inflation that could become self-reinforcing after a financial crisis because falling inflation, or deflation, boosts the real return of holding cash. This is why central banks need to supply extra liquidity after a crisis to avoid a dangerous self-reinforcing deflation that further exacerbates the run into cash.

Responses to Financial Crises

A financial crisis, like that of 2008, sharply elevates uncertainty about the future path of the economy. Economic policy, especially monetary and fiscal policy, is meant to reduce uncertainty by providing liquidity (monetary policy) and demand (fiscal policy and monetary policy) to stabilize the economy when households and firms are sharply cutting outlays in the face of sharply elevated uncertainty. However, as Frank Knight observed in *Risk, Uncertainty, and Profit*:

> The use of resources in reducing uncertainty is an operation attended with the greatest uncertainty of all. If we are uncertain as to the results of ordinary business operations, we are doubly so as to the results of expenditures along any of the lines enumerated looking to the increase of knowledge and control.[5]

A shock as substantial as the 2008 financial crisis presented policymakers with a sudden disaster for which obvious solutions did not exist. The Fed and the Treasury proposed the Troubled Asset Relief Program (TARP) shortly after the September 2008 Lehman collapse to help recapitalize banks. Congress at first rejected this proposal as a bailout for those who caused the crisis. Resulting intensification of the crisis, abetted by a jump in uncertainty tied to rejecting the TARP proposal, caused Congress to relent and pass TARP.

Early 2009 brought what turned out to be a poorly designed fiscal stimulus package that both underestimated the crisis' severity and misapprehended its nature. The large transfers to government employees and hastily devised public works projects were far from optimal responses to the large wealth losses in the midst of elevated uncertainty that occurred late in 2008 and early 2009. Business-as-usual, temporary measures like the Cash for Clunkers incentive program were initiated abruptly and then revoked, sometimes just as abruptly, compounding the uncertainty attached to such ad hoc policy. Payroll tax cuts and extensions of unemployment benefits were considered, rejected, and then enacted a year later at a time only after the economy was losing the temporary momentum it had gained and then lost in the wake of stop-and-go fiscal stimulus measures.

Monetary Policy Uncertainty

The Fed had to contend with uncertainty surrounding extemporaneous policy measures once it pushed interest rates to zero early in 2009. Quantitative easing was controversial and experimental, with some opining that it would lead to hyperinflation while others, seeing it as too limited in scope, predicted deflation. The Fed had to feel its way from QE1 in 2009 to QE2 in 2010, with the latter partly driven by signs of emerging deflation. The Fed implemented Operation Twist, aimed toward lowering long-term rates, in September 2011 and QE3 in August 2012, introducing yet another experimental phase of monetary policy that included targeting unemployment and committing the Fed to leave stimulus in place longer than usual after the economy had recovered. The Fed hinted strongly at a greater tolerance for higher inflation. At the least, its target level for inflation became more uncertain.

As the Fed struggled with its own postcrisis extemporaneous monetary policy, uncertainty was further elevated by two additional policy measures. The Dodd-Frank legislation designed after the crisis to further regulate the financial system introduced massive uncertainty surrounding bank operations that remains very much in place today. Much of the intent of the legislation has yet to be fleshed out with operational interpretations.

Second, Congress raised uncertainty, as already noted, by constantly bickering about whether and when to extend tax cuts and other stimulus measures. In mid-2011, it threatened not to extend the debt ceiling, managing to lose a AAA rating for US Treasury debt. As if this was not enough, Congress legislated a huge collection of tax and spending measures that expire simultaneously on December 31, 2012, creating a so-called "fiscal cliff." If they are not modified, the measures expiring will subtract 4 percentage points from the tepid 1.5 percent growth rate now in place, throwing the US economy decisively into recession in early 2013.

Since the expiration date follows a presidential election and coincides with a lame-duck Congress, uncertainty has surged concerning what action the government might or might not take to mitigate the fiscal cliff. Add to this the recession in Europe and a rapidly slowing Chinese economy, and it is little wonder JPMorgan reports that global business equipment spending looks set to have declined at a 4 percent annual rate during the third quarter. It is hard to imagine a pickup in the fourth quarter, given the looming fiscal cliff and uncertainty about the policies the next administration and Congress will follow.

Crises and Uncertainty

Economic crises elevate economic policy uncertainty because they occur infrequently and unexpectedly. Policymakers do not know how to react because in most cases they have spent precrisis months denying a crisis is coming. Onset of a crisis forces rapidly formed policies and actions that, at least in hindsight, are far from optimal.

The substantial wealth losses for households and financial institutions that have followed the crisis have prolonged its negative impact, save for well-managed firms that have been able to sharply reduce costs and boost profits at the expense of labor. Policy uncertainty, especially tied to the new health care legislation, makes it difficult for firms to estimate the cost of adding to labor, so they tend to substitute capital as a means to enhance productive capacity.

We have had four years of extemporized monetary policy—some of it well executed but now being pushed into a highly experimental phase—and ad hoc fiscal measures financed with low-interest debt that Congress and both presidential candidates say has to stop growing. Economic uncertainty is choking the economy simply because there is no clear path toward the next steps for monetary or fiscal policy, let alone the morass of regulatory changes embodied in Dodd-Frank and Obamacare.

To say that the effect of economic outcomes will occur in 2013 and beyond cannot be estimated in November 2012 is something of an understatement. If uncertainty is not substantially reduced by early 2013, there is little doubt that an uncertainty-induced global recession will occur. Whoever is elected president must understand this and induce Congress to follow a path to lower tax rates paid for by a simpler, less uncertain tax code. Beyond that, the United States must move to steady expenditure reduction and a stable, predictable path to a smaller debt-to-GDP ratio. The Fed needs to commit to low and stable inflation and abandon its flirtation with higher inflation aimed at helping improve labor markets. Let lowered policy uncertainty and a simplified tax system that boosts growth help labor.

The most effective economic stimulant in 2013 would be reducing the high level of economic policy uncertainty that has built up since the 2008 financial crisis. Less social engineering with the tax system, less complex regulation for the financial system, less government management of health care, and monetary policy aimed at price stability would help lift the US economy back toward 3–4 percent growth by 2014.

Notes

1. The Dodd-Frank Wall Street Reform and Consumer Protection Act was financial reform legislation passed during the Barack Obama administration in 2010 as a response to the financial crisis of 2008. It established a number of new institutions and imposed new regulations and rules designed to avert a similar crisis.

2. The Affordable Care Act was a massive overhaul of the nation's health care system intended to extend health care insurance to millions of Americans.

3. The Car Allowance Rebate System (CARS), otherwise known as Cash for Clunkers, offered financial incentives to car owners to trade in cars that were not fuel efficient.

4. On December 31, 2012, a number of tax cuts were due to expire, and across-the-board federal budget cuts were to become effective. The fear was that the confluence of these two events would undermine the already shaky economy but was averted when Congress passed the American Taxpayer Relief Act of 2012.

5. Frank Knight (1885–1972) was a University of Chicago economist who was one of the main founders of the "Chicago School." Frank Knight, *Risk, Uncertainty, and Profit* (Boston, MA: Houghton Mifflin, 1921).

Endogeneity: Why Policy and Antibiotics Fail

FEBRUARY 2014

Looking back at the policy measures implemented by governments, central banks, and various institutions over the turbulent years just past, Makin suggested they are losing their power to respond effectively to economic shocks. He wrote that just as bacteria can adapt and evolve to become resistant to antibiotics, firms and households can anticipate and adapt to the Federal Reserve's target-based movements and that a paradox results from this anticipatory adaptation: As the economy strengthens, the Fed reacts by withdrawing stimulus, which pushes investors out of stocks and into bonds and weakens the market. As a result, he said, the Janet Yellen Fed would have to decide whether to enact another round of stimulus and risk an asset bubble or continue to taper as stock prices fall.

Quantitative easing (QE) and fiscal stimulus are becoming less effective. Why is that? The reason is the same as the reason that antibiotics, overused in an attempt to cure infections including common colds, are becoming less and less effective with more intensive use: endogeneity.

Endogeneity is a property of endogenous systems—be they biological, sociological, or economic—in which changes have an internal cause or origin. Biological endogeneity, helpful for understanding economic endogeneity, refers, in one popular and widely discussed case, to the enzymes that evolve to protect bacteria against being attacked by antibiotics.

The Centers for Disease Control and Prevention has recently decried the excessive use of antibiotics to deal with common colds. Such use deadens their effectiveness in combating more serious illnesses such as pneumonia. After repeated treatments, the cold bacteria, with the antibiotic-resistant gene, survive and thrive. A population of bacteria emerges that cannot be killed by antibiotics. Newer antibiotics might work for a time, but only until the bacteria evolve with new enzymes that destroy the newer antibiotics. Medical science ends up in a race to develop new antibiotics at an accelerated pace, running faster and faster just to stay in place, like Alice in Wonderland in the Red Queen's race.

Economic Endogeneity

How do such anti-immune dynamics apply to economic systems? First consider monetary policy in normal times. The Federal Reserve follows a rule, usually the Taylor rule, that ties the Fed's target interest rate (the federal funds rate) to the difference between actual and target inflation and growth rates. Some versions replace the growth rate target with a target rate of unemployment. Given the rule, changes in the federal funds rate, the Fed's instrument of monetary policy, are expected to be tied to the changes in growth and inflation relative to their target values. Households and firms that are best prepared for changes in the Fed's policy adjustments—those best at predicting growth and inflation—will, given rational expectation, already have responded to the Fed's actions that are predictably driven by the Taylor rule. Therefore, the actions themselves produce a less discernible impact on growth and inflation.

Repeated rounds of Fed responses to nontarget levels of goal variables make it easier for more households and firms to accurately anticipate the Fed's behavior. Fed policy changes come to be endogenous, having an internal causal origin, and produce a less discernible impact on the economy. The Fed's antibiotic—changes in the federal funds rate—is rendered powerless by the anticipatory adaptation to such changes by the households and firms it is trying to affect.

Such endogeneity and the lack of responsiveness to policy-driven rate cuts that it implies eventually forced the Fed to push the federal funds rate to zero in late 2008, when the economy continued to collapse even as the rate was cut rapidly from 2 percent in September down to virtually zero in December 2008. As recently as September 2007, the federal funds rate had been far higher, at 5.25 percent. In 2010, the Fed turned to QE that tied its purchases of Treasury securities and mortgage-backed securities to the inflation rate, to the unemployment rate, and de facto to changes in the level of stock prices.

As households and firms adapted to this policy, a regime that came to be called "the Bernanke put" because the Fed was so predictable in its support of financial markets, QE became less effective in boosting the economy. Successive rounds of QE continued to boost stock prices because zero interest rates kept forcing investors seeking income from investments to keep taking more risks. As QE persisted and zero interest rates were described by the Fed as likely to stay at zero "for a considerable period," income-hungry investors kept buying more risky investments such as junk bonds and dividend-paying stocks.

Repeated, increasingly larger rounds of QE became less effective at boosting the economy over time until, by May 2013, Fed Chairman Bernanke hinted that QE might be gradually phased out. Tapering obsessed markets all throughout summer 2013. Having adapted to the prospect of rising QE, markets responded negatively to tapering hints until the threat of it was temporarily, as it turned out, withdrawn in September 2013. By December 2013, tapering had been so widely discussed and QE so widely accepted as ineffective that the initiation of actual tapering produced little, if any, discernible impact on either markets or the economy. QE had become endogenized and therefore nearly powerless, an impotent ecobiotic. In its place, the promise of sustained low interest rates for an ever-expanding period—until the unemployment rate drops to 7 percent, then to 6.5 percent, and more recently to 6 percent or lower—is also becoming endogenized and therefore less effective as an economic stimulant.

The Power of Surprises

Of course the concept being described here is an operational counterpart to the concept of rational expectations. That concept, introduced in the 1970s, postulates that only surprise (unexpected) policy changes produce any impact on real economic indicators such as the pace of growth or the unemployment rate.

Endogenous measures are those that are fully anticipated because they are predictable responses to deviations from actual target values of inflation, growth, or some other policy objective. On the other hand, policy surprises are exogenous, determined outside the ecosystem. As such, they are not anticipated (endogenized), so they can have real effects on output or unemployment.

The September 2008 Lehman Brothers collapse and the immediately ensuing full-blown financial crisis were truly massive exogenous shocks. These shocks produced large negative impacts on growth and employment.

The Lehman shock was actually a policy change insofar as it resulted from a decision by the Department of the Treasury and the Fed to not rescue Lehman as they had rescued Bear Stearns just six months earlier in March 2008. The massive policy responses to the late 2008 financial crisis—such as the Troubled Asset Relief Program, cutting the federal funds rate to zero, and eventual QE—exceeded the expectations of households and firms and therefore helped stabilize the economy. They had an exogenous component. By March 2009, markets had begun to recover. Subsequent measures such as QE produced diminishing returns on markets, growth, and employment as they became endogenized by markets. The ever-enlarging rounds of QE2 during 2010–12 boosted markets, but not the economy.

While anticipated, the initiation and subsequent enlargement of QE3 in September 2012, to a pace of $85 billion per month in Fed purchases of Treasury and mortgage-backed securities, signaled to investors that more risk-taking (buying stocks, junk bonds, and emerging-market assets) would be required to earn higher returns. As rent-seeking behavior was anticipated by more and more investors, prices of stocks and junk bonds kept rising during 2013. The same was true for house prices, another popular household asset favored by investors at low interest rates and low prices.

The endogenization of the Fed's support for risk-taking carries with it a paradox. As repeated rounds of stock and junk-bond buying boost prices and the wealth of their owners, spending rises, and the economy improves. Then, as investors begin to anticipate self-sustaining growth and observe a falling rate of unemployment, the prospect of further Fed encouragement of risk-taking atrophies. This change was reinforced when the Fed began tapering asset purchases in December 2013. Paradoxically, better economic news may well produce lower stock prices in 2014, just as worse economic news boosted stock prices in 2013. Both apparent paradoxes result from eco-endogeneity, which ties the search for returns on risky assets to predictable Fed efforts to boost a persistently weak economy.

The policy endogeneity problem also arose with the repeated rounds of fiscal stimulus that began in January 2009, which were repeated on a virtually annual basis until early 2013. These fiscal stimulus measures turned into fiscal drag after the tax increases of January 2013 and the "sequester" of spending begun in March 2013.

Interestingly, the sharp 2013 reversal of US fiscal policy from boost to drag probably contributed to slower growth during the first half of 2013. But by the second half, the economy grew faster, partly in response to continued firm signals of support from the Fed and partly in response to the wealth increases that had resulted from the search-for-yield boosted stock, junk-bond, and property prices.

The Fed's Dilemma

Endogeneity and the diminishing effectiveness of countercyclical monetary and fiscal policy measures are more pronounced after large exogenous shocks such as the 2008 financial crisis. This is because the size of the negative shock forces repeated rounds of monetary and fiscal stimulus that, as they are endogenized by households and firms, have progressively less impact on their behavior. The only thing that "works" is the pressure from zero returns on owners of low-risk, low-return assets to acquire riskier assets that will provide more income. The rise in the price of those assets produces the wealth effect that in turn stimulates spending. Unfortunately, higher stock and house prices leave such riskier assets vulnerable to price drops if investors' still-tepid appetite for risk vanishes in the face of exogenous bad news like emerging-market crises such as Argentina's January 25 currency devaluation and rising fears over China's financial sector.

Eventually, even the positive impact of zero interest rates on stock prices atrophies as asset prices are stretched beyond normal levels and the economy is boosted by positive wealth effects. The market comes to expect a withdrawal of Fed efforts aimed at boosting risk-taking. The Fed—some Federal Open Market Committee (FOMC) members have already said so—may risk creating a bubble if such efforts are seen to boost stock prices above "fair value." Better economic news and endogeneity signals a reversal of Fed support for markets. Asset allocators then may even sell stocks and buy bonds in the face of economic strength, which portends less Fed support for markets. Commentators marvel at the paradox of a better economy that emerges alongside weaker stock prices and lower interest rates (higher bond prices) as asset allocators switch out of stocks and into bonds.

The emerging 2014 endogeneity-driven paradox of a better economy coupled with a weaker stock market will confront the Janet Yellen–Stanley Fischer Fed with difficult choices. Under one scenario, the Fed continues to moderate QE as stock prices fall in the face of a stronger economy. In this case, the Taylor rule holds, and employment and inflation closer to target levels signal a need for less stimulus. Under an alternative scenario, the Fed re-boosts QE in response to falling stock prices, pushing those prices into bubble territory. The risk of higher inflation—so troubling to FOMC hawks—intensifies, and if inflation actually does rise, the Fed confronts a need to tighten.

The first scenario—in which the Taylor rule combined with lower unemployment and the risk of higher, stable inflation—drives the Fed to reduce QE faster or hint at an earlier increase in the federal funds rate and may be emerging in the first quarter of 2014. Should this scenario continue to play out, risky assets—especially emerging-market stocks, currencies, and bonds—will weaken further. Stock prices in advanced economies may fall as well, as investors move from stocks back into high-grade bonds. This shift would be intensified by continued falling inflation.

The second scenario, in which rapidly falling US stock prices frighten the Fed (wealth losses, weaker spending, and an economy relapse), would elevate market volatility. A drop in house prices would compound the Fed's fear of recession. The drop in stock prices in scenario two is interrupted once the Fed determines that the pace of implied wealth loss jeopardizes growth and risks further negative inflation and outright recession. If it boosts the stock market, the eventual Fed ease—reverse tapering and a longer-term pledge of zero rates—would signal the birth of the Yellen-Fischer put.

It is too soon to tell which scenario will play out, but under either, stock prices will probably fall during the first half of 2014. What happens after that is up to the Yellen-Fischer Fed.

Stay tuned.

APPENDIX

Figure A1. Global Stock Markets and Key World Events

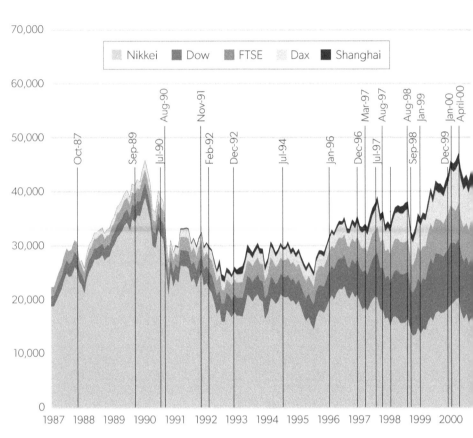

Date	Event	Date	Event
Oct 1987	Black Monday	Mar 1997	DVD Player Is Released
Sep 1989	Apple Mac Laptop Is Released	Jul 1997	Asian Financial Crisis
Jul 1990	Gulf War Recession	Aug 1997	Netflix Is Founded
Aug 1990	Gulf War	Aug 1998	Russian Devaluation and Default
Nov 1991	Fall of the Berlin Wall	Sep 1998	Google Is Founded
Feb 1992	Maastricht Agreement	Jan 1999	BlackBerry Pager Is Released;
Dec 1992	First SMS Message Is Sent		Euro Is Introduced
Jul 1994	Amazon Is Founded	Dec 1999	T-Mobile Is Founded
Jan 1996	Motorola Releases First Flip Phone	Jan 2000	Peak Surplus ($236 Billion);
Dec 1996	Alan Greenspan's Irrational		Dot-Com Bubble Bursts
	Exuberance Speech	Apr 2000	Verizon Is Founded

Source: American Enterprise Institute.

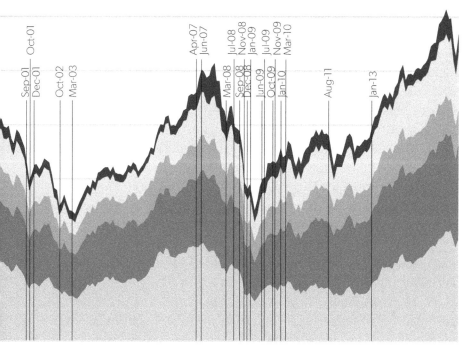

Date	Event		Date	Event
Sep 2001	9/11 Attacks		Nov 2008	Citigroup Bailout
Oct 2001	Apple iPod Is Released		Dec 2008	Fed Cuts Rates to 0 Percent
Dec 2001	Enron Collapses		Jan 2009	Bank of America Bailout
Oct 2002	Dot-Com Bubble Crash Ends		Jun 2009	General Motors Files for Bankruptcy
Mar 2003	Iraq War		Jul 2009	Cash for Clunkers
Apr 2007	Century Financial Files for Bankruptcy		Oct 2009	US Unemployment Rises to 10 Percent
Jun 2007	Apple iPhone Is Released		Jan 2010	Eurozone Crisis
Mar 2008	Bear Stearns Collapses		Mar 2010	Affordable Care Act Enacted
Jul 2008	IndyMac Collapses		Aug 2011	S&P Lowers US Government's Credit Rating
Sep 2008	Global Financial Crisis		Jan 2013	Fiscal Cliff

John H. Makin: A Life in Three Acts

John H. Makin, PhD, was fond of saying he'd had three careers. A University of Chicago–trained economist, he began his first career after writing his dissertation on the risk involved in the composition of international reserve holdings. For the next decade, he held positions at several research universities, including the University of Wisconsin–Milwaukee, the University of Virginia, and the University of British Columbia. During this time, he also held research appointments at the Federal Reserve Bank of Chicago and the Federal Reserve Bank of San Francisco.

In 1976, he moved to the University of Washington, and in 1978, he was named the director of the Institute for Economic Research there, a post he held for many years. As a professor of economics at the university, Makin frequently commented on national and international economic policy debates. He served as a consultant to the International Monetary Fund and the US Treasury and held a post as a research associate at the National Bureau of Economic Research. During this time, he also began his long-running relationship with the American Enterprise Institute (AEI), first as a visiting scholar, then, in 1984 as a resident scholar and director of fiscal policy studies. His tenure at AEI was his second career.

After serving as a member of the Panel of Economic Advisers for the Congressional Budget Office for a decade, holding posts at AEI, and consulting for the Bank of Japan, Makin moved from academia and the think tank world into financial markets, working closely with Caxton Associates for two decades. This was his third career. During Makin's time as chief economist at Caxton Associates, the fund returned, on average, 21 percent per year, one of the best in the industry. In 2010, Makin returned to a full-time position at AEI while serving as an adviser to Cornwall Capital.

During his career in Washington, he also served as the director of the Japan–United States Friendship Commission and as a consultant to the US Treasury Department, the Congressional Budget Office, and the

International Monetary Fund. He specialized in international finance and financial markets, with emphasis on Japanese and European economies.

Makin wrote widely about the US economy on topics related to monetary policy and tax and budget issues. He began a series of widely read monthly essays titled *Economic Outlook* for AEI in 1995. This book includes many of those essays. He was also the author of numerous books and articles on financial, monetary, and fiscal policy.

Makin's untimely death in 2015 was a great loss for AEI and for so many who treasured his economic commentary and insights. He is survived by his wife, Gwendolyn van Paasschen, and his daughter, Jane.

For a full list of Makin's publications, please visit his AEI scholar page: https://www.aei.org/profile/john-h-makin/.

Many of Makin's scholarly publications are also available on his Google Scholar page: http://scholar.google.com/citations?user=BefXfzYAAAAJ&hl=en&oi=ao.

Index